innovation
ALCHEMY

LORI GLOVER, J.D.

MANAGING DIRECTOR, GLOBAL STRATEGIC ALLIANCES,
MIT COMPUTER SCIENCE & ARTIFICIAL INTELLIGENCE LABORATORY

Innovation Alchemy

HOW TO BUILD
STRONG INDUSTRY
ENGAGEMENT PARTNERSHIPS
FOR **IMPACT** AND **ECONOMIC GROWTH**

WILEY

Copyright © 2025 by John Wiley & Sons. All rights reserved, including rights for text and data mining and training of artificial intelligence technologies or similar technologies.

Published by John Wiley & Sons, Inc., Hoboken, New Jersey.
Published simultaneously in Canada.

No part of this publication may be reproduced, stored in a retrieval system, or transmitted in any form or by any means, electronic, mechanical, photocopying, recording, scanning, or otherwise, except as permitted under Section 107 or 108 of the 1976 United States Copyright Act, without either the prior written permission of the Publisher, or authorization through payment of the appropriate per-copy fee to the Copyright Clearance Center, Inc., 222 Rosewood Drive, Danvers, MA 01923, (978) 750-8400, fax (978) 750-4470, or on the web at www.copyright.com. Requests to the Publisher for permission should be addressed to the Permissions Department, John Wiley & Sons, Inc., 111 River Street, Hoboken, NJ 07030, (201) 748-6011, fax (201) 748-6008, or online at http://www.wiley.com/go/permission.

The manufacturer's authorized representative according to the EU General Product Safety Regulation is Wiley-VCH GmbH, Boschstr. 12, 69469 Weinheim, Germany, e-mail: Product_Safety@wiley.com.

Trademarks: Wiley and the Wiley logo are trademarks or registered trademarks of John Wiley & Sons, Inc. and/or its affiliates in the United States and other countries and may not be used without written permission. All other trademarks are the property of their respective owners. John Wiley & Sons, Inc. is not associated with any product or vendor mentioned in this book.

Limit of Liability/Disclaimer of Warranty: While the publisher and author have used their best efforts in preparing this book, they make no representations or warranties with respect to the accuracy or completeness of the contents of this book and specifically disclaim any implied warranties of merchantability or fitness for a particular purpose. No warranty may be created or extended by sales representatives or written sales materials. The advice and strategies contained herein may not be suitable for your situation. You should consult with a professional where appropriate. Further, readers should be aware that websites listed in this work may have changed or disappeared between when this work was written and when it is read. Neither the publisher nor authors shall be liable for any loss of profit or any other commercial damages, including but not limited to special, incidental, consequential, or other damages.

For general information on our other products and services or for technical support, please contact our Customer Care Department within the United States at (800) 762-2974, outside the United States at (317) 572-3993 or fax (317) 572-4002.

Wiley also publishes its books in a variety of electronic formats. Some content that appears in print may not be available in electronic formats. For more information about Wiley products, visit our web site at www.wiley.com.

Library of Congress Cataloging-in-Publication Data is Available:

ISBN 9781394307210 (Cloth)
ISBN 9781394307258 (ePub)
ISBN 9781394307265 (ePDF)

Cover Design: Wiley
Cover Images: © ArthurGraphix/stock.adobe.com, © Kazim/stock.adobe.com

SKY10109636_060325

Contents

Foreword .... *vii*
Introduction .... *ix*

PART 1
Step 1: Understand the Fundamentals 1

PART 2
Step 2: Define Your Strategy 63
Step 3: Know Your Stakeholders 80
Step 4: Map Your Connection Points 126
Step 5: Understand Possible Paths of Engagement 146

PART 3
Step 6: Create Your Plan 171
Step 7: Build Your Team for Success 182
Step 8: Execute the Plan 186
Step 9: Track Successes and Learn from Mistakes 197
Step 10: Innovate 200

PART 4
Toolkit 205
Additional Resources 237

Notes *239*
Acknowledgments *247*
About the Author *249*
Index *251*

Foreword

As Director of MIT's Computer Science and Artificial Intelligence Lab (CSAIL), I can say with certainty that today's rapidly evolving technological landscape has led to the need for closer relationships with industry. As global challenges become increasingly complex, the traditional silos that once separated educational institutions from the business world are giving way to collaborative partnerships that harness the strengths of both sectors.

Innovation Alchemy explores the transformative potential of industry–academic partnerships, highlighting how these alliances can catalyze groundbreaking research, accelerate the commercialization of new technologies, and create a skilled workforce equipped to meet the demands of a dynamic economy. In sharing strategies we have used at CSAIL, along with contributions from other universities and companies, this book illustrates principles that have enabled these partnerships to flourish and the tangible, as well as intangible, benefits they bring to businesses, educational institutions, the broader innovation ecosystem, and regional economic communities. Additionally, there have been many lessons learned, and this book also addresses the challenges that can arise when trying to bridge the gap between academic inquiry and industry application. By understanding the motivations, goals, and language of each sector, we can foster an environment where creativity thrives and impactful solutions are born.

In an era where knowledge is power, the partnership between industry and academic sectors is not just beneficial – it is essential. Together, we can bring dynamic new technologies from research to reality, enhance global competitiveness, increase job opportunities for economic growth, and ultimately shape a future that is innovative, inclusive, and resilient, crafting a brighter tomorrow for all.

—Prof. Daniela Rus

Introduction

This book is designed to help frame approaches to innovation engagement partnerships between the academic sector and the industrial sector. Some parts speak to industry, others to academia. Academic institutions, companies, nonprofits, start-ups, accelerators, research labs, and community organizations involved in innovation can leverage this book to help create *mutually* beneficial partnerships and collaborations. These partnerships are symbiotic in that each partner has something the other needs but can't provide on their own. A common example of a symbiotic relationship in this context is the workforce. Companies need skilled workers, and those workers are educated and trained by colleges and universities as well as professional associations, trade groups, and others. The skills and knowledge delivered to the learner in the academic setting translates to the talent needed by companies to make a commercial impact.

The terminology in the book falls into two main classifications of "industry" and "academia" but applies to the alignment of all the units in the innovation ecosystem. Similar to the periodic table of elements in chemistry classes, the following illustration plugs the organizations in the innovation ecosystem into the table in place of the chemical elements. The white and light grey squares are more aligned with industry or commercialization/impact, while the darker grey squares are more aligned with academic/research/creation. This is the *periodic table of innovation elements* containing the various organizations needed for *Innovation Alchemy*.

52 **Bt** Business & Technical Trade Groups 127.6								
51 **Rp** Research Parks 121.76					84 **Po** Workforce Development Groups 208.98243	8 **Na** Non-academic Education Providers 15.999
7 **Cu** Colleges & Universities 14.007	115 **Sg** Student Groups 290.196	83 **He** Healthcare entities 208.9804		34 **Ed** Economic Development Organizations 78.97	116 **F** Foundations 293.205	16 **Np** Non-Profits 32.07
15 **Ps** Policy & Standards Groups 30.97376200	6 **Su** Start-ups 12.011	14 **Ic** Innovation Centers 28.085	32 **Ng** NGOs 72.63	50 **Fo** Family Offices 118.71	82 **Lf** Law Firms 207	114 **Cw** Co-working Spaces 289.191
35 **Fc** Federal Centers of Excellence 72.63	2 **Ci** Company/Industry 10.81	13 **A** Accelerators 26.981538	31 **Vc** Venture Capital 69.72	49 **P** Publishers 114.82	81 **F** Foundries 204.383	113 **Pp** Public–Private Partnerships 286.183

All of these organizations are part of what I call the *innovation supply chain*, which we explore in Part 1. Connecting industry and academia is the fuel for the innovation supply chain. There really is no one size fits all, but understanding the foundations is essential. This book will explore key issues to be aware of, critical considerations in form and function of planned partnerships, and best practices for success. There are also worksheets, forms, and planners to help you get started (a functional toolkit!), regardless from which organization you are approaching collaboration plans.

The basis of mutual benefit is essential. Innovation engagement partnerships are built on value. They are built to benefit the institutions involved and foster innovation that will impact the broader community. Academia and nonprofit research centers don't sell a product. Instead, they can offer vision further up the innovation curve without the constraints of daily corporate operations. For industry or commercial organizations, there is value in connecting with the talent, new ideas, new technology awareness, and start-ups from the academic elements. It has been well established that in today's world, one must, according to Peter Drucker, "innovate or die," and not all innovation can come from within. New ideas, fresh perspectives, and challenges from outside the box help companies stay on top of the ever-changing landscape (technological, policy, talent, etc.) and connected to those nascent developments that can cause the next seismic shift in their industry sector.

Similarly, for academia, partnership opportunities with industry offer employment pathways for students, research partnerships on impactful challenges, support for mission-critical programming, and a customer base for newly spun-off start-ups. Academic institutions need to understand industry's challenges to best prepare the next generation workforce to help industry thrive and to help solve pressing problems for which no commercial solution exists today.

Years of budget cuts and a shrinking federal investment in research has increased academia's need for student support, research funding, and programming assistance. Additionally, many institutions are facing "the cliff,"[1] a projected 15% decline in college students from 2025 to 2029. This will impact the talent supply and the creation of new innovations as well. Consequently, many more academic institutions are trying to figure out pathways to connect with industry for new educational opportunities to help industry upskill the workforce they have, funding for research, and a commercialization pathway for new technologies. However, innovation is happening at lightning speed. Companies can't realistically invest in every research sector that could impact their business. Focusing on the core internally and developing ties with external institutions working on new innovations is an approach that leverages resources and can deliver broad value. As technology and new business ideas move from the university or research center to the marketplace, industry plays a key role as customers, funders, and partners to help start-ups grow and strengthen the greater economic region.

If your company is large or small or your academic organization is a community college, undergraduate, graduate, medical or non-profit institution, you have the ability to create strong, impactful, and mutually beneficial partnerships. The key to building strong collaborations is to not only understand the value proposition and impact opportunity, but also to align well on needs and deliverables. This book can help start, or refine, the process of building the engagement structure.

Several excellent professional organizations exist to expand knowledge in these areas as well as help you develop a professional network of people, in both industry and academia, who work in this space:

- University Industry Innovation Network (UIIN)
- University Industry Demonstration Partnership (UIDP)
- National Association of Corporate Relations Officers (NACRO)
- National Association of Colleges and Employers (NACE)
- University Professional and Continuing Education Association (UPCEAA)

- Association of University Technology Managers (AUTM)
- American Association of Engineering Education College and Industry Partnership Division (ASEE CIPD)

Industry and academia need each other more now than ever before. Times are changing rapidly. New technologies burst onto the scene and explode the status quo. The need for a skilled workforce that can adapt and move a company forward is increasingly essential. Connecting with research to envision entirely new markets and possibilities, as well as with the start-ups bringing the latest from research labs to the commercial marketplace, ushers in continued innovation and possibilities. Every economy can benefit from strong engagement partnerships for new technologies, preparing the next generation of workers and building strong economic centers. These collaborations are vital to a thriving economy and positive societal impact that can benefit people around the globe with helpful new products, new economic pathways through education and jobs, and flourishing innovation systems for better living and environmental impact.

This book examines the 10 steps to successful innovation engagement partnerships for both the industry and academic organizations in the *Periodic Table of Innovation Elements*. In short, they are as follows:

1. Understand the fundamentals.
2. Define your partnership strategy/frame ROI.
3. Know your stakeholders.
4. Map your connection points.
5. Understand possible paths of engagement.
6. Create your plan.
7. Build your team(s) for success.
8. Execute the plan.
9. Track your successes/learn from mistakes.
10. Innovate.

In this book, the 10 steps are divided into four parts:

- **PART 1** provides the necessary background to understand perspectives from different institutions and includes step 1 to understand the fundamentals.
- **PART 2** examines the key factors to help you frame your engagement including steps 2–5.
- **PART 3** helps scope a vision and a roadmap for creating your own innovation engagement partnership framework and includes steps 6–10.
- **PART 4** is the toolkit. It includes materials I have developed over the years building different engagement partnerships. The worksheets and checklists are to help you in planning. There are also tip sheets on best practices and lessons learned to help you in building and establishing an impactful innovation engagement partnership.

Together we can build thriving ecosystems that move revolutionary breakthroughs, and skilled talent, out of labs and into the commercial marketplace for impact and economic growth.

Focus Features

Additionally, there are focus features and case studies from industry, academia, and others on different forms of engagement partnerships in practice. There are also interviews with people who are at the heart of some of the most important features of successful innovation collaborations.

Side Note

This book focuses mainly on the building of engagement programs through a US-focused lens. It does not, however, address the role that the US government and its agencies have in assisting industry-academic partnerships. There are other forms of partnerships and engagements that include various models where government can be a successful component such as the National Science Foundation's Industry-University Cooperative Research Centers (IUCRCs), but that topic is beyond the scope of this book. Additionally, with a US focus, the book does not address models that may exist in other countries that have different rules on funding and intellectual property, etc.

In this book, "CSAIL" refers to the Massachusetts' Institute of Technology's Computer Science and Artificial Intelligence Lab. It is mentioned frequently in examples.

Part 1

Step 1: Understand the Fundamentals

Why Partner?

Today competition is extreme. The need for new innovative technologies, top talent, and novel disruptive processes all contribute to a rapidly evolving economic landscape. The intersection of industrial and academic sectors (which include nonprofits, research organizations, business trade groups, workforce development organizations, etc.) has emerged as a critical nexus for fostering innovation and driving economic development.

Increasingly the organizations in the ecosystem, that *periodic table of innovation elements*, all play a vital role in the *innovation supply chain*.

The Concept of the Innovation Supply Chain

All of the organizations identified in the *periodic table of innovation elements* are critical to manifesting ideas and bringing them to commercial impact. As traditional supply chains start with raw materials, the innovation supply chain starts with ideas. Groundbreaking ideas often come from America's colleges and universities. "America's innovative and entrepreneurial culture is often regarded as one of this country's greatest national advantages in an increasingly competitive world. This innovation infrastructure includes a large number of universities and colleges, research institutions, laboratories, and start-up companies all across the United States – from major cities to rural areas."[1] See Figure 1.1.

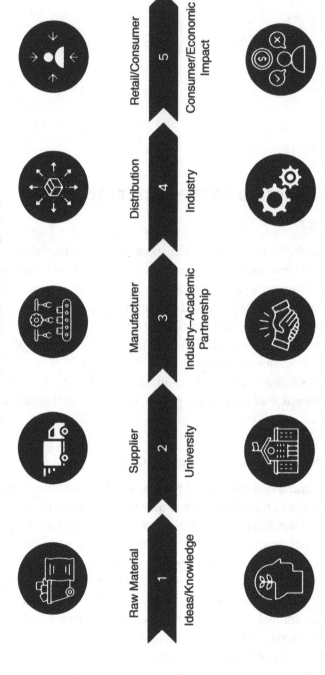

Figure 1.1 The innovation supply chain as compared to a traditional supply chain

The role universities play in igniting innovation is well established. Probably one of the first examples of innovation from university labs having direct commercial impact is the story of Vitamin-D milk. In 1919, Professor Harry Steenbock from the University of Wisconsin – Madison conducted research in his lab, which led to Vitamin-D – fortified milk. That product helped benefit millions of people, and the patents from that discovery generated approximately $14 million before they expired.[2]

In 1965, the University of Florida's football coach, Dewayne Douglas, was troubled by his players experiencing difficulty in the Florida heat and approached the university's researchers for help to replace body fluids lost by physical exertion. The result: Gatorade, a drink aptly named for the mascot of the football team it helped. Gatorade generated $6.7 billion in sales in 2023.[3] And in 1980, the federal government enacted Bayh–Dole, also known as the Patent and Trademark Act Amendments, enabling universities to retain the ownership of inventions funded by federal research dollars. This was the catalyst that really established universities and research centers as the source of the raw material for the *innovation supply chain*. However, as Harvard researchers Maria Roche and Justine Boudou wrote in their July 2024 study,

> *Academic institutions incubate novel ideas and are important innovation partners for companies, but getting products out of universities and onto the market can be challenging.*[4]

Moving from the labs to the commercial market is very important. Even former President Barack Obama made reference to this in his comments on November 17, 2010:

> *The key to our success . . . will be to compete by developing new products, by generating new industries, by maintaining our role as the world's engine of scientific discovery and technological innovation. It's absolutely essential to our future.*[5]

The commercial benefits are well documented. A 2019 report from Venture Well finds:

> *The benefits for companies continue to stack up, including access to a network of faculty, key opinion leaders, and lead scientists, and the ability to team up with other companies interested in the same research. University-industry partnerships provide excellent opportunities to expose students to industry culture, so when students graduate, they are better prepared to start working at these companies.*[6]

Universally, everyone agrees the end product is desired. Bright creative minds, technologies with never before seen capabilities, and disruptive new start-ups that ignite whole new industries for growth are all goals we want realized today. But how does it all start? What fuels it? How can all the players in the ecosystem benefit? How can these partnerships be built for success and sustainability?

Groundwork for Success: Exploring Possibilities, Understanding Constraints

Most innovation engagement partnerships are anchored by a college or university, and the ecosystem that develops involves start-ups, companies, related nonprofits, accelerators, venture capitalists, and more to turn ideas into economic impact. One of the first fundamentals to recognize in exploring engagement partnerships is that the academic sector and the industry sector are structured very differently. Companies are generally for profit, focused on delivering value to shareholders, meeting financial targets, creating products/services customers need, and staying ahead of the competition. The academic sector, on the other hand, is generally nonprofit, focused on education and research, having a positive community impact, with their "product" being new ideas/knowledge. The two potential partners come with very different perspectives. Understanding how those perspectives frame that sector's approach to engagement partnerships can help strengthen the foundation upon which the partnership will be built.

Most organizations seek partners based on their needs. There are many reasons behind why an organization would seek to partner. Some are obvious, and others more nuanced. Motivations may include: acquiring new technologies/capabilities, leveraging the other's expertise, acquiring new customers, bringing a new value to your organization and/or your customers, reducing costs, building/expanding brand awareness, uncovering new opportunities, accelerating innovation, or offsetting research and development costs, among others. Recent examples of successful partnership models involving companies, as well as universities, include the following:

Industry/Industry: Co-branding for clear market alignment with Go-Pro and Red Bull

A great example of co-branding for market alignment is the partnership of two powerful brands in the "adrenaline" space: Go-Pro and Red Bull. They are popular brands, and each brand evokes action, adventure, and excitement. Their partnership leverages their complementary customer bases and expands their respective market reach, not to mention solidifying their brands' recognition as synonymous with an "adventure lifestyle."

Academia/Academia: Cross-registration for courses with MIT, Harvard, Wellesley, and MassArt

Full-time students at Massachusetts Institute of Technology (MIT) may cross-register for classes at Harvard University, Wellesley College, and the Massachusetts College of Art and Design (MassArt). Students from those colleges and universities may also cross-register at MIT. Cross-registration is available among the schools for full-time students in the spring and fall semesters. This enables the students to take classes of interest that may not be offered at their home institution, thus forwarding the academic mission of education and expanding reach. This partnership enables each of the participating institutions to offer a broader range of options to its students than any one institution could do alone.

Industry/Academia: The Procter & Gamble Company (P&G) and the University of Cincinnati (UC) simulation center

P&G funds a simulation center at the University of Cincinnati. Both parties have a staff person responsible for coordinating projects at the center. All projects are from P&G and involve UC students and faculty in research. The center was founded in 2008 and is an example of a long-term strategic engagement. P&G has had many industrial problems solved, new technologies created, and hired students who can hit the ground running. UC has had interesting research projects, published leading papers in the discipline, and received the funding to make this type of commitment possible. The partnership's successes are marked by the collaboration's continued growth.[7]

Successful partnerships, such as those described, are not merely transactional. All of these examples are built for long-term success. They address a specific shared goal and leverage multiple connection points for win-win collaborations. As Harvard's Rosabeth Moss Kanter has stated, "In the global economy, a well-developed ability to create and sustain fruitful collaborations gives companies a significant competitive leg up."[8] It helps universities too!

Successful partnerships are strategically designed. One of the main reasons engagement partnerships fail in fueling the *innovation supply chain* is because of inconsistent approaches and misaligned vision. There is a company (not to be named) that has been the poster child of inconsistency and a perfect example, from my experience at CSAIL, of what not to do.

Case Study: What NOT to Do

Company X declares they want to enter into a research partnership. The company joins a research initiative, is very active, and even sends an employee to be embedded in a lab and conduct research side-by-side with university researchers. This goes on for more than two years. Close relationships are built. Shared knowledge helps advance not only the research but also the company's framing of the problem. There is mutual respect and appreciation.

Then Company X has a reorganization. The embedded researcher leaves. Communication with the company is disrupted because no one was appointed to be the liaison to continue collaborations. Another year passes, and then Company X terminates the relationship as "no longer achieving value."

Two years later a new department at Company X decides to engage broadly with the lab through a different program. This program connects Company X to research highlights, students, conferences, professional education, and start-ups. This time Company X is focused on start-ups. They are very engaged in start-up connections over the next two years. Then there is another management shift, a new direction, and another break in connections.

Four more years go by and Company X attempts to engage again, this time with research, start-ups, and talent as goals. Much has been lost due to the erratic nature of Company X's engagement. In the intervening years, relationships have fallen apart, and people who had positive work experiences on the research projects have moved on. Company X has no ongoing presence, so students and start-ups are not familiar with them. By being transactional, they have lost out on the good momentum that was built, including the goodwill that would have been there from students and start-ups, but most importantly they did not see the fruits of the research turn into successful applications that addressed the challenge. The path to commercialize the research, hire the students skilled in addressing the problem, and fund/

(continued)

(continued)

partner/acquire the start-up that spun out was all lost to Company X. And without Company X engaged in the lab, students lost the real-world perspective on the value of the work they were doing, other sources of funding were required to complete the work, and trust/goodwill suffered.

This does not mean every engagement partnership has to last 30 years with unlimited funding. But to do this successfully, it should be well thought out from the beginning to ensure consistency and a shared understanding of what success should look like for both sides. This is the basic blueprint for a one-year engagement or a 30-year engagement. The *periodic table of innovation elements* represents the various types of organizations in the ecosystem and is not only inhabited by companies and universities. There are a variety of other neighbors: nonprofits, nongovernmental organizations (NGOs), incubators, accelerators, maker spaces, innovation centers, venture capital firms, local community business organizations that partner on jobs/job training, etc. Everyone in that ecosystem is looking for partners to address their needs that they can't satisfy with internal resources alone. Despite differences in structure, form, mission, and function, everyone in the ecosystem wants the same thing: growth. Understanding how to leverage what you have to get what you need is fundamental to building strong partnerships that get all connected parties to the overarching goal. The cooperation of the different organizations in the ecosystem fuels growth, which is critical for the economic development of the respective regions engaged and the smooth operation of the *innovation supply chain*.

Recently, research from BPI Network stated that "Alliances for new ideas, insights and innovation" are sought by 44% of businesses and 85% say alliances are "vital to growth."[9] *Harvard Business Review* notes "94% of tech industry executives consider innovation partnerships a necessary strategy."[10]

So, it's pretty clear engagement partnerships are desired. But how do we make them work? And work well?

In order to make an impact, you have to solve somebody's problem in the real world.
—Prof. Hari Balakrishnan, MIT

Culture

An organization's culture governs its behavior and it runs the entire spectrum. Some cultures are purpose driven, others value teamwork and support, some are fast paced and highly adaptive, others are fiercely competitive, some are authoritative, and others are entrepreneurial. Both industrial organizations and academic institutions bring value to the table, but the cultures they bring with them are often at odds.

On the academic side, organizations tend to have very independent units. Faculty can set their own agendas, consensus building is valued, and there is generally a culture of openness. Universities train the students that become the next generation of employees and company leaders, create new technologies that are integrated into new products, conduct fundamental research that is the genesis of entirely new fields and capabilities, and spin out start-ups that take research to reality. Independence enables creativity; faculty acquire tenure and with that career security at their institution. Publication of research results is not just encouraged, it's required. The success of the students reflects on the faculty and the institution. The overarching mission is societal improvement through education, research, and positive economic impact.

On the industry side, the culture is usually aligned with the vision of the CEO and board of directors (if the organization has one). Companies need to stay competitive and need to make a profit to stay in business. Rarely would a company undertake an endeavor for exploration or curiosity. Its expenditure of funding and people needs to help it achieve its goals.

However, industry has employment opportunities for university students, offers a commercialization path for newly developed technologies, aligns well as a partner in research, and is both a customer and funder of exciting new start-ups. Culturally, the CEO sets the strategic vision, and the workforce is more fluid. According to the

October 2024 report from the Bureau of Labor statistics, the average time a person stays at a job in 2024 is 3.9 years.[11] It is important to recognize cultural differences and how they can impact the intersection of an engagement partnership. Some of the biggest challenges are rooted in the opposing cultures of the two communities. For example, companies have to try to get an edge on their competition, be the first to market, or own the intellectual property on a product to keep market advantage. The academic/research community, on the other hand, is open with the mission to share knowledge and discovery. In academia the governing mindset is "publish or perish" with the sharing of knowledge fundamental to the overarching mission. And intellectual property is a whole different animal (more about that in a later chapter).

This cultural divide can derail a research engagement partnership if the two sides cannot come to an understanding over the right to publish findings. In many cases, there are ways for industry's need to protect confidential information and academia's need to share results to both be satisfied. In some cases, however, the culture clash cannot be overcome. Conversely, there are other intersection points where cultures and needs align well, such as recruiting or capstone projects. Culture has nuances, and where an engagement partnership is considered as a whole, not a transactional one-off, beneficial alignments can be identified and leveraged.

Motivation and reward metrics are also very different between industry and academia. In industry, people advance their careers in taking on new responsibilities, developing expertise, leading new product development, etc. In academia, faculty could spend their entire career becoming an expert in a specific area and advance their careers through publication, training students, sharing expertise, etc. Securing patents or commercializing technology is not generally how faculty are evaluated for tenure or other career promotions. And to my knowledge, very few universities weigh industry engagement into any faculty career evaluations. Understanding these core motivational factors affecting the people building the engagement partnerships is significant and fundamentally necessary to form win-win engagements.

At the heart of any partnership, after all, are people. In general, most people pay attention to things that are important to them because of duty, reward, joy, etc. People involved in building and maintaining engagement partnerships need to understand the metrics applied as well. I was at a conference recently where an industry leader was hosting a session and he posed a question to the audience about how to engage faculty effectively. Participants from both academia and industry offered ideas on different programs of engagement (i.e., faculty grant programs, industry sabbaticals, etc.) Then one person raised their hand and asked how to engage faculty, not the programs but how to get them interested in collaboration. This question goes to the heart of metrics and motivation. Some faculty are very entrepreneurial and enjoy working with industry (there is a section on that later), but others are not sure how or why to engage industry.

A key factor in this issue is how faculty are measured for their careers. They have academic careers first and foremost. They are measured on their contributions to their field, papers accepted at conferences and published in leading journals, the students they teach and advise, the courses they design, and the books they write. These are factors that help with tenure, promotion, and advancement in academic careers.

Industry partnerships and start-ups generally do not count toward tenure or any measure of commendation at their institutions. It's unfortunate! If a faculty member is early in their career, they are focused on the steps they need to take to get tenure. Their mentors are coaching them on the pursuit of tenure, not industry connections. At a strategic level, there is value placed on industry engagement partnerships from universities as a whole. Industry partnerships are widely recognized as a necessity for innovation commercialization and as a key economic driver, but the academic reward system is not well aligned.

In industry, some leading companies put a great deal of thought into how they approach academic relationships and have key people and departments to carry out the vision for engagement. Alternatively, in other situations, the management of the engagement partnership is given to someone who was not involved in creating it, doesn't know what the strategic value is, and has a full-time job doing something else. If your company is in the first category, you are in good shape. If you are in the second category, your reward system is not as well-aligned. If you are investing time, money, and effort into creating an engagement partnership, make sure it is someone's job to manage it and its success is part of their reward metrics. In Part 4, there is a "Readiness Quiz," which can help companies, non-profits, research centers, academic organizations, and others thinking about starting an innovation engagement partnership get a handle on where they are in terms of readiness and what they may need to do to get the proper foundations in place. The quiz is online at www.innovationalchemy.net and can be accessed by the code in Part 4. By answering each question on a scale of 1–5, your "readiness" level to launch, or revise, your own innovation engagement partnership can be determined. The test also refers you to specific areas of the book and tools in the toolkit that can be helpful.

In my experience building CSAIL Alliances at MIT, one factor I weighed carefully was faculty time. Within the first few weeks of starting my role, the multiple pulls on faculty time became very apparent. I needed faculty to engage with industry partners, but I also needed them to do the research that attracted industry in the first place. It became clear I needed to develop a program that would make the best use of faculty time *and* resonate with the companies looking to engage the lab. It took some time, but in CSAIL Alliances, we created a process that works for both the faculty and the companies. We align the factors for success. Faculty want to meet with organizations that have synergy with their research. Companies want to meet the faculty working on the latest advances in areas applicable to their interests and connect with the students in their group for future talent.

However, time is something no one ever has enough of, and this can hamper partnership development. Faculty may not be familiar with the company looking to engage and may not have the time to research potential alignment. For companies, time is equally important. Instead of investing hours searching websites and reading papers to determine which faculty member may work in the area of interest, or emailing into a black hole with the hope of a response, CSAIL Alliances was built to deliver efficient results for both and save time.

At CSAIL we have more than 130 faculty researchers and multiple researchers in any given discipline. It takes time to determine where the matches could be, and the Alliances team knows what area each faculty member works in, what their current projects are, whether they are able to take on new work or are on sabbatical, the best timing to start a project, and the recent papers that align with the challenge area. Alliances is also well versed in industry trends and needs, proactively producing industry alignment reports that map to research going on in the lab. Leveraging Alliances helps both faculty and companies save time and reach connection points faster. Alliances is one example of an engagement partnership and how such a program can deliver value (more on CSAIL Alliances in Part 4).

If the cultures are so diametrically opposite at the core, how can they ever partner? Answering this and identifying the key bridges to partnership is crucial. Understanding of, and respect for, the cultural differences is key to getting any collaboration off on the right foot. As my colleague MIT Prof. Hari Balakrishnan sums it up, the academic community has "a set of tools, techniques, and expertise" and looks to industry to share your problems. Together we can do great things!

But, to get it right, it's important to set appropriate expectations. Some of the cultural issues have been highlighted, but other factors in how organizations operate such as sharing culture, speed/time horizons, and return on investment (ROI) metrics should also be examined in more detail. Before we move on, another example of culture is the organization's calendar. There are several types of calendars: academic operational, corporate fiscal, yearly, academic fiscal, etc. Setting expectations around something as simple as the calendar is important for alignment.

For example, in universities, colleges, and the nonprofits affiliated with them, the summer is generally not a very active period. Faculty are on nine-month contracts with unpaid summers, so often, those months are when they do research, create start-ups, or write books. In many universities faculty are often not on campus, though this is not the case with independent research labs and some medical schools with faculty on 10-, 11-, or even 12-month contracts. Similarly, students often do internships in the summer. Starting a collaborative project in June is likely to be very frustrating to industry partners as things will not generally progress until everyone is back for the new academic year. Summer, however, could be a great time to partner for pipeline programs for talent. Summer "academies" that align with a company's core business draw graduate, undergraduate, and even high school students.

For industry, the calendar they work with is equally important in establishing alignment. It may take months for academic and industry counterparts to build a relationship and identify a topic for collaboration. Then getting the contracts in place with the respective legal departments can take several more weeks. If the calendar slips away during this time, the funds that were budgeted for the project at the beginning may no longer be available. Similarly, if at the end of the fiscal period an engagement partnership is established, implementation may be delayed if funding was not allocated in the current operational budget. Everything is about alignment.

Sharing

Sharing is hard. Sharing is at the very root of the cultural differences between the industry and academic sectors. Academia wants everything to be open, freely available, and published, but industry generally does not. Industry needs to secure competitiveness.

For faculty to advance their careers, they must publish in top academic journals. When research is published, it is shared with the research community, which includes universities, research centers, and industry researchers. One of the challenges in research-based engagement partnerships is negotiating publishing for industry-sponsored research projects.

For many academic institutions, refusal to allow publication is a nonstarter. At the core, universities must support the free exchange of ideas among faculty and students. If it is valuable, research will need to be published and shared with the larger community. Any constraint on publication can be seen as a threat to the academic researcher's independence and put the project and/or project data in question.

When negotiating publication, it's important to understand that as much as a research university wants to share the work, they also do not want to put the industry sponsor in a detrimental situation. If they did, would any industry sponsor work with a university? Not likely. If industry did not sponsor research, it would not only negatively impact the research and learning at that university (and likely the greater field) but also harm the *innovation supply chain*. Publication is a balance. Industry proprietary information should be protected, but the research must be shared with the broader community.

What about companies practicing "open innovation"? In a podcast with Nokia, the founder of the concept, Henry Chesbrough, stated that open innovation ". . . means that organizations that used to do everything from the laboratory to the market, inside their own four walls, are instead doing things much more openly and collaboratively along that journey. And that has two primary flows. One from the outside in; from the outside to our own innovation process and markets. And then the second set of flows from the inside out; from our internal technology and research to other pathways to market. So those are the two main flows of open innovation. Outside in, inside out."[12] But a company subscribing to the open innovation philosophy does not mean it has no interest in intellectual property or is willing to put its trade secrets on display for the world to see. Publication can still be a sticky point even for companies practicing open innovation. Why? Because for many companies it makes sense in some areas but not necessarily all areas. In the interview with Nokia, Chesbrough uses Tesla as an example. Tesla has announced it will provide its patents to others who want to use its charging stations, but it will keep its battery technology research buttoned up. Open sometimes, closed others.

Another area where open sharing is prevalent is in the open-source code community. The academic community contributes substantially to the open-source movement. According to Wikipedia,

"The open-source-software movement is a social movement that supports the use of open-source licenses for some or all software, as part of the broader notion of open collaboration. The open-source movement was started to spread the concept/idea of open-source software. . . . The term *open-source* requires that no one can discriminate against a group in not sharing the edited code or hinder others from editing their already-edited work. This approach to software development allows anyone to obtain and modify open-source code."[13]

In the open-source community, there are two main types of licenses: **copyleft** and **permissive**. The exact license under which the open-source code is granted is important. Mendio.io gives a very straightforward explanation of the difference:

A copyleft license makes a claim on the copyright of the work and issues a statement that other people have the right to use, modify, and share the work as long as the reciprocity of the obligation is maintained. In short, if they are using a component with this kind of open-source license, then they too must make their code open for use by others as well. Whether this applies to all of their code or just the modifications they've made to the licensed code depends on the license (ex. GNU General Public License [GNU GPL]).

A permissive open-source license is a non-copyleft open-source license that guarantees the freedom to use, modify, and redistribute, while also permitting proprietary derivative works. Permissive licenses place minimal restrictions on how others can use open-source components. This type of license allows varying degrees of freedom to use, modify, and redistribute open-source code, permitting its use in proprietary derivative works, and requiring nearly nothing in return with regard to obligations moving forward.[14]

There are now more than 80 types of permissive licenses (see Figure 1.2). Some of the most common are Berkeley Software

Distribution License (BSD), MIT license (Massachusetts Institute of Technology), Apache License 2.0, and Internet Systems Consortium (ISC) License. The Apache 2.0 license and the MIT License together make up over 50% of the open-source licenses currently in use.

Sharing code was actually the norm in the early days of computers in the 1950s and 1960s. However, as the computer software industry grew, more and more proprietary programs were developed and commercialized. Many open-source projects have actually become commercial enterprises and are extremely valuable such as Linux (from Red Hat), Git (from GitHub), MySQL (from Oracle), and Hadoop (from Cloudera). Together these companies have a market value of approximately $23 billion – quite an economic impact for freely shared software.[15] At CSAIL, Alliances maintains a database of open-source code that is searchable by application, software used to write it, and license use it is granted under (mostly MIT open-source license). This can be valuable to companies that engage because though none of it is commercial grade off-the-shelf software, it can

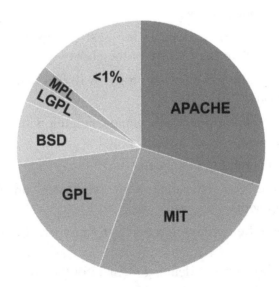

Figure 1.2 Representation of the respective shares of the open-source licenses currently in use

Part 1 Step 1: Understand the Fundamentals

often be spot-on in addressing a core problem a company is looking to solve, and leveraging open-source code can greatly reduce the effort and spend in building a solution but still enable the company to gain proprietary rights as they customize.

When evaluating a research connection point in an engagement partnership, it is important to consider not only what areas are appropriate for engagement, but the nuances of the engagement. Look for opportunities to find common ground. Sharing can be difficult, but it can also be beneficial.

Time Horizon and Speed

We know the cultures are very different in the commercial community versus the academic community. Consequently, in partnering, there are some key timing questions for the industry members of the ecosystem that will help define the best path for alignment:

- What are you looking for from an academic engagement?
- What is your timeline?
    - Something to be done in the next few months? Immediate impact or further out? All of the above?
    - A more applied research project with less than a year's time horizon?
    - Or something potentially game-changing with a longer time horizon of 5, 7, or even 10 years?
- Are you acquiring new talent?
- How are you educating your workforce on the newest developments?
- Will there be consulting services from experts in the field?

The time horizon is a defining element of the engagement. If the need is in the near term, outsourced engineering, engaging with start-ups, capstone projects, consultancy, training, etc., may be the first rung of the engagement ladder for that organization. There may also be longer-term needs and more strategic considerations, but step 1 can be to connect with the most immediate need. For any innovation engagement partnership to be win-win, it must be strategic, *not* transactional. In Part 4 there is a worksheet to help you think through how to structure engagement partnerships. Elements that are short term in nature may be with one institution, yet longer-term research may be with another. There are many factors to consider. All the needs of your company are not likely to be served by just one organization in the academic sector. Starting to build engagement partnerships should map out the possible pathways to connect and then evaluate which institution serves those needs best.

In addition to the time horizon of an engagement, the speed at which the engagement "delivers" is also a factor. For both industry and academic communities, clarity on the length and pace should be clear to set a solid foundation for the engagement. As for speed, academia will never be accused of being the rabbit in the race. Things move slowly in academia. The culture is all about building consensus and committees rule the day. Ideas need time to ripen. Launching a new program can take many months from idea to operation. For industry, speed and the goal of being first to market is often essential. Delivering a product before competitors is a market advantage. Industry is better at trying new things and "pilot" programs. In today's world, change is always increasing. In 2023 Bill Gates posted on his blog "Artificial intelligence is about to accelerate the rate of new discoveries at a pace we've never seen before."[16] And since Chat GPT came on the scene the advances in applications across all types of businesses and industry sectors has been amazing. Furthermore, quantum, nanoscale, and other technologies are just coming into play. They are still in their infancy, but progress is moving quickly. It is an optimal time to build engagement partnerships to understand capabilities, create use cases, and shape the direction needed for positive impact and economic success. Industry needs the research labs to advance these new technologies, and the academic community needs industry to commercialize them and make them available to people. But what are the best models to engage? Looking at time and speed, the following are a few examples.

Short Term

Let's examine some short-term (less than 1 year in duration) examples. Capstone projects in engineering, a case project in business school for MBA students, co-ops or even a project-based consultancy with a faculty member are good places to start. For talent, Northeastern University in Massachusetts engages with companies in cooperative learning experiences that alternate semesters between academic study and full-time work. These experiences enable students to work full-time for a company for a period of six months while still in school and on track to earn their degree. The connection point may be short term, but the engagement partnership as a whole is strategic.

Capstones are fairly common undergraduate requirements in engineering programs in the United States. For them to be most effective, industry partnership is needed. At MIT, our New Engineering Education Transformation program partners with industrial sponsors on senior capstone projects. In Focus Feature 1.1, my colleague Dr. Amitava "Babi" Mitra shares how the program has partnered with Aurora Flight Sciences, a division of Boeing that works on autonomous systems, propulsion technology, and manufacturing processes for valuable short-term capstone projects. There are many benefits reaped by both MIT and Aurora Flight Sciences, but there have been challenges too.

Focus Feature 1.1 Capstone Projects Success

How Aurora Flight Sciences and MIT's New Engineering Education Transformation (NEET) program are working together to develop and implement industry-oriented projects for cross-departmental teams of MIT seniors majoring in aeronautics and astronautics, electrical engineering and computer science, and mechanical engineering.

By Amitava "Babi" Mitra, PhD, founding executive director, New Engineering Education Transformation (NEET) and Gregory L. Long, PhD, lecturer and founding lead instructor, NEET Autonomous Machines, Massachusetts Institute of Technology.

Introduction

MIT's mission is "to advance knowledge and educate students in science, technology, and other areas of scholarship that will best serve the nation and the world in the twenty-first century." Universities and academic departments have evolved on timescales of decades to centuries amid various forces that have influenced their development, with departments historically being organized around educational disciplines. Yet, societal challenges, opportunities, and many modern technologies and systems are integrative and require close collaboration across a wide range of disciplines. Individual departments/disciplines (and even joint majors) inherently do not (and cannot, in a four-year undergraduate degree program) capture the full spectrum of expertise demanded by many of today's challenges or systems.

The New Engineering Education Transformation (NEET) program was launched in 2017 by MIT's School of Engineering with the goal of reimagining engineering education to "better prepare students to address critical societal challenges in the 21st century" and to "strengthen MIT's contribution to engineering education worldwide." Students join this three-year opt-in, opt-out program as sophomores, pursue the major of their choice, and earn a NEET certificate in the usual four years, in one of these four high-impact threads: autonomous machines, climate & sustainability systems, digital cities, and living machines.

Students are voting with their feet. NEET has grown from about 40 sophomore when it was launched as a pilot in 2017–2018 to a vibrant community of 227 sophomores, juniors, and seniors in the 2024–2025 academic year, making it MIT's fourth largest undergraduate academic cohort. The program has evolved into an academically and demographically diverse community of students who are pursing 31 majors from 16 departments across 4 schools. There are now over 175 NEET alumni across the world.

(continued)

(continued)

"NEET is about more than engineering" says Dr. Amitava "Babi" Mitra, founding executive director of NEET. "It's about nurturing the world's toughest challenges with heart and curiosity. Watching students thrive and grow and why this program matters so deeply."

The NEET Autonomous Machines Thread

NEET Autonomous Machines was launched as a pilot in 2017–2018. It is based on the well-known Conceiving, Designing, Implementing, Operating (CDIO) international initiative that offers an innovative educational framework for producing the next generation of engineers.[17]

Sophomores, juniors, and seniors in the NEET Autonomous Machines thread are exploring and learning how to apply autonomy and robotics technologies to addressing real-world problems such as monitoring air pollution, inspecting public infrastructure, and removing litter/debris from public areas and streets. Our students typically major in aeronautics and astronautics, mechanical engineering, electrical engineering, and computer science.

Gregory L. Long, lecturer and founding lead instructor of NEET Autonomous Machines, explains the student learning journey from sophomore to senior year. "Our sophomores begin the program with individual projects that help them develop basic robot design, computer programming, and mechanical fabrication skills. As they progress through their junior year, our students (working in small groups of 4–6) focus on projects that involve computer control algorithms, object recognition, and high-level decision making which require more time, knowledge, and resources. During their senior year, our students are expected to work on a multifaceted project from the ground up and make decisions that might be required in a small start-up company."

The Senior Capstone Project in NEET Autonomous Machines and Its Evolution

In their senior project, students develop a multifaceted autonomous/robotic system that solves a real-world problem with real-world applications. Beginning with student-inspired project ideas as well as project ideas offered by our industry partners, students select a specific class project where they work collectively as an engineering team. Through a complete process of conceiving, designing, and implementing, students learn how to synthesize previous studies/knowledge in autonomous systems/robotics to solve a meaningful problem in the field.

The 12-unit senior capstone project class is titled "16.84 Advanced Autonomous Robotic Systems." It was offered for the first time in spring 2020, and then again in spring 2021 and 2022. We learned from those experiences that NEET Autonomous Machines seniors wanted a challenging project that involved them in a constructive engineering activity that reached beyond their previous coursework.

Challenges Faced
Developing and implementing a project that focused on addressing a real-world problem had several challenges. Identifying a project that was both suitable and feasible within the given time frame of one semester proved the most challenging. Although the students had taken previous courses in robotics, they universally had gaps with implementing a project that required expertise in several fields in addition to the logistics of project management. Along with these project-specific challenges, the students, being seniors, were also preoccupied with satisfying graduation requirements in their majors, so the NEET project, although interesting, was not necessarily a top priority.

How NEET and Aurora Flight Sciences (a Boeing Company)
Are Working Together to Address the Challenges
Boeing is a founding co-sponsor of the NEET Autonomous Machines thread. The need to create and offer industry-relevant projects for students led to discussions between the MIT-NEET team and experts from Aurora Flight Sciences. Discussions started in early spring 2022, leading to collaboration in establishing the

(continued)

(continued)

redesigned 16.84 senior spring project class offered in spring 2023 for the first time. We understood from prior experience that seniors needed to be better prepared to start their capstone project on day one. To address the challenges identified, the 16.84 class offered in spring 2024 added a 3-unit seminar class in the fall prior to offer a set of focused activities and determine the autonomous system they would design. This included outlining materials, facilities, and resources needed to create the system. NEET worked with Aurora experts to propose five industry-related projects in the fall of 2023 that were suitable and feasible for our students to accomplish. This move was a good first step because it narrowed potential projects to the areas of expertise of course staff. Also, in our industry-related slate of proposed projects, we narrowed down issues with software and hardware to ensure the students had the resources to complete the project.

With these changes in the delivery of our senior project, during the first year of collaboration with Aurora, our students were able to work through all of their software and simulation issues. Unfortunately, however, hardware implementation issues were still present primarily due to logistic issues (the required components arrived late or when the students were away on break). During our second year of collaboration with Aurora, we made the acquisition of hardware a high priority by securing all the components throughout the previous fall semester. This additional move allowed our students to satisfactorily complete their stated project goals by the end of the spring semester.

As part of the program, Aurora experts participate in weekly design classes, facilitating group discussions, and giving demonstrations and guest lectures. Throughout our two-year collaboration, Aurora-led lessons have focused on developing requirements, selecting projects, setting up subteam structures, and learning project management skills.

Benefits for Aurora Flight Sciences

Dr. Jessica Edmonds, director of Applied Research at Aurora Flight Sciences, spearheaded the company's effort to get involved with the program. "Aurora was founded by an MIT graduate, and we have enjoyed a close collaboration with the university for many years," said Edmonds. "The NEET program is a great way to be involved with MIT. I'm excited to have this opportunity to work with the NEET students and give them the chance to work on a real-world aerospace application."

Dr. Luke Burks, AI/ML research scientist at Aurora, serves as a mentor for the MIT students in the NEET Autonomous Machines program. "Being a part of the NEET program has been a real growth experience for me. I love having the opportunity to help prepare these students for their transition out of academia and into industry," said Burks. "It's a bit humbling, and hopefully I can teach them a few things I wish I'd known before graduating. My favorite part of giving a lecture is hearing the questions I get at the end of it," said Burks. "Once the students start asking questions, you can see them engaging with the problem and trying to understand it for themselves. Sometimes they'll ask questions I haven't thought about or don't have the answer to. These are the best type of questions because I get to learn something, too."

Benefits to the NEET Program

Dr. Mitra notes the value derived from this collaboration:

- NEET graduates are valued by industry as they "job-ready." They spend their sophomore through senior years working collaboratively with students from different majors. Students in the NEET Autonomous Machines thread, for example, typically major in aeronautics and astronautics, electrical engineering and computer science, and mechanical engineering. They immerse themselves in a community that's passionate about exploring, learning, and applying autonomy and robotics.

(continued)

(continued)

- We've been fortunate to work with a terrific team of engineers at Aurora who are excited and passionate about what they do, and who enjoy igniting that passion in undergraduates. The Aurora team helps with project design, development, guidance, and mentorship. In turn, the students learn about the culture and programs at Aurora, which can help them determine if this is a career path they want to pursue. It's truly a win-win scenario.[18]

Dr. Amitava "Babi" Mitra is the founding executive director of New Engineering Education Transformation (NEET), Massachusetts Institute of Technology, a program that was launched in 2017 to reimagine and transform MIT's undergraduate engineering education. Prior to this he was the founding dean, School of Engineering & Technology, BLM Munjal University, India, where he launched "Joy of Engineering," a first-year hands-on course designed to get students engaged with engineering. Mitra was the senior vice president, Knowledge Solutions Business, NIIT Inc. Atlanta, Georgia, USA, and founding member of the Board of Governors of the Pan Himalayan Grassroots Development Foundation, Kumaon, India. He is regularly invited to deliver keynote addresses in conferences focusing on engineering education. Mitra has co-authored papers presented at the 2018 through 2024 annual conferences of the American Society for Engineering Education and is co-editor, special issue on Interdisciplinary Learning and Transforming Engineering Education, European Journal of Engineering Education (2025). Dr. Mitra earned a PhD in chemical engineering from BITS, Pilani, India, and conducted his research at the department of chemical engineering, MIT, under the guidance of Professor Adel F. Sarofim.

> Dr. Gregory Long is a lecturer and lead instructor of the NEET Autonomous Machines thread at MIT, where he currently teaches design, fabrication, control and programming of robotics devices and autonomous machines. Dr. Long has taught mechanical engineering design, mechanism design, dynamics and controls as well as a variety of mathematics courses for over three and half decades. Dr. Long received his doctoral degree in mechanical engineering and applied mechanics, with an emphasis in robot mechanics, from the University of Pennsylvania where he worked in the GRASP Laboratory with robot kinematics pioneers Richard Paul, Vijay Kumar, and J. Michael McCarthy. He has published research in robot mechanics and engineering education as well as a textbook entitled "The Fundamentals of Robot Mechanics."

■ ■ ■

The NEET/Aurora Flight Sciences example is a win-win-win. The company, the students, and the academic institution all benefit. This program is focused on undergraduate (sophomore through senior) students bringing four academic disciplines together in multidisciplinary teams and helping them to be as career ready as possible upon graduation. There are other models too.

For instance, at Texas A&M, capstone projects with industry are offered in 10 different disciplines. They are capstones that bring together teams of seniors to work projects sponsored by industry, government agencies, and others. The sponsor sets the requirements. The projects may take one or two semesters, depending on the major. Capstone deliverables can include conceptual designs, engineering analysis studies, hardware or software prototypes, and test data.[19] Companies that participate in capstone projects can benefit from new design concepts and prototypes. Texas A&M University offers several contractual options to accommodate industry needs for confidentiality, intellectual property, and deliverables.

Business schools also have industry-sponsored projects. Carnegie Mellon works with companies and nonprofits on capstones and projects. The value connection is simple: the company or nonprofit provides the business challenge, and the university provides the students to deliver "innovative and analytics-based insights."[20] In addition to deliverables, organizations that get involved also get connected to student talent.

Capstone and project sponsorship generally involves a fee and a time commitment on behalf of the sponsor. These programs often involve sponsors in guest lectures, student mentorship, and program design.

Longer Term

For research engagements, the term is typically 3–7 years and with strategic engagements often in the 10+ year range. Other examples with longer-term elements include those involving executive and professional development that can last for decades. Research collaborations with interdisciplinary centers can be very valuable in looking at longer-term engagements. The next model, shared by Christie Ko, executive director of the Digital Economy Lab @ Stanford, illustrates benefits and challenges of a broader scope of engagement (see Focus Feature 1.2).

Focus Feature 1.2 The Interdisciplinary Academic Center

Engagement with Interdisciplinary Centers

By Christie Ko, executive director of the Digital Economy Lab at Stanford

I begin with this caveat: my experience has been limited to two institutions: MIT, where I worked for 12 years, and Stanford, where

I've worked since 2020. I recognize my perspective is highly specific to these elite universities. Also, my views obviously do not reflect those of MIT, Stanford, or any of the groups with whom I am or have been affiliated.

When I was a college student, I thought of universities as the venerated keepers of knowledge and innovation – ivory towers where professors in tweed were pontificating about a newly unearthed manuscript or discovering a new behavior of a subatomic particle that would transform physics. But over the course of 16 years working in multidisciplinary research centers, I've realized the important other roles the universities play in the economy and society.

Universities are now expected to go beyond education, discovery, and innovation. We are called to share knowledge freely with diverse audiences, guide public discourse, and address the most pressing issues of our time. Our role includes creating engaging marketing materials, hosting professional-quality conferences, and producing content for a wide range of audiences including K-12 students, educators, policymakers, industry leaders, and retirees, to name a few. Our research must demonstrate global awareness and relevance, and we must respond swiftly to emerging developments. Leaders in government and industry frequently reference our reports, and our faculty are often invited to testify before Congress. In short, universities are a public good for more than teaching: they are an on-call service for unbiased expert opinions and knowledge, which must also buoy our society with the workforce, innovations, and entrepreneurs that uplift and drive our economy.

As the world looks to academia for knowledge and educated opinions on issues ranging from climate change to artificial intelligence, social media, policy, and economics, I've come to see that the traditional structures and processes of higher education

(continued)

(continued)

(publishing academic papers, tenure processes, and so on) are often strained and struggle to meet these immense expectations. One of the key ways universities are able to fulfill these expanding roles is through partnerships with industry. In fact, the groups I've worked with could not have accomplished a fraction of their work without these critical industry relationships.

While some universities receive significant public funding, my experience has primarily been with labs and centers that receive a large portion of their funding from the private sector. Industry funding (memberships, gifts, or sponsored research) supports faculty, students, staff, events, experiments, and every other aspect of our activity. Those gifts and grants from companies have some advantages over government funding, including the following:

- **Agility:** Where a National Science Foundation (NSF) proposal can take many months to come together, then many more months before funding is awarded, a corporate gift might happen in a matter of weeks, providing urgent funding for researchers who have a new opportunity or idea. (We, of course, continue to write for, and occasionally win, NSF grants, but we don't primarily rely upon them.)
- **Flexibility:** While there are many potential grant-making organizations, researchers are sometimes writing grants for calls that aren't a perfect fit for what they want to do or for their time frames and budgets. If you have a good match with an industry sponsor, they can support work that might not be in high demand from traditional grant-making organizations at the time.
- **Size:** In boom years, the private sector sometimes has an appetite to push the envelope and be ambitious with their academic support, encouraging big projects with large budgets that might otherwise have received only a series of smaller grants from different sources.

It should be noted that there are downsides to industry funding. In a down economy, industry memberships and support for universities often contract. Companies can experience workforce churn that can orphan projects and groups, and universities have to contend with public accusations of being "too connected to industry." All of these are rational concerns, but as I'll lay out in the paragraphs that follow, it is more than worth it to work with industry.

Perhaps more important than funding, industry partners also provide essential knowledge to the universities with whom they work. Early in my career, I worked for Dr. Ernest Moniz (who later became the United States Secretary of Energy 2013–2017) at the MIT Energy Initiative (MITEI); our mission there was (and remains) to transform the world's energy systems. Over many years working across a number of teams, I saw the amount of useful information that flowed in both directions. Companies brought forward the actual problems they faced, whether in engineering solar panels, formulating new concrete, testing new lubricants, or finding ways to capture carbon. Companies shared where the pain points were in their processes – knowledge that pointed to real opportunities for impact. Furthermore, MIT researchers were given feedback on ideas in real time with practitioners who understood how a technology could be applied in certain settings. All of this equates to keeping the university research relevant by drawing from industry expertise, and accelerating research that is better positioned for successful applications.

When I moved from MITEI to the Sloan School of Management's MIT Initiative on the Digital Economy (IDE), I worked directly with senior leaders from financial services, insurance, pharmaceuticals, retail, and other sectors to better understand how digital technologies were changing business and the economy. Instead of seeing mostly engineering challenges, I saw the same phenomena, but with questions around organizational behavior, economics, business models, and digital platforms. Senior leaders would explain the challenges they face trying to transform their businesses for the digital age, helping our researchers learn about adoption,

(continued)

(continued)

best practices, and culture that fed many academic projects and papers. Whether in management or engineering, one thing all of the researchers with whom I've worked have in common: they want to have an impact on the real world. The magic happens when researchers fully understand the problems that need to be solved. That can't happen without counterparts in business.

Relatedly, and perhaps of equal importance, is that industry partners can be an excellent source of data for academic research projects. Students and faculty are eager to gain access to new datasets to fuel projects. Proprietary datasets, while often cumbersome to tap, can be incredibly rich sources of information; information that benefits the public good while maintaining the privacy and security of everyone involved. For example, at the Stanford Digital Economy Lab, we work closely with Automatic Data Processing (ADP) on the jointly produced National Employment Report. This report draws from ADP data and the research team includes members from both our group and theirs, to analyze trends and produce monthly reports on wages and employment. Simultaneously, ADP data is also helping our researchers explore several academic projects on labor, skills, wages, and more broadly helping us to better understand how artificial intelligence (AI) is impacting employment.

For companies with an appetite for deeper engagements, we also partner with them to run experiments. Today, for example, many business leaders are trying to understand how and when to use generative AI within their firms. At the most basic level, they are looking for use cases. At a more advanced level, they are thinking about how to transform their whole enterprise. Between where we are today and where companies want to be in 5 years, there are a lot of unknowns and a huge need for good data. By working with us to run experiments within their firms, we can test and measure the productivity impacts of generative AI in the real world. This knowledge is crucial not just for business leaders, but for academics, policymakers, economists, etc. When companies partner with us, they get our help with their rollout, measurement, and analysis. And we get to share the results with the world.

Now we've touched on one of the key ways the industry can benefit from universities. And much of what I've mentioned as benefits to the university (save funding) flows the other way, too. Companies learn a great deal from universities. In the previous example of running an experiment rolling out generative AI within a firm, the company benefits from the expertise of academics who eat, sleep, and breathe generative AI and economics. In the experiment scoping process alone, the company gets a crash course on how to run experiments, the previous relevant literature on the topic, and a framework for how to think about the transformation of their workforce in relation to the latest AI tools. Additionally, our academic researchers are motivated not by a paycheck or contract renewal, but by the opportunity to generate the best peer-reviewed paper they can; to do that, they must be unwaveringly rigorous in their approach and analysis.

The relationships that are formed in this process (whether through a membership, sponsored research project, experiment, or otherwise) are themselves a core benefit to both parties and can be of special value to firms hoping to recruit talent out of universities. At the MIT Energy Initiative, I watched energy firms compete with big tech for the same engineering students. The energy firms who managed to recruit the really talented engineers had gone above and beyond the annual trip to the job fair. They were building relationships with departments and faculty on campus. They were seeding interesting projects with faculty that drew the attention of other respected academics and sharing useful datasets that brought more researchers to their doorstep. They were sending their technical leaders to engage with academics at regular intervals, providing frequent opportunities to be seen and heard on campuses and at research conferences. In short, recruiting top talent from elite universities is a contact sport, and one that requires a long-term,

(continued)

(continued)

pipeline mindset. Partnering with labs and centers on research and through memberships can provide the opportunities and programmatic scaffolding needed for successful talent acquisition.

Industry can also benefit from sending their talent into universities through partnerships. Many university programs, including several with whom I've worked, offer visiting scholar appointments to qualified industry representatives. These individuals set aside their professional obligations for a period of time to focus on the research their company is supporting with the university. These engagements can be fruitful for both parties; the visitor gets training and experience alongside our researchers and a profile-boosting affiliation, as well as opportunities to network with university faculty, staff, alumni, etc.; the university benefits from not only having a talented team member but also by having a direct relationship to a member of the firm who can help advocate for the projects, inform the researchers of useful information about the firm, and identify more opportunities to engage.

Not all firms have the bandwidth to let their star players take a year for this kind of engagement. But universities also form less intensive but equally valuable relationships with industry leaders. The Advisory Group for the Stanford Digital Economy Lab, for example, brings together key thinkers like James Manyika (Google), Sarah Friar (OpenAI), Reid Hoffman (Greylock Ventures), Dario Amodei (Anthropic), and many others for regular discussions about how AI is developing and what we should be focused on. Their guidance helps shape the research portfolio at the Lab, and we keep them informed of the latest developments coming out of our projects.

I've not touched upon what most firms probably expect to be the largest benefit to working with universities: IP. While this was a key ROI for many engineering firms with whom I've worked, having transitioned into economics and management science almost a decade ago now, the desire for the creation of IP comes across my desk less often. But I would be remiss not to note the incredible benefit in jointly owning or licensing IP out of universities. This is, no doubt, of significant value.

Finally, I'll remark upon something related to our research that will help frame the last benefit I'd like to highlight: the idea of scarcity in a world of digital abundance. The ability of anyone, now powered with AI and more compute than ever before, to produce massive quantities of instantaneous, highly customized information, is staggering. Everyone has an opinion. Everyone can be an influencer. In short, our digitally abundant world is noisy. And what's scarce are the trustworthy, knowledgeable, and credible voices. The voices that don't rush to judgment or bluster with opinions that aren't supported by data. Universities can and should be a source for credible, rigorous research that benefits all of society. Partnering with universities, companies demonstrate their commitment to the unbiased pursuit of knowledge – a shared value that is worth more than any immediate return on investment.

> Christie Ko is the executive director of the Stanford Digital Economy Lab (S-DEL). She works closely with Professor Brynjolfsson to lead the development of S-DEL's programs, activities, and events. Prior to joining S-DEL, she was the associate director for the MIT Initiative on the Digital Economy, where she managed corporate fundraising and stewardship and spearheaded events, communications, and oversaw the research portfolio. She was previously head of Member Services for the MIT Energy Initiative, where she worked closely with corporations, foundations, and individuals supporting research, symposia, events, and educational programs. Christie sits on the Advisory Boards for the Centre for Work-based Learning (University of Strathclyde) and the Centre for Relationship Marketing and Service Management (Hanken School of Economics). Christie received a BA in literature from Boston University and an MS in writing and cultural politics from the University of Edinburgh.

■ ■ ■

Part 1   Step 1: Understand the Fundamentals

Something in the Middle

Where a capstone or course project may involve a semester or two and can be completed within a year, multiyear broad-scoped endeavors such as Amazon's newly announced $25 million, 10-year partnership with the University of Washington, the University of Tsukuba, and NVIDIA focusing on AI research and workforce development[21] is at the longer multiyear range.

At CSAIL, we have created a consortium-like path of engagement. These are called *initiatives*. They are somewhere in the middle because they are meant to have a 3–5-year time commitment, not as short as a semester but not as long as an interdisciplinary research center. Technology changes so quickly, and initiatives are not designed to last 20 years. Initiatives at CSAIL are similar to a consortia model but with some key differences. Where CSAIL is at the cutting edge of computer science and artificial intelligence research and this is a core principle held at CSAIL, the engagement model needed to be responsive to make contributions to the field, address real problems, and share insights with our member companies.

Initiatives are created in partnership with industry and are very collaborative by design. They form around a theme when the research in the lab is at the point where it can deliver a positive impact to the industry members on current problems they face. They are research based and strive to invent innovative solutions for real problems for which there is no current commercial solution. Every industry member funds the initiative at the same amount and receives the same benefits as all the others. Initiatives are small groups of companies, usually between 8 and 12. Each industry member has a seat on the governing board along with the faculty director(s), the lab director, and me. We discuss the challenges faced by industry, the research that may address those challenges, and then, as a group, we create "problem statements." These problem statements are not that Company X needs a solution for Y but more fundamental challenges to problems facing a variety of industries represented by the member companies. The problem statements are sent to the whole lab, all 130+ researchers spanning 60 research groups and a wide variety of disciplines. Researchers whose work aligns with the challenges send in proposals (how the researcher would address the problem in a one-year time frame) to be considered for funding. The board, as a whole, receives all the proposals (usually 15–30 of them) and reviews them with their internal team. The company teams rank the proposals in terms of alignment for funding from the initiative. In reviewing all the proposals and how different faculty researchers from different disciplines would approach the problems, much can be learned regardless of which ones are selected for funding.

In the past decade of running these, the top two are usually unanimous. Then there are trade-offs. For industry, one benefit of this structure is that instead of one project, typically 5–10 are funded each year. And, if a proposal was not selected to be funded by the initiative, it can still be a collaboration between the researcher and the company sponsor under a traditional sponsored research agreement (SRA). This structure enables the industry members to address not only what is most important to them in the initiative but also explore some areas they may be curious about but could never justify funding a project in that area.

Additionally, the connection points are amplified through initiatives. Instead of a traditional research project with one faculty member, one research discipline perspective, and one research group's students, initiative members connect with 5–10 faculty researchers, multiple research disciplines addressing the problem, and students across 5–10 research groups.

Initiatives are a blend of tangible benefits, intangible benefits, and seeded research – so they don't fit squarely in one bucket. Initiatives seed research but include all the benefits of Alliances Affiliate such as conferences, workshops, assistance with recruiting, executive education discounts, and so much more. Seeding research in this type of structure is generally less costly than sponsored research and can be used to amplify a research vein. Seed projects such as these often provide the data researchers need to be successful in securing much larger government grants for further research. That expanded research is funded by the government and, under Bayh–Dole, encouraged to be commercialized by industry. Models such as Initiatives can be useful for leveraged benefit. In being part of an initiative, the member companies know the projects are addressing current challenges and they follow, in real time, the progress made in developing solutions, whereas companies that are not involved do not have this knowledge. Additionally, a research project may yield an exciting solution with potential as a start-up. Companies involved in initiatives can see the evolution of the new technology from genesis to application. Over a 3–5-year period, many benefits can be achieved.

Benefits for Industry

- Learning and information exchange from the proposals. Each team has access to all the proposals and ideas on how to address the problems. Even proposals that are not funded can yield valuable insights.
- The projects can be useful to industry members, and often the code is released to them under MIT open-source license in the initiative report.
- Talent is trained in areas of interest to that industry group and may be employed in the future.
- Exposure to not just one but 5–10 faculty researchers and the students in their groups. Funding research at a university is one of the most impactful things a company can do to build brand awareness and attract future talent.

Benefits for MIT

- Initiative projects have a much better chance of receiving funding because only the researchers in the lab reply to the call for proposals.
- It is easy to collaborate internally with researchers from other groups.
- Funding for truly novel ideas and approaches enable researchers to obtain data needed to apply for federal grants with

substantially more funding – and that enables the research to continue and industry does not have to fund it to benefit from it.

- It provides critical funding for students that enable research groups to "soften the peaks and valleys." Researchers secure government grants and bring on students but then grants get reduced, or canceled in some cases, yet the faculty has made a commitment to the student and has to fund that student. Initiatives help to keep the research going and soften the steep peaks and valleys of government funding for research groups.

Initiative-Funded Project: SCRAM

Secure Cyber Risk Aggregation and Management (SCRAM) was funded through our FinTech@CSAIL Initiative and continues to be an ongoing project. SCRAM brought together researchers in finance, cryptography, cybersecurity, and policy. The goal was to allow multiple entities to compute aggregate cyber-risk measures[22] without requiring any entity to disclose its own sensitive data on cyberattacks, penetrations, and losses. The project results from two computations in a pilot study with six large private-sector companies resulted in: (1) benchmarks of the adoption rates of 171 critical security measures and (2) identifying links between monetary losses from 49 security incidents and the specific subcontrol failures implicated in each incident. These results provide insight into problematic cyber-risk control areas that need additional scrutiny and/or investment, but in a completely anonymized and privacy-preserving way. For participating companies, they gained new information about the defensive failures that led to the largest monetary losses. These findings could help all firms direct their investments in cybersecurity to defenses that have the highest return.

Not every type of engagement is available at every institution in the academic sector. For a front row seat to the latest innovations and enabling positive economic growth in your region, being involved is not only important but can be consequential in economic impact. Alternatively, academic institutions may seek industry partners for different parts of their innovation engagement partnerships. In Part 4 there is a worksheet to help evaluate and align potential partners.

ROI and Metrics

The terms *ROI* and *metrics* are common in business terminology. Return on investment (ROI) is a key measurement of successful partnerships. But unlike standard commercial partnerships where Company X invests Y and yields Z, Innovation engagement partnerships often involve tangible and intangible elements. And investment can be in several forms: money, time, expertise, etc. The academic community also looks at ROI with industry engagement. Faculty are often a key component to an innovation engagement partnership with time and expertise being investment factors universities weigh when evaluating ROI with an industry partner. Where these partnerships cover many different areas, there can be different investment factors in each one. However, they all have two buckets in common: tangible benefits and intangible benefits. Virtually every element of an innovation engagement partnership can be placed into one of those buckets.

Tangible Bucket

If Company A has a discount code it can use for professional education programs, that savings can be directly tied to the code provided. If Company A then puts 50 employees through professional development programs at $2,800 each ($140,000 total face value) and uses its 20% off code, it is easy to demonstrate the $28,000 savings. It's real money. Instead of a bill for $140,000, the company has a bill for $112,000.

There are also very tangible benefits that can be measured that are not monetary such as talent acquisition. A company may engage a university, workforce development center, or professional association with the goal of hiring to support a new area or an expansion. If a specific path is designed to draw talent, the effectiveness of that path can be measured against its outcome. If Company B wants to hire undergraduate students, it may attend a college career fair as part of its engagement plan. The cost (time and money) of attending the career fair is measured against the results: Did they hire any good candidates who applied through that career fair? Since hiring costs and training costs are well studied, the company has a good idea if the investment in the activity yielded a positive ROI.

Intangible Bucket

This bucket is also valuable and can significantly impact the tangible bucket. However, it is hard to measure with concrete metrics. When we think of things like branding, visibility, and reputation we generally agree they are intangible and hard to quantify. The value of those factors is significant though. Take the tangible bucket example of the career fair. If Company B invests time and money to send recruiters to a career fair only to have few students show interest, that would not be a positive ROI. If the students are not aware of what Company B does (as well as its values and reputation), students may not seek out Company B at the career fair crowded with companies whose names and opportunities are familiar. It's a completely missed opportunity for the intangible bucket to align with the tangible bucket for positive ROI.

Innovation engagement partnerships provide both the corporate community and the academic community with tangible and intangible benefits. Some of the best intangible benefits are the connections, new thinking, shared knowledge, and exposure to different challenges and potential solutions discovered.

The exploratory engagement that seeds innovation is one of the most impactful yet hard to measure benefits. There is a story here I love to tell. I believe it is an amalgamation of a few stories woven together, but the message is important. The story goes that years ago a researcher at MIT's Media Lab had a problem to solve. His mother had to take multiple pills each day, but she was losing her eyesight and could not read the labels. Faced with this challenge, he went on to design a small, lightweight sensor that could be placed on the bottom of each pill bottle. The sensor had to be small and thin enough so it would fit on the bottom of the pill bottle without causing it to be unstable. He created the sensor and, so his mother could distinguish one bottle from another, he made it capable of recording a message. He had the sensor on each pill bottle play a different song: "ABC," "Twinkle Twinkle Little Star," etc. The sensors worked perfectly, and the problem was solved!

The researcher worked to solve a problem he was aware of, but when a company visited campus and saw the device, they immediately saw a new product that would distinguish them from competitors. Universities do not know the needs of every business, but when a company engages with a university, it is introduced to a variety of novel approaches and can identify game-changing innovations. The wisdom of Socrates underlies the intangible benefit here: "You don't know what you don't know." Being engaged at the university, being present in the labs, meeting faculty and students, guest speaking in classes, etc., all bring opportunities for positive intangible ROI.

One of the hardest things to do is track all the connection points that impact ROI. For both academia and industry, it's important to track and quantify, where you can, the efforts that impact ROI. I always refer to innovation engagement partnerships as a "handshake," not "hand up." These collaborations are not philanthropic in nature, though philanthropy may play a role in the overall plan. Successful innovation engagement partnerships are based on *mutual* benefits.

At MIT CSAIL, we use Engagement Reports as a tool to help keep track of the activity among the faculty, students, companies, startups, and affiliated MIT units we work with. It's not perfect, but we try to capture at least the activity in the larger areas of engagement. The document addresses both the tangible bucket items and the intangible bucket items. We look at activities that are of value to both the company and us as the university. The following are items that could be tracked in an industry engagement report:

Tangible	Intangible
Amount saved by discount codes used for savings in professional education	List of meetings, workshops, talks invited to or have access to
How many people used discount codes for professional courses or conference attendance	Early access to see research before it is commercialized
Amount saved by free or discount conference passes used	Opportunities for branding and visibility on campus/on-site
Number of students/people attending tech talk	Conversations with faculty on state of the art in various areas/thought leadership
Connections made to start-ups for partnerships or investment	Networking opportunities
Benefit from pilot testing	Open-source code connections
Leverage use of space for meetings, events, interviews, etc.	Posting jobs or internships
Appearance as conference speaker or workshop lead (not pay to play but a tangible benefit of being involved and connected through the innovation engagement partnership)	Connecting with students or organization members via guest lectures, tech talks, student clubs
Mentions in social media, website post traffic, news articles	Connecting with alumni

(continued)

(continued)

Tangible	Intangible
Career fair attendance and number of resumes received/interviews completed	Visibility with early-stage start-ups
New technology or insights from sponsored research	Newsletters and briefings with updates
Licensed technology that became part of a product or improved business processes	Opportunity to join working groups to explore challenges that align with research
Co-published papers in academic journals	Neutral convening capability
White papers produced	Reputational value increased as being involved in specific areas
Named centers, co-location, and development	Opportunity to join industry advisory boards
Leverage use of equipment	Opportunity to see variety of projects and scout innovations

These are just some of the many possible connection points that could make up an engagement report, which would provide a good overview of where and how the partners interact. At your company or academic institution there may be other connection points not mentioned above. You can customize your lists to reflect your specific programs and operations. A sample engagement report is included in the toolkit in Part 4.

> *What most academics want is to do something impactful.*
> —*Prof. Sam Madden, Dept Head*
> *MIT Computer Science*

Some companies have recognized the value of engagement partnerships for a long time. They connect with the innovation ecosystem in a variety of ways and with academic institutions, they are strategically aligned. A well thought out vision and execution of that plan is illustrated by Sony Interactive Entertainment (see Focus Feature 1.3).

Focus Feature 1.3 Industry Perspective on Long-Term Engagement for Impact

Sony Interactive Entertainment: Academic Engagement Case Study

By Sony Interactive Entertainment

Sony Interactive Entertainment (SIE) has a long-standing tradition of collaborating with academia globally to drive innovation across its product portfolio.

As a case study currently, there is a group within SIE that aims to revolutionize gaming experiences through bold innovation and technical creativity. To achieve this, the group has developed a 7–10-year strategy centered around three foundational research themes. This long-term vision enables the formation of enduring academic partnerships beyond traditional sponsored PhD models such as knowledge exchange placements, academic sabbaticals, research fellowships, sponsored labs, and shared ideation spaces. All have the aim of creating a win-win engagement model.

To deliver this effectively, the group employs academic development managers across three continents to develop unique research relationships with the academic community to co-create projects that will help accelerate the research themes. The following are the key features of these projects:

- **Acceleration:** Actively seeking collaborations with academic institutions can advance research in key technologies.

(continued)

(continued)

- **Long-term impact:** Developing technologies and products can have a lasting impact on the industry and society, aligning with SIE's long-term strategic goals.
- **Innovation and creativity:** Collaborating with academia brings fresh perspectives and innovative ideas, helping to push the boundaries of what's possible in technology and entertainment.
- **Access to cutting-edge research:** Academic institutions often lead in pioneering research. These partnerships provide SIE with early access to the latest advancements and breakthroughs.
- **Flexibility and adaptability:** Long-term partnerships allow for more dynamic and flexible collaboration models, enabling both parties to pivot and adapt to the rapidly changing technological landscape.
- **Enhanced problem-solving:** Combining the practical expertise of SIE Engineers with the theoretical knowledge of academic researchers can lead to more effective and innovative solutions to complex problems.
- **Research visibility:** Publication is a primary goal for universities and researchers; it also provides measurable outputs for SIE and is a motivator for all parties.

Furthermore, SIE aims to establish strategic partnerships with selected universities, which are characterized by the following:

- Multiple long-term collaborations across various disciplines
- Deeper relationships, greater trust, and more effective working dynamics
- Increased ability to shape research to SIE needs and pivot more quickly

By focusing on these key areas and establishing strategic partnerships, SIE are committed to driving innovation and achieving their long-term goals.

Research and Development

> *Research is creating new knowledge.*
> —Neil Armstrong, Astronaut Apollo 11,
> Aeronautical Engineer

According to the Carnegie classification of Institutions of Higher Education, there are approximately 266 research universities in the United States.[23] The Cap20 report of 2012 notes that the World Economic Forum classified the United States, in the twenty-first century, as an "innovation-driven economy." This means that "the creation of new wealth depends not just on traditional inputs like natural resources, land, or labor – or on increasing the efficiency of existing capabilities. Rather, new wealth in an innovation-driven economy requires the discovery and development of new ideas to solve old problems and the seizing of new opportunities with technology and ingenuity."[24]

Research is at the heart of innovation. It spurs new technologies, creates new companies, and helps expand the thinking and experiences of students. Universities are often leaders in research, both fundamental and applied. The classification framework developed by the Carnegie Commission on Higher Education in the early 1970s categorized colleges and universities as R1 and R2, "very high" and "high" research activity, respectively. The research universities grant PhDs. But research and innovation are not restricted to R1 and R2 institutions. Many universities and colleges have scholarship as part of their mission. Scholarship can take different forms aside from fundamental or applied research and instead include things such as literary authorship creating new knowledge, new analyses, or creative activity in the arts.

For many years, research was considered the domain of institutions of higher education, but industry has taken on more and more of the applied research activity. Each year, the top 2,500 or so international R&D spenders collectively invest more than $1 trillion in R&D.[25] Since the 1960s, federal government investment in research has declined and industry investment has grown. Figure 1.3 from the National Center for Science and Engineering Statistics illustrates the trend.

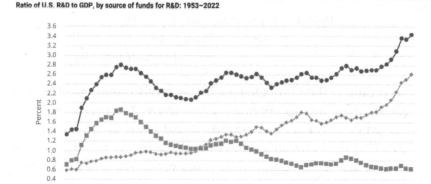

Figure 1.3 This chart from the National Center for Science and Engineering Statistics shows the ratio of U.S. R&D to the GDP by source of funds for R&D from 1953 to 2022.

Note: Some data for 2021 are preliminary and may later be revised. The data for 2022 include estimates and are likely to later be revised. The federally funded data represent the federal government as a funder of R&D by all performers; similarly the funded data cover the business sector as a funder of R&D by all performers. The "other" category includes the R&D funded by all other sources-mainly, by higher education, nonfederal government, and nonprofit organizations. The gross domestic product data used reflect the U.S. Bureau of Economic Analysis statistics of late October 2023.

Source: National Center for Science and Engineering Statistics/Public Domain.

Recently, Dr. Neil Thompson, who holds joint appointments in MIT CSAIL and MIT Sloan School of Management's Institute for the Digital Economy (IDE), dove into the connection between industry and academia specifically for innovations. According to his research, two-thirds of firms surveyed (320 firms with 500M+ revenue across 8 countries) sourced innovations from universities and in the last few years, while 9% of those firms had their single most successful innovation projects come from universities.[26]

However, as we discussed previously, commercial and academic timelines are often very different. Industry, often, seeks innovations to be available in 6–12 months. In some cases, research has progressed enough so that is a possibility, but in many cases, the availability of an innovation is years away.

Take the fax machine, for example. In 1959, former MIT student Shintaro "Sam" Asano was on the phone trying to explain a concept to a colleague across campus. Sam was frustrated that they couldn't just draw pictures and instantly send them to each other. Therefore, he created a technology to transmit scanned material through phone lines to solve the problem. His "facsimile machine" was licensed to a Japanese telecom company before becoming a worldwide phenomenon in the 1980s.

The equation is simple:

existing problem + research to solve problem = innovation

But innovation without the industry partner to scale the technology and bring it to market would not accomplish impact and economic growth. Both university research and industry commercialization are needed to bring innovations out of the lab to benefit people and the economy as a whole.

The Tiny Surgeon

There is another story of creative innovation I'd like to share. CSAIL is an interdisciplinary research lab with faculty researchers from many different departments across the institute. We have robots of all shapes and sizes. There are robots that fly, swim, sort objects, help humans with heavy tasks, and even humanoid robots that can drive a car and use power tools. So what happens when a mathematician focused on folding properties teams up with a roboticist? The mathematician's research is akin to origami in using folding to make things smaller and smaller. The roboticist recognizes this capability as an interesting application in her research. Together they create an origami ingestible robot, smaller than a fingernail, that folds up on itself, can be encapsulated in ice, swallowed, and perform stomach surgery or deliver a drug injection.

And it's made out of sausage casing, so it's easily eliminated through the digestive system when its tasks are complete (Prof. Daniela Rus and Prof. Eric Demaine). In this case, the problem was more general (avoiding invasive surgery), but it was research that led to an impactful solution that will benefit people's lives. The project is currently in trials, and we hope it will be able to be used in the coming years.

These examples are stories of innovations from research that can have a positive impact on the lives of people everywhere. But there remains a challenge in fueling research. Everyone wants the end product of research: the talented students, the new innovative technology, or the disruptive new start-up. But research takes funding. As shown in Figure 1.3, federal funding today is less than half of what it was in the 1960s. Industry has become a funding partner to advance research, but the speed of innovations over the past 10 years dwarfs the prior 50 years. Innovation engagement partnerships addressing research are a critical component to the innovation supply chain. Investing in research for innovation pays off in many ways that benefit industry, their customers, the public, and the greater economy! Not only are new technologies, inventions, approaches, and pioneering methods created, but students who work on those innovations are highly trained and poised to help the company when hired. Start-ups that spin out of a university setting test the prototypes and validate performance often providing industry with a shortcut to advancement. Research is the essential building block not just for technical and scientific disciplines but for business, medicine, financial models, psychology, social sciences, economics, and more.

Industry often funds university research through sponsored research agreements (SRAs). For universities, sponsored research involves a project that is "sponsored," or funded by a company. Typically, these agreements are between one company and one researcher and include the following:

- Specific scope of work
- Financial accountability and/or reporting (the funds must be separately budgeted and accounted for)

- Fixed time for performance on the project (usually three years but can range from one to five years)
- List of deliverables which can be code, a working prototype, a paper or report, etc.

Sponsored research is a very effective way for industry to partner with academia to explore the creation of a solution to an industry problem for which no commercial solution currently exists. And, unlike outsourced engineering, the problems are broader than just one product or enhancement.

There are also master agreements for sponsored research that can involve many researchers on different projects. The agreement sets out the terms for the engagement with the company but there can be several different statements of work (SOW) that are covered by the master agreement.

A Safer Ride

An example from CSAIL involves a sponsored research engagement with Toyota to create a car that will never be the cause of an accident. In 2015, Toyota created a joint research endeavor with MIT and Stanford to focus on computer science and human–machine interaction with the immediate goal of reducing highway injuries and fatalities.[27] The project's key program areas are collaboratively addressed by MIT and Stanford working with Toyota, both at their respective campuses and at the Toyota Research Institute (TRI) in California. Collectively, research is focused on improving the ability of "intelligent vehicle technologies to recognize objects around the vehicle in diverse environments, provide elevated judgment of surrounding conditions, and safely collaborate with vehicle occupants, other vehicles, and pedestrians."[28] MIT led on the robotics research, while Stanford took the lead on computer vision research. Researchers from the universities spent time working at TRI, and researchers from Toyota spent time at the universities. This was governed by a master research agreement that spelled out the terms, timing, projects, intellectual property rights, deliverables, and all the details of the collaboration. These agreements are drafted and managed through a university's Office of Sponsored Programs or similar department. They are a stakeholder in the innovation engagement partnership ecosystem (more on that in Part 3).

Another method of engagement for research and development is through centers specifically for outsourced engineering. For example, Rose-Hulman Institute of Technology in Indiana has "Rose-Hulman Ventures,"[29] which helps companies with professional projects including prototyping, software app development, and new product development. This center focuses on short-term deliverables to meet the engineering needs of companies. Students can work on the project, but there are also professional staff and faculty involved. This structure addresses a very specific component that is not necessarily a traditional offering of an academic institution. Universities have had to expand and many offer creative new ways to engage. Win-win successful innovation engagement partnerships involve several components, recognize multiple connection points, and are strategic not transactional. Understanding what is available to build your engagement partnership is just the start. In the toolkit in Part 4 there are worksheets to help frame a strategy.

Ultimately, no discussion involving research can be had without mentioning intellectual property (IP). Looking back at the culture differences, where industry tends to be protective of new discoveries and the academic community tends to be open with publishing, IP is definitely one of the most difficult factors in establishing innovation engagement partnerships. But it does not have to be. Looking deeper into the motivations that govern IP ownership can be helpful in crafting options to deal with IP in sponsored research agreements (SRAs).

Seeing Through Walls – The Rise of the Invisibles

To illustrate the root tension over IP ownership, I like to share the story of Prof. Dina Katabi's research. Back in 2011–2012, she was working on a system using wireless technology to provide extremely accurate indoor geolocation. Her group created what she called "WiTrack" technology. This technology used wireless signals 1,000× smaller than cell phone signals to ping off a person in an indoor space and then display where that person was located within that space accurately to within a few centimeters. This new technology worked through walls and without the person having to wear anything to pick up a signal! By 2013, this technology could do what she had set out to do: accurately locate and display the location of a person inside a building. Think of all the potential use cases from first responders to video games! This was 2013, before the massive acceleration in machine learning (ML) and artificial intelligence (AI). Consequently, in the following years, her lab worked to extract different types of data from the wireless signals such as heart rate and breathing rate at medical grade quality, without the attachment of any devices. Soon machine learning features were leveraged, and the project could measure gait and motion, enabling it to tell the difference between a person falling, consciously sitting, or walking with difficulty. Put all that together with the health vitals measurements and you have a very useful way to monitor health remotely without invasive video cameras or wearables that need to be attached to the person. For Prof. Katabi, the future is invisibles not wearables. In 2013, a company interested in accurate geolocation could obtain a license for that technology but not ownership of that IP. If IP ownership was transferred, the groundbreaking work leveraging ML and AI would likely not have happened. The accurate indoor geolocation work was background IP to the work done in later years, so if it had been given up, all the new technology, and the start-up Emerald, which helps elderly people stay in their homes, would likely never have come to be.

Universities don't create products to compete with companies and start-ups often perfect the prototyped technologies (thereby reducing risk for industry) before they partner with or are acquired by the larger companies. However, companies looking to sponsor research engagements may view the project as a means to acquire IP. Companies do not want competitors to be able to obtain the research insights, especially when that company is paying the university for the work. That is all very reasonable. Consequently, if the research yields valuable information, IP licensing is always on the table, and in most agreements, the university grants the company a nonexclusive royalty-free (NERF) license to use the work product for continued internal research. Where the university owns the IP and the company licenses it, both parties win: the company can leverage the new insights effectively, and the university can continue the research vein, often yielding even more interesting innovations that the company could come back to license in the future. No one knows what the future will bring. But university labs are on the cutting edge and enabling them to keep driving pioneering research keeps the innovation supply chain functioning well and furnishing industry with new innovations at limited risk to their own core operations. It's a perfect symbiotic relationship.

Now, I'd like to share one example of where IP and the concept of proprietary information stopped a collaboration cold before it could even start. A few years back, I had a series of positive discussions with leaders of a group in a large multinational company and had provided the group leaders with an agreement to join an initiative (the consortium-like model described earlier). There are several companies that join and many faculty who work on projects within the initiative. There is no specific scope of work for one company and no confidential or proprietary information gathered from any company to complete projects in the initiative. Additionally, the projects address several different areas under a common theme. Most project results are published in open source. The leaders of the business unit understood this model and were interested in becoming involved. However, their legal counsel could not wrap her head around an agreement where no one wanted their confidential information and the company would not receive IP for their investment. The attorney was clearly used to dealing with vendors and other partners where either one or both, confidential information or IP, was part of the deal. Where the initiative was neither contracted engineering to obtain IP nor a process-specific consultancy where confidential information would be necessary, she ended the discussions. The company had never done something like this and she was not about to let them start now. How sad for innovation! A company who had never engaged with a university for research insights and whose leaders saw the value was stopped because the engagement plan didn't fit the prescribed ways the company was used to partnering. *To be innovative, you cannot let processes prescribe pathways of collaboration.*

Managing Expectations

The negotiations for IP licensing are handled through a university's Technology Licensing Office (TLO), Technology Transfer Office (TTO), or similar department. In other academic or research organizations, the legal department may handle this similar to industry. The TLO/TTO also handles intellectual property for the inventors and are critical to the success of the start-ups being spun out of the institution. Most of these departments have a database of technology that is available for licensing as well. But universities are not the best at marketing, and many times it is hard for companies to discover what is available to license.

Innovations are happening in colleges, universities, and research labs all over the country. Connecting on revolutionary approaches to industry problems is vital for economic growth. We need to solve those problems, create new technology, generate novel discoveries, and launch new companies to stay competitive and keep the gears running in the innovation supply chain. If research is involved as part of an innovation engagement partnership, exploring entirely new ground can take a time. It's important to understand the timeline, deliverables, and costs, to manage expectations accordingly.

Universities are not usually focused on near-term research. Conversely, industry is often focused on time to market, being the first, making clear quick decisions, and moving at a much faster pace. If there is no discussion about expectations and agreement to a framework, any collaboration will be faced with frustration if not failure.

It is important to note that not all research results in a new innovation. Sometimes the answer is that the problem cannot be solved in that way. Other times, the problem at hand cannot be solved by the research undertaken, but an entirely different problem can. It's important to frame expectations and accept that sometimes research does not always yield a stunning result.

It has been said that industry focuses on today, industry research labs address tomorrow, and universities address the day after tomorrow.[30] Broadly, research can be viewed in that way, but it's not fixed silos. Research is new knowledge. It may focus on addressing a problem for which there is no current solution or it could be to push boundaries of understanding. Research engagement can be viewed as a broad spectrum ranging from the most theoretical to the most applied. Theory does not have immediate applicability, but it is so important because it is theory that tests the outer limits of what is possible. Take quantum computing, for instance. The first theory of what would become quantum mechanics was introduced by Max Planck in December 1900 when he presented his theoretical explanation involving quanta at a conference in Berlin, Germany. Despite having invented quantum theory, he did not understand it himself at first. Nevertheless, he received the Nobel Prize for Physics in 1918 for his achievement. Though he made the historic quantum announcement, he played only a minor part in the further development of quantum theory. This was left to Einstein, Poincaré, Bohr, Dirac, and others.[31] Now, in 2025, you could say we are in the race to "quantum reality." There are only a few quantum computers today, and they do not have the capacity, yet, to bring about revolutionary changes. However, research is moving quickly, and it all began with a theory that could explode computer security, blockchain, and other technologies we have come to rely on. There are theories today that could become the answer to new security protocols and platforms that could expand post-quantum applications. Theory is at one end of the spectrum.

At the other end is applied research. When researchers engage in applied research, it is solution based, focused on a specific problem and often readily actionable. Often examples of applied research can be found in business schools, the social sciences, and some technical disciplines. When charting an innovation engagement partnership, the scope of research at an institution and its alignment to needs, present and anticipated in the future, is important to the innovation economy and creating growth. Just because it may not be useful in the next three months does not mean research shouldn't be part of the overarching plan.

Additionally, it's important to understand the various paths, or structures, to enable the connections. As mentioned, models include traditional sponsored research that typically involves a specific faculty member or group of researchers, a clearly defined scope of work with specific deliverables, an agreed upon timetable, IP terms, publication terms, and other items specific to that engagement. There are also consortia models that tend to be precompetitive in nature focused on a topic that is important to all the industry members who join. In consortia, there is not a specific scope of work between any one faculty member and a company. Instead, consortia are governed by the consortia agreement. Related to research, and aligned with talent acquisition, are student sponsorships. If PhD students conduct research in a company's area of interest, that company may consider a student fellowship. Student fellowships are usually philanthropic in nature and support a student during their work on their PhD. These three examples (research, philanthropy, and other fees) are the main three buckets of funding between universities and industry partners. There is a difference in how these models operate. In the next section we'll take a look at the "color of money."

Color of Money

No, not the Martin Scorsese film. When it comes to strategically planning an innovation engagement partnership, understanding how funds are treated is important. The "color" of the funding to an academic or nonprofit institution brings different costs and benefits for each partner. In some cases, there could be tax benefits for a company; in other cases there are significant overhead charges for a university. The elements within an engagement partnership can each fall into one of three general categories: gifts, sponsored research, and other fees.

Gifts

Let's start with gifts. There is no specific benefit tied to giving a gift. There are no deliverables, no budget, and no reporting of how funds were used. And often, gifts are tax deductible as most academic institutions are nonprofit organizations (check with your tax advisor, of course). With gifts there is stewardship, or the relationship building that happens when a gift is made. Stewardship often involves meetings with the gift recipients, the donor being kept informed of the impact of the gift, and the progressively deeper relationship between the donor organization and the academic institution or nonprofit supported by the gift. A common example of a gift as part of an innovation engagement partnership with a university is a student fellowship. A student could be the recipient of funds to cover all or part of tuition. Some academic institutions allow for named fellowships, which has the added benefit of name recognition and branding within the university department for the company that sponsors the student. Gifts can also be a very important component in innovation engagement partnerships in terms of brand building, awareness, and unrestricted gift funds to help the research advance.

Another type of gifts are in-kind donations. In-kind gifts are win-win and very useful because they are usually needed and well branded by the donor. This form of gift is nonfinancial and can be either goods or services. Some examples, and their impact, include the following:

- Oregon State University received electrical testing and measurement equipment for its electrical engineering fundamentals teaching laboratory from Keysight Technologies. This enabled the college to adjust and expand its curriculum to take advantage of the capabilities of the new equipment.[32]
- Cleveland Metropolitan School District received 1,900 new computers donated by KeyBank as part of an initiative to support STEM education. The computers impact more than 4,000 students at three high schools and nine elementary schools.[33] K-12 is where the future begins. Enabling students to gain digital skills plants the seeds for tomorrow's workforce.

For other nonprofits, gifts can support operations, specific programming, purchase equipment, and so many other activities that are essential to their operations. Gifts can also be made to support faculty and research, but the arrangement for a gift in support of research is very different from sponsored research.

A gift letter is often the document used to record a gift. This document should never include things like IP terms, research product rights, or requirements a student commits to employment if a fellowship is accepted. Those terms go against the definition of a gift and are likely to cause issues.

Sponsored Research

On the opposite side of the spectrum, there is sponsored research. Mainly this category is an important consideration at R-1 or R-2 research universities[34] and research labs/centers in the academic community. For the purposes of this book, I will highlight individual-sponsored projects, sponsored research programs, and master research agreements with industry partners.

What makes a project sponsored research? A project is sponsored research if an external party provides funding for a research project that

- Has a specific scope of work. This is referred to as a statement of work (SOW) and is crafted by the sponsor and the faculty to be involved in the project. The SOW directly impacts the resources and budget of a sponsored research agreement.
- Sets out specific deliverables.
- Establishes a time table for when those deliverables are to be conveyed to the sponsor
- Includes a set budget.
- Requires an explanation of how funds were expended against that budget.

Generally these agreements will be negotiated by an organization's attorneys and, in the case of universities, staff from the university's sponsored research office and/or legal department will be involved. The agreement terms will likely also address the following:

- **Publication:** The importance of publishing research results cannot be stressed enough. For many research universities, any curtailing of publication is a nonstarter. Publication fuels innovation, and it can be done while protecting an industry sponsor's confidential information when required.

- **Intellectual property (IP):** This can be a thorny issue as previously mentioned. In many sponsored research agreements (SRAs), the university will retain IP but grant the sponsor a nonexclusive royalty-free license (NERF) for continued internal research. NERFs allow the sponsor to use intellectual property generated from the collaboration for research purposes without having to pay any royalties.

- **Specific deliverables:** The deliverables of a sponsored research agreement could be a paper, an analysis, a prototype, a proof of concept, code, etc. Research can be applied or fundamental in nature, but it is *not* outsourced engineering. It is broader than a quick solution that will apply to only one company's specific set of challenges (like enhancing a piece of software).

- **Time frame:** SRAs can cover any time frame but generally are three years in term. Research in novel areas takes time and PhD students do much of the work.

- **Confidential information/proprietary data:** This is a very important consideration. It should be spelled out in the agreement how the information will be shared, marked, stored, etc.

- **Export controls:** In the United States, any research agreement needs to be aware of export control laws. Two key regulations are Export Administration Regulations (EAR) under the Department of Commerce Bureau of Industry and Security (BIS) and International Traffic in Arms (ITAR) under the Department of State Directorate of Defense Trade Controls (DDTC). These laws are federal regulations that restrict the release of certain items, information, and software to foreign nationals in the United States and abroad. In a globally connected world, these are very important to know.

- **Funding amounts:** The amount of funding can vary depending on the scope and duration of a project. A single project may be $50,000 or $500,000. The scope, length, faculty involvement, student involvement, equipment needed, etc., are all taken into account to determine the cost.

The structure of the SRA can also take several different forms. It can be an agreement for one project with a single researcher or a group of projects with multiple researchers that addresses components of a problem. The components can be 2–3 projects or 20+. If the structure is with a single researcher, the typical process is to establish a scope of work, set of deliverables, and all the governing terms for that project. If there are several projects, that typically involves a master research agreement. The master establishes all the governing terms of the agreement (IP, publication, cost, etc.), but each project has its own scope of work and deliverables. If a company is looking to work with a research organization in several different areas, a master agreement can be very useful in speeding up the process of getting everything aligned and the work started. Other types of agreements that may be used in partnership agreements are materials transfer agreements and data use agreements in addition to SRAs.[35]

Another topic that often comes into play with sponsored research is overhead charges. Overhead is what the research institution, college, university, or nonprofit may charge to cover expenses that support the research. This can vary quite a bit and there could be a whole chapter on this topic. Generally, it's the fee that goes to cover the operational costs and it is deducted from the amount researchers receive for the research. Understanding overhead charges at the beginning of research discussions is important.

Other Fees

Finally, let's look at other fees. In this bucket, most of the other items that any organization would pay to an academic institution, aside from gifts or sponsored research, fall. These fees are often "fee for service." There are, of course, tuition dollars, but there are many other connection points involving fees such as fees for professional or executive education, career services support, capstone projects, affiliate programs, student group events, hosted events, consortia memberships, innovation sessions, facility rentals, and dozens of others. Tuition funds or membership fees do not cover all the costs faced by universities and other nonprofits. Additionally, many state institutions are further constrained by shrinking state budgets. In some states, whether the sponsor is for-profit or nonprofit can make a difference as to how the funding can be categorized. With this "color of money" there is flexibility in how an engagement partnership can be structured. Industry is a very important partner to academic, research, and nonprofit organizations. "Other fees" enable more creative collaborations and further innovations.

In Part 4, there are worksheets to help you think through and roadmap possibilities for engagement partnerships. Most importantly, remember there are many different avenues with many different connection points. These partnerships are all about building relationships, driving innovation, and moving novel technologies and approaches out of the labs and into the commercial marketplace. They are not merely transactional. They are transformational.

A great example of a transformation, rather than transactional, impact can be found in Uganda. I was recently at an event to celebrate the Playing for Change Foundation. This organization provides music and cultural programs to children around the world as well as supplies essential needs in the communities that their programs operate. At the Bidibidi refugee camp in Uganda where they have music programs, the World Food Programme (WFP) was supplying food rations. But in 2020, they announced a significant reduction in food distribution. Playing for Change stepped in and bought 20 hectares of land and helped the residents learn how to farm the land and create a sustainable food source.

Key Takeaways from Part 1

- There are clear benefits in partnering, both tangible and intangible.
- Communication and respect for culture/motivations are critical.
- It's all about relationships and proper alignment.

Part 2

Step 2: Define Your Strategy
Step 3: Know Your Stakeholders
Step 4: Map Your Connection Points
Step 5: Understand Possible Paths of Engagement

Step 2: Define Your Strategy

How do you think about innovation engagement partnerships? It depends on your vantage point!

Whether you look at the partnership from the academic vantage point or corporate vantage point, determining where the value maps to your internal needs is critical for an effective engagement. It's not always clear on first pass, especially when academic institutions and industry come from such different worlds. The first step is to do some value mapping to help define your strategy.

Figure 2.1 illustrates how the same partnership goal may be viewed by someone on the industry side and someone on the academic side. How does each party map the value to its internal needs?

Now, think back to Part 1 and align the goals into tangible versus intangible benefits of engagement partnerships. Not every partnership is solely financial. Thinking about how an alliance can map to needs, goals, value, and ROI are all important factors. There is a worksheet in Part 4 to help you with this mapping.

Looking at the chart in Figure 2.1, it's clear there are many possible connection points for an innovation engagement partnership.

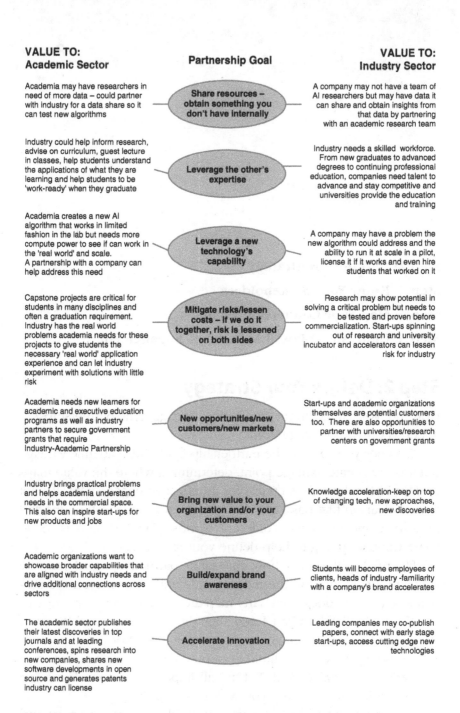

Figure 2.1 Various partnership goals and the benefits that can be recognized by both the academic sector and the commercial sector

However, it is not "build it and they will come." Win-win engagement partnerships take work to create and maintain on both sides (more about building effective teams in Part 3).

Establish Clear Goals

Clarity in what you want to achieve with the engagement partnership is essential for success. Make sure you establish clear goals and a framework to understand what success looks like. Examine why you want to partner in the first place. Where will you see the benefit? How will you measure/recognize the benefit? A mismatch wastes valuable time, effort, and money. It can also derail a relationship. Strategic alignment from the start is essential.

Let's take a look at a partnership between Syracuse University and JPMorgan Chase (JPMC). The two institutions came together in 2011 to create the Institute for Veterans and Military Families (IVMF). The vision for IVMF was to "advance the post service lives"[1] of the 25 million US veterans and their families through a variety of programs, education, research, and policy work. JPMC was already working with Syracuse in other areas and became a founding corporate partner in IVMF.[2] At first glance, this may seem an unlikely alignment. After all, Syracuse University is in rural upstate New York far away from any financial hub, and JPMC is one of the largest financial services firms in the United States headquartered in New York City, more than 250 miles away from Syracuse. But dig a little deeper.

Syracuse University has had a long history of working to support the military, veterans, and their families. This history dates back to World War I with the establishment of the Students Army Training Corps in 1918. This would become the Reserve Officers Training Corps (ROTC) in 1919. The following decades would bring even closer and expanded collaborations with the military as well as programs for veterans and their families. In 2011, the 100,000 Jobs Mission was formed to hire 100,000 veterans by 2020. JPMC was one of the 11 leading companies that signed on to this mission. Looking at the foundational factors of timing and alignment, the two institutions aligned extremely well in *this specific area*. Both had a mission to connect and support veterans. Together they formed a center that fulfilled both their goals.

In terms of seeing the benefit and measuring the success of the partnership against its goals, just look at the impact statement of the center:

> To date, more than **200,000** transitioning service members, veterans and military family members, were impacted by IVMF programs. In 2007, when we launched our very first program – before the IVMF was even founded – that number was **17**. Those numbers matter because they speak to our mission, and the commitment of our people, our funders, our partners, and our world-class advisory board to take action **to advance and positively impact** the post-service lives of this nation's veterans and their families.[3]

The testimonials and success stories inform the benefit measurement. Both institutions achieve their goals through this engagement. Syracuse has set up the infrastructure, houses the center, creates the programs (no cost career and entrepreneurship training), and conducts the research. JPMC supports this center not only financially with more than 30 million dollars in grants but also in hiring veterans.[4] As of last October, JPMC has hired more than 18,000 veterans and 3,100 military spouses since they first took the pledge and partnered with Syracuse on the IVFM. This example is a long-term win-win engagement partnership. Additionally, this partnership benefits the veterans and their families, upskilling the workforce for economic benefit to spread out beyond just New York state.

However, not all engagement partnerships have to be on a large scale. There are examples on a smaller scale as well. In 2019, the University of Tampa (UT) established the Southard Institute for Sales Excellence to provide professional development opportunities for UT students. There is a sales minor within the Department of Marketing for students interested in sales. Though less than 3% of all colleges in the United States offer a recognized sales program, research from the Sales Education Foundation found almost 60% of all college business majors begin their professional careers in entry-level sales positions.[5]

The Southard Institute for Sales Excellence works closely with corporate partners who offer lunch-and-learns, participate in reverse career fairs, help coach students, and judge competitions. The goals are aligned with talent. UT provides learning opportunities in an important and underserved area, the corporate partners can connect with students interested in sales, and both the university and the corporate partners benefit when trained students are hired by the companies.

The importance is understanding your goals and establishing clear alignment. If there is misalignment, there will likely be mutual frustration. We've already covered the different benefits each side can receive from a common partnership function in Figure 2.1, and we've looked at both the tangible and intangible buckets of benefits. Aligning all those factors to concrete goals builds the framework of the engagement partnership on a solid foundation. Once the foundation is strong, the partnership can grow, and both parties can derive the benefits.

I think one of the simplest ways to illustrate this is to look at the Engagement reports I mentioned earlier. At CSAIL, a company may engage with us on research, student connections, professional education, start-up connections, etc. When a company is onboarded, we ask specifically about goals and how they would define success after the first year. There are many opportunities for companies to engage in a variety of ways and the client relations coordinator (CRC) assigned to them proactively sends them information about activities that align with their stated objectives.

For example, let's say a top objective for Company X is student recruitment. Over the year the activity of the company engaging with the lab is tracked, and they are offered time slots and assistance to host tech talks to connect with students. At the end of the year when the report is created, a pattern emerges. It turns out no one from the company went to any of the student-focused events, no one gave a tech talk, no jobs or internships were posted, and there was virtually no engagement with students at all even though that was stated as a top goal. Instead, the research engagement was significant. Many people from the company attended conferences, workshops, and symposiums. A company researcher and a lab researcher met at a conference and were in talks to write a paper together. Even some of the open-source code was being looked at for development and possible inclusion in a new product. The company was engaged, but just not along the original goal stated.

If you asked the university relations/recruiting team, they may not see this as a successful engagement, but if you talk to people in research, engineering, or the CTO's office, you would get a different opinion. Setting the goal and having the right people engage is critical. The first step is often the most difficult. But if a solid foundation is built (step 1), the engagement partnership can grow in many ways, and everyone involved can build on successes and harvest the benefits.

Understand What You Have to Work With

Achieving a goal depends a lot on what you have to work with. Once the fundamentals of alignment have been addressed, it's time to assess this and define your strategy. Whether you work in the academic community or industry, there are people, organizational structures, funding sources, policies, and politics to consider. This is a partnership, so the first question is "What can I bring to the table?" This may seem obvious, but there are factors that need to be considered before you can confidently establish your framework. For the academic side it could be delivery of an executive education program only to find out faculty are not available in the time frame. Alternatively, it could be a new high-performer recruiting and training program in your company that has the budget pulled before it can be put in place. There are always circumstances beyond control, but before establishing a plan, be sure the underlying value factors are set.

Next, people and the organizational structures are important to consider. I've shared previously the story of the partnership that never got off the ground because, despite high-level engagement, the organizational structure put the legal department in the position of not just advising but making the call on what could or could not be done. Unfortunately, too, the lawyer involved had never seen a university partnership and was not inclined to explore new territory. The people in both organizational structures need to understand the value of engagement and what benefits the partnership can bring.

In another example, a hurdle often faced in crafting comprehensive innovation engagement partnerships is determining who pays for what. Both industry and academic sectors have budgets to adhere to. As an example, it may be that a company wants to engage in a low-cost affiliate program to better understand the research, get to know the faculty and students, and take some time to explore potential collaborations before undertaking a more extensive engagement. Organizationally it could be a challenge to determine which budget supports this. Is it research? Human resources recruiting? The individual business unit that initiated the engagement? In some cases, it may make sense for units to share the expense, but there are cases where the connections don't happen because the organizational structure doesn't support it.

Organizational structure is challenging on the academic side as well. Universities are not known for being easy to navigate. Their websites are a maze of information and generally crafted for the student and the academic-focused audience. From the home page of most universities, there are links for current students, prospective students, parents, faculty/staff, alumni, visitors, etc. Where is the industry link? You generally have to dig deep into the site or the sites of other departments, labs, or centers. It's not easy to find who to talk to, never mind what types of programs may be available. If you want to build engagement partnerships with industry, make the starting point easy to find.

Resources

Next a constraint that cannot be overlooked is the resources needed to run a partnership once it is in place. Building it is one thing. Running it is another matter altogether. If the engagement partnership is small, maybe three to five organizations engaged, it could be possible to have one or two people do the building and managing. More likely, the engagements will involve more organizations. If that is the case, tending to the needs of an active partner is a separate job from seeking new additional partners. Partners will not stay partners if they do not feel valued, listened to, and involved.

Ingredients

The next piece to examine in defining your partnership strategy is taking a close look at your ingredients. What do you have to work with to secure a partnership? What don't you have that you need? Partnership ingredients go to the essence of *innovation alchemy*. There are many types of combinations that pull together various organizations in the ecosystem to create the clusters. Ingredients can include the following:

- People/talent
- Research
- New technology
- New processes
- Funding
- Equipment
- Start-ups
- Datasets
- Materials
- Educational programs
- Workforce training programs
- Conferences/workshops
- Advisory boards
- Curriculum development

And so much more. . ..

There is a worksheet in Part 4 to help you take a closer look at ingredients you have to work with now, how to map them into an innovation engagement partnership, and what you may need to acquire as you develop your roadmap.

To illustrate mapping goals to value, needs, ROI, and what you have to work with, Natascha Ekert, former head of Siemens Global Academic partnerships, shares her approach as a "boundary spanner" in Focus Feature 2.1.

Focus Feature 2.1 Industry Perspective on Strategic Engagements

Craftsmanship or Fine Art? Confessions of a Boundary Spanner Between Industry and Academia
By Natascha Eckert

Boundary spanners: individuals within an innovation system who have, or adopt, the role of linking the organization's internal networks with external sources of information.[6]

I was a long-standing boundary spanner at the intersection of Siemens and its strategic external research partners for more than 15 years. That does not at all mean I'm automatically an expert in successful university–industry collaboration. Nevertheless, as for any kind of partnership, there are some key ingredients for success (or at least for not failing...): be open, be honest, be adaptive. Sounds easy, right? I can tell you; it isn't. At least not always. Sometimes I was an artist; more often I was a craftsperson. Let me tell you a bit about my journey.

Siemens, with its 50,000 R&D employees, its €6.2 billion investment in R&D, and its 11 defined Core Technologies, has always been active in terms of collaborative research with universities and research institutions. Activities range from fundamental research on lower Technology Readiness Level to engagements in university start-ups, from capstone projects with students to co-creation in joint labs, from expert exchange at all academic levels to sustainable investments in new professorships: Siemens knows how to play the open innovation fingerboard. And this "knowing how" includes the whole bandwidth of opportunities and challenges, success stories and frustrating failures, highs after new joint endeavor signing ceremonies and lows during endless rounds of slow-moving IP negotiations.

For more than 20 years now, Siemens has followed a strategic approach when collaborating with universities. Strategic typically

(continued)

(continued)
means long-term, aligned, trusted. But it also means having the distinctive competencies needed to keep a partnership up and running. We'll come to them later.

We started around the turn of the millennium with a university-centric partnership model. We agreed on a long-term strategic partnership with a handful of mainly technical universities (referred to as first-tier Center of Knowledge Interchange = CKI and second-tier Principal Partner). The partnership worked with defined research areas and also appointed liaison managers on both sides for our CKIs. Over the years, we added new partners and denominated others due to portfolio shifts on our side (in terms of technology and business). Overall, we were able to build a couple of sustainable and trusted partnerships collaborating on cutting-edge and hands-on technologies and innovations.

In 2022, we decided to take university collaboration within Siemens to the next level – the Siemens Research and Innovation Ecosystems. The university-centric approach was displaced by a more ecosystem-oriented scheme. It's natural for both companies and universities to interact with different stakeholders. Navigating through an increasingly complex environment, with its technical and social challenges, necessitates bundling the forces of all stakeholders to develop impactful innovation. We now count a total of 16 Siemens Research and Innovation Ecosystems (RIEs) comprising universities, national labs and research institutes, technology incubators, academic start-ups, political institutions, and industrial peers and customers.

So much for the theory. Now, let me take you behind the scenes.

As with any good partnership, whether bi-/tri- or multilateral, a few key ingredients are needed to navigate through all kinds of economic downturns, geopolitical tensions, and even paralyzing pandemic situations:

1. **Make your strategic partnership unique:** When targeting a strategic partnership with HEIs, you have to drive some decisions

early on. Do you want to assign single parts (e.g., Faculties) as partners or the whole university (with a view to interdisciplinarity)? Do you want to focus on special topics or technologies, or do you follow a more holistic approach? Do you want to assign fixed budgets? How do you want to interact with the partner – through your own dedicated intermediaries or as a partner of University Liaison Offices? With our Siemens RIEs, we address whole organizations while focusing on certain technologies, topic areas, and even formats. Furthermore, we assigned RIE Managers for each or our 16 Siemens RIEs. Together with intermediaries on the Siemens side, they drive their research and innovation ecosystems in a unique style – locally anchored and globally connected (taking the regional differences of the HEI landscapes into account). Furthermore, think about the purpose of your strategic partnership scheme: Do you want to foster tech transfer, are you hunting for top talents, do you want to engage in education? We decided to follow a comprehensive approach, leveraging the full power of our company while reflecting its needs.

2. **There's no lack of good intentions, but . . . :** Even if both parties agree to common goals in their relationship, it is an ongoing balancing of expectations, benefits, and – more often than you'd think – even disappointments. We have established a transparent governance structure and clear operating processes for our Siemens RIEs to keep our strategic partnerships productive and innovative, trusted, and resilient. Collaboration within (and even across!) an ecosystem is driven by our dedicated liaison managers: They define and adjust the scope of engagement, orchestrate the partner network, and foster new research and innovation projects. But even with a proper structure and governance, the crucial part remains management of the expectations of all different stakeholders. From the beginning on, and throughout the entire period of strategic partnership. This means communicating openly about your

(continued)

(continued)

own expectations, listening to your partners' expectations, and being able to carefully balance the two.

3. **Put yourself in your partner's shoes:** When I look at the list of "opportunities and challenges" that I discussed with the university–industry community as much as 10 years ago, the mutual understanding of different "business" constraints, incentive schemes, and performance measures was always at the top of the list. And not much has changed. My recommendation: Let the various people tell their stories and you will figure it out. While academic researchers are measured primarily by the number and quality of their publications, industrial researchers are driven by creating applicable technologies and innovations, that is, their focus is more on patents. Normally, businesses receive their R&D budgets on a yearly basis (in tight times, on an even shorter cycle), whereas faculties need long-term sustainable funding of their PhDs (minimum three years) supporting industrial collaboration. And you'll even find differences at the management level: Running a company is not the same as running a university. Make your collaborating parties on all levels understand each other.

4. **Money makes the world go round:** When starting a strategic partnership program, your partner wants to see your commitment to long-term engagements – and investments. So, make sure that you have the internal resources needed to drive a strategic partnership program with HEIs: resources for sponsored research, resources to invest in publicly funded projects, resources to manage the partnership. Having an extra budget to seed-fund or financially match research project proposals can help boost new topics and kick-start collaboration with new partners. Siemens has used both approaches successfully. But even if money plays a crucial role in fueling the partnership, you should also think about options for less conventional engagements: low-cost investments in student challenges,

talent projects, summer schools, donation of products (hardware and software), training material for education, engagements as advisor, lecturer, mentor, and nonfinancial support of academic start-ups. Ask university partners what they need, learn from your peers, and be creative.

5. **Trust is good, but (trusting) control is better:** Even if you feel like you're on a cozy honeymoon, you need to have a solid foundation of terms and conditions for your strategic partnership – from the beginning. We have Master Research Agreements with all our strategic partners when it comes to facilitating tech transfer from universities to our businesses or Corporate R&D. MRAs set the legal framework for any kind of research collaboration. IP is and will remain the most challenging part of all these agreements. As universities increasingly engage in the start-up sector, IP is becoming crucial to the commercialization of results. You need case-to-case options, adaptable and flexible solutions, reference cases, and you need patience. Over the years, experience has shown me that some challenges will remain challenges – and IP is one of them. Again, understanding each other's pain points and bringing diverging positions closer together. There's no winner in the end, but there is a successful project/collaboration.

6. **Open innovation needs an open mindset:** The idea of innovating openly by inviting others is appealing and in the meantime state-of-the-art for nearly any organization. But driving innovation openly requires tearing down a lot of established, even firmly ensconced thinking. You will struggle to conduct an open innovation contest and require at the same time strict confidentiality and exclusivity of all results. You will struggle to collaborate on an interdisciplinary research project and exclude your own experts working in another division, department, or function. Ask yourself to what extent you are ready and willing to really share knowledge openly. Working in ecosystems

(continued)

(continued)
forces you to think in more open spaces because negotiating complex multilateral agreements by optimizing all different interests can be the end of open innovation.

7. **Find the right balance between bottom-up and top-down:** Within Siemens, we never start a strategic partnership from scratch, that is, without any collaboration history we can build on. We often have long-lasting relationships between academic and industrial researchers in a specific field of technology. Or we've already supported education programs with our SW licenses for many years. But even if you have a successfully proven interaction at the project level, you need buy-in and commitment from top-management. To me, there is no better way to win the commitment of top leaders than by involving them actively in our partnership scheme. Each of our Siemens RIEs has a dedicated top manager as executive sponsor for the whole ecosystem. Top leaders pave the way to multilateral collaborations, encourage our experts to leverage the full innovation power of ecosystems and act as thought leaders for ecosystem management. This is often connected with an active engagement in one or the other advisory board or university council. Also, on the partner side, we involve the CEO or VP level in order to guarantee high relevance and awareness for our partnerships.

8. **Make sure that you can do the splits:** The broader the network gets, the more diverse the interests can become. Even within HEIs, some people have a more industry-friendly mindset than others. Research institutions have different funding structures and often are more competitors than partners of big corporations. On the other hand, academic start-ups might need the companies' infrastructure for a scale-up of their prototypes. As a boundary spanner your competence as orchestrator of different requirements, interests, and expectations is required all the time. And you have to get the commitment of the different stakeholders to the joint objective of developing

technology and innovation for the general benefit of society. Both sectors need to remain agile and adaptive: Business portfolios can change, universities reinvent themselves, new countries enact new tech transfer policies, alliances might change, and partners may move.

Our Siemens RIE scheme – what a crazy ride so far! It's amazing to observe the ecosystem growing every day, to see new partners entering, new alliances being born. Innovation often happens when you don't expect it. To foster a resilient ecosystem spirit and tie our partners closer together, we recently issued our Siemens RIE Manifesto, a written statement of beliefs, aims, and values. We created a shared gateway for start-ups to address Siemens as a technology partner, mentor, or sales channel. And we look for cross-ecosystem engagements, such as trilateral or multilateral seed-funded research engagements or overarching mentorship and student exchange programs – the fine art of collaboration (or, simply, the art of managing increasing complexity!). In the future, the scheme may be grown by adding new ecosystems and fostering more cross-ecosystem programs and initiatives. Multilateral funding across regional borders might facilitate this cross-ecosystem research – even if increasing administrative, legal, and protection policies show an opposing trend. Freedom of research and open innovation are becoming more endangered...

It was a real privilege to work with so many smart people over these 15 years. Nevertheless, being a boundary spanner between industry and academia calls for a lot of staying power. Budget cuts and the myth of universities as ivory towers on the industry side, prevalent scientific measurement of performance, and the myth of companies as big spenders on the university side. As a boundary spanner you have to continuously translate and juggle values, languages, and priorities. Nevertheless, facilitating transference across sector boundaries is one of the best jobs I ever had.

(continued)

> *(continued)*
>
> *Natascha has many years of experience in the University–Industry–Business sector and currently manages Siemens' global strategic partner programs with universities and research institutes (Siemens Research and Innovation Ecosystem Program). Natascha holds several seats in University Councils and Strategic Advisory Boards. She is a member of the UIIN Practitioners Committee and an active member of UIDP. Natascha holds a PhD degree in Business Administration/Strategic Management from Ludwig-Maximilians-University Munich.*

■ ■ ■

Acknowledge Weak Points and Constraints

There are always weak points, constraints, contrarians, and obstructions. It is important to acknowledge them from the outset and take measures to deal with them head on. Sometimes they are real, but sometimes they are just perpetuated myths. I share this because, years ago at a prior institution, I was working to establish a partnership with a company and was repeatedly told not to work with them. I was surprised as I had had positive interactions with the individuals. I decided to try and get to the root of this belief because if the general attitude was not to work with Company X, I was not going to get the support from the other departments needed to create the partnership. It turned out, 20 years prior, a prominent faculty member had had a falling out with one of the company's leaders. And though neither that faculty member nor that individual was still employed by the respective organizations, the myth still persisted.

This example is helpful to also illustrate the need for support. Unless you are in a position to direct other departments to provide support, you are going to need to work to get their support. In the previous example, I needed the cooperation of faculty, legal, sponsored programs, and more to get this partnership in place. If they didn't support me, it would never have happened. Moreover, support is necessary up and down the hierarchy, as well as across, the organization. If the proposed innovation engagement partnership is not supported by leadership, or conflicts with their direction, it will not succeed. Once there is a clear direction and support is secured, you need to motivate your team.

Building successful innovation engagement partnerships is a team sport. Your team can be people who report directly to you, people who have been tapped to come together and work on the partnership from various units, or people within other departments that you need to create the partnership but do not report to you. In past roles, I have worked with leaders in sponsored research and philanthropy to build comprehensive engagement maps for organizations involved with the university. It is extremely helpful to map out the various connection points, collaborations, and people involved. In this case, we called it the "Stakeholders Group," and it included people from various internal departments engaging with industry. Everyone brought information on their respective engagements to the meeting and we were able to build a comprehensive map of the engagement partnership for each organization. This was extremely useful on the academic side because we could identify holes and opportunities for additional collaborations, but it was also useful to the companies because they got a good sense of which units were engaged and how. It is probably the number-one thing I hear from companies: "I know we have some collaboration with you, but I don't know the extent of it." At the UIIN annual conference two years ago, I was speaking with a company representative who was trying to meet administrators from their partner schools to gauge the scope of the engagement. It's not usually a clear map for anyone so the more an innovation engagement partnership can be strategic as opposed to ad hoc connections, the more effective it can be in helping both partners involved understand the value and benefits derived.

Point of Contact (POC)

Another important consideration is an organization's culture as it relates to engagement. For example, in the industry sector, there is usually a champion or someone charged with building innovation engagement partnerships. In some cases where the relationship management of the partnership is the job of the POC, their organization's culture can factor into the success of an engagement partnership. How is that POC measured? What is their metric for success? In some cases, the culture lends itself to putting the POC in a position to be the "keeper of the knowledge." In these cases the POC is the only person who interacts, receives information, and ultimately determines who within their organization gets information about the partnership. This can be tricky politically as important information may not be shared with perceived rivals, etc. Though the role of the POC should definitely be someone's job, the culture should support sharing of the information received or it will be challenging.

On the opposite end of the spectrum is the internal culture of sharing new developments from partners broadly and especially with those units that can readily benefit. If there was a best-practice rule book for being a successful POC, it would follow the guidance of Steve Whitacker from British Telecom (BT). In his role, he was actively involved in many areas, built fantastic and respected relationships with faculty, and synthesized the information he gathered into succinct monthly reports distributed throughout BT. He would share many reports and postings broadly on internal BT listservs so all could see the benefit. Everyone had visibility into what was happening and how to take advantage of the partnership.

Step 3: Know Your Stakeholders

1. **Entrepreneurial faculty:** Conversations with Mike Stonebraker and Daniela Rus
2. Legal Departments, *Intellectual property*, sponsored research, Research Administrative Services (RAS), and Technology Licensing/Transfer Office
3. Students as Stakeholders
4. Corporate Business Units

In visualizing the engagement partnerships, think of the partnership at the center of the wheel in Figure 2.2 and all the blocks that make up the wheel represent potential stakeholders in what you

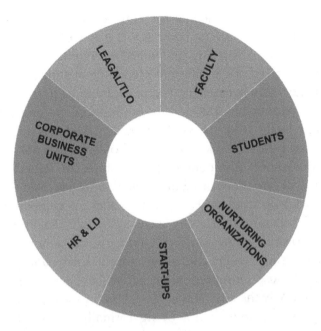

Figure 2.2 Stakeholders from various groups in an innovation-focused engagement partnership

want to build. The drawing is not meant to be all inclusive. There can be many other stakeholders involved too. Mapping to acknowledge and include the various stakeholders will help your innovation engagement partnership to get set on the proper foundation for growth, impact, and economic value.

As mentioned in Part 1, *people matter*! Knowing who needs to be involved and building those relationships is fundamental to the success of any innovation engagement partnership. The roles of individual stakeholders are necessary to build and maintain collaborations. These varying roles will need to collaborate on some level to get the most value out of a partnership. This can be tricky in both academia and industry.

Many units in an academic organization may be involved in building innovation engagement partnerships. Similarly with many large companies, many units may be involved: university engagement, research/R&D, engineering, marketing, finance, human resources for recruiting, learning and development for workforce upskilling, the innovation arm that scouts for new technology, start-ups, and innovations that can help the company. It may well be that no one in university relations knows anyone in R&D. Aligning stakeholders that need to be involved at the different phases of creating *and* maintaining the engagement partnership is crucial. Putting effort into building an amazing partnership, but not lining up people to engage, extract value, and manage it for the goals to be achieved is a wasted effort.

Let's take a closer look at the stakeholders in Figure 2.2. At the heart of innovation engagement partnerships for impact and economic growth are entrepreneurial faculty. These are the faculty members who do it all: research, teach, start-up companies, advise companies, mentor, etc. Faculty have incredible demands on their time, and most often, engaging with industry and launching start-ups is not factored for tenure and promotion. It seems almost counterintuitive that these entrepreneurial faculty have such an enormous impact in not only the commercial world but in society more broadly, and they do it despite it not being formally "counted" for their academic career advancement.

Entrepreneurial Faculty

There are many examples from colleges and universities across the country, but, being from MIT, I am most familiar with entrepreneurial faculty from my university, so I will share some highlights and interviews here.[7]

A Conversation with Professor Daniela Rus, MIT Professor and Director of MIT's Computer Science and Artificial Intelligence Lab

Prof. Rus is currently the Andrew (1956) and Erna Viterbi Professor of Electrical Engineering and Computer Science and Director of the Computer Science and Artificial Intelligence Laboratory (CSAIL) at MIT. Her research areas include robotics, mobile computing, and artificial intelligence. Academic honors include her being a member of the Class of 2002 MacArthur Fellows; a fellow of ACM, AAAI, and IEEE; and a member of the National Academy of Engineering and the American Academy for Arts and Science. On top of all that, she is an avid entrepreneur. Her companies include Venti Technologies, which automates logistic and shipping hubs, and Liquid AI, which aims to build an entirely new type of AI powered by a liquid neural net. Professor Rus is not only a highly regarded expert academic but also a savvy entrepreneur moving her breakthrough technology from her lab to real-world applications.

1. From your experience, what are the most significant benefits that you as a faculty member, and universities broadly, gain from collaborating with industry partners in the field of technology and data management?

Industry collaborations can provide funding for research projects, student fellowships, and lab infrastructure. This funding allows faculty to expand their research agenda, purchase new equipment, and support postdocs for PhD students, all while reducing reliance on limited government research grants. Industry partnerships also give faculty access to large, real-world datasets and current challenges in the industry vertical, for example, in technology and data management, and this can lead to more relevant problem formulations and solutions, and higher research impact. Collaborating with companies provides practical problems and data that align with industry needs. This allows academic research to connect to practical applications. Industry collaborations expand faculty members' professional networks and provide exposure to corporate R&D teams, engineers, and business leaders. These relationships can lead to additional research partnerships, speaking engagements, or consultancy opportunities.

2. In your opinion, what are the key factors that make a university–industry partnership successful, particularly in the context of research and development in technology?

Successful partnerships have strong leadership support from both the university and the industry partner. Both must align on the goals of the partnership and the area of focus. From a university perspective advancing fundamental research and developing new technologies is the most important objective, although in some cases there are also explorations for commercializing the innovations. From a company perspective, universities allow the companies to "see around the corner" and in turn, this gives the company competitive advantages.

Clarity on the purpose of the collaboration is important in order to ensure that both sides have aligned expectations. The partnership should offer tangible benefits to both parties. For universities, this may mean access to industry resources, data, and funding, while industry partners benefit from cutting-edge research, innovation, and access to a talent pool of students and researchers. Consistent and transparent communication is important for tracking progress, addressing challenges, and adapting to challenges. Defining ownership of the intellectual property early in the process is necessary to prevent conflicts later. The university IP standard is: if invented at the university it belongs to the university. If invented at the company, it belongs to the company. If invented jointly it belongs jointly.

3. How many companies have you been involved with that spun out of your research? Can you talk a little about them? What was the process like?

I've spun out four companies: LiquidAI, Venti Technologies, The Routable Company (TRC), and ThemisAI.

Each of these companies started as a research project in my lab. Exploring what could be possible. As we were successful in proving it could be done, commercial applications were identified, and I spun them out as start-ups. Venti Technologies, based in Singapore, provides autonomous logistics (vehicle & operational efficiencies) for industrial and global supply chain hubs in closed-campus environments such as ports, airports, warehouses, factories, and depots.

My latest spinout is LiquidAI. As we all know, AI and LLMs (large language models) use vast amounts of energy and are unwieldy, difficult to explain, and so large they cannot be deployed on edge devices. In my lab we set out to build a form of AI that would be energy efficient, explainable, and small enough computationally to be deployed on edge devices. We took inspiration from nature: a roundworm that functions its whole life on nine neurons. We developed a new type of AI: once a LiquidAI model is trained, the set of digital neurons the new model employs are smaller and more capable than a traditional LLM. LiquidAI means less energy needed and less compute needed but capable of delivering at the scale of much larger LLMs.

4. Can you provide examples of successful university–industry collaborations that you have been involved in or observed, and what lessons can be learned from these examples?

The Toyota–CSAIL joint Research center started with the vision of creating a car that will never be responsible for a collision and become the owner's friend. This vision was inspiring for the faculty and students involved in the project and allowed for a wide range of research topics to be developed as part of this program. The program started nine years ago and contributed many important findings to Toyota.

5. In your experience, how have universities nurtured start-ups and spinouts? How can industry partnerships enhance these efforts?

Universities have been nurturing start-ups by creating dedicated courses and ecosystems that support the entrepreneurial journey. These include incubators, accelerators, and innovation hubs where start-ups can access mentorship, shared workspaces, and networking opportunities with investors and other stakeholders, for example, MIT's Martin Trust Center for Entrepreneurship. Universities also create training programs for entrepreneurship, for example, MIT's Start 6 course that started as an EECS program and expanded to a university-wide program. Universities also invite start-ups to present at key events, for example, for MIT CSAIL@60 we invited 60 start-ups to present as part of the program.

6. From a start-up or spin-out perspective, what are the most valuable types of support or resources that can be accessed through university–industry collaborations?

University–industry collaborations provide start-ups with critical resources, including financial support, technical expertise, access to markets, computation, and talents. Industry partners can provide financial support through investments, grants, data, compute offerings, or corporate venture capital funds. In some cases, start-ups have gained direct funding from industry sponsors that are interested in co-developing technologies or acquiring cutting-edge innovations. Industry partners can offer start-ups early access to markets, customers, and supply chains. Start-ups also benefit from access to a steady stream of well-trained talents from universities, including students, postdocs, and faculty advisors.

Start-ups often struggle with the cost of R&D infrastructure (e.g., access to manufacturing tools, laboratories, and other specialized equipment). University–industry collaborations can provide access to facilities, research labs, and other technical resources that would otherwise be prohibitively expensive for early-stage companies.

7. How can universities and industry partners work together better to create a sustainable ecosystem that fosters innovation, supports start-ups, and drives broader economic development?

Establishing joint innovation labs and research centers where academic and industry researchers collaborate on cutting-edge technologies allows both parties to share resources, expertise, and infrastructure. This encourages interdisciplinary explorations. For example, the **MIT-IBM Watson AI Lab** is a collaboration where IBM researchers work alongside MIT faculty to develop AI technologies that benefit both academia and industry.

Universities should lower the barrier to starting a venture by making it easy for the professors to take time off to devote to the venture, by allowing professors to have leadership and executive roles at their start-ups, and by simplifying the licensing of IP.

Sustainable ecosystems are built on long-term relationships rather than transactional engagements. Universities and industries should seek strategic alliances that align the university research agendas with the long-term industry trends, in order to create long-lasting win-win programs.

A Conversation with Dr. Michael Stonebraker, Professor Emeritus at UC Berkeley and Adjunct Professor of Computer Science and Engineering at MIT

Dr. Stonebraker is credited with inventing relational database management systems such as Ingres and Postgres while at UC Berkeley, as well as C-Store, H-Store, SciDB, and DBOS while at MIT. Academically he is a recipient of prestigious awards including the IEEE John von Neumann Medal, the first SIGMOD Edgar F. Codd Innovations Award, and the ACM Turing Award (the Nobel prize of computer science). Additionally, he is a Fellow of the Association for Computing Machinery and a member of the National Academy of Engineering for the development and commercialization of relational and object-relational database systems. He has founded or co-founded 10+ companies including the Ingres Corporation, IL lustra, Paradigm4, StreamBase Systems, Vertica, VoltDB, Tamr, Hopara, and his latest venture, DBOS, which has developed novel application and system software.

1. From your experience, what are the most significant benefits that you as a faculty member, and universities broadly, gain from collaborating with industry partners in the field of technology and data management?

The most significant benefits I feel faculty/academics get from industry are sharing the problems they are seeing which are of interest to enterprises in the real world, being a sounding board for new ideas, and testing new prototypes.

2. In your opinion, what are the key factors that make a university–industry partnership successful, particularly in the context of research and development in technology?

In my opinion, the single most important factor is enabling smart people from industry, who understand the technical problems, to participate and connect with researchers. Conferences are one way to get technical people from industry and academia together – whether they are large research-based conferences such as ACM SIGMOD (association for computing machinery special interest group on management of data) or conferences on campus that bring industry and academic researchers together, it's important to have the conversations that can spark impactful work for both parties.

3. How many companies have you been involved with that spun out of your research? Can you talk a little about them? What was the process like?

At MIT there have been (I think) seven. Each one has been a commercialization of open-source MIT software prototypes. When I joined MIT, I had a substantial track record at Berkeley; I knew how to get a VC-backed start-up off the ground.

4. Can you provide examples of successful university–industry collaborations that you have been involved in or observed, and what lessons can be learned from these examples?

Probably one of the most successful collaborations I have had is with the Intel Corporation. The Intel–MIT partnership in data science started back in 2012 when CSAIL's BigData Initiative was selected by Intel to be one of their Science and Technology Centers. That connection not only provided funding and resources for researchers but brought an Intel employee (Nesime Tatbul) to MIT as a visiting researcher. She is in the lab working with our research groups. Her contributions have been tremendous, and this connection was key to making things happen.

5. From a start-up or spin-out perspective, what are the most valuable types of support or resources that can be accessed through university–industry collaborations?

From my experience spinning companies out based on university research, the most important thing industry can provide is the validation of the ideas.

6. How can universities and industry partners work together better to create a sustainable ecosystem that fosters innovation, supports start-ups, and drives broader economic development?

Remember, I have been able to spin out companies from open-source MIT projects. Releasing the software as open-source makes it much easier to start companies than working through the TLO (technology licensing office). Also, working through structures like the CSAIL Initiatives brings industry in to work with researchers around specific areas of focus. That structure enables us to respond to real world problems and develop solutions that can be used to address those problems.

In the previous interviews, the entrepreneurial faculty share their thoughts on the importance of collaboration with industry and how they have been able to move research from the lab to the commercial space. But both of the interviews are with computer scientists. Often, computer science does not involve patents such as the life sciences.

Robert "Bob" Langer, The Langer Lab, MIT Department of Chemistry

Professor Langer has been granted more than 1,400 patents. He is one of the world's most highly cited researchers with more than 427,000 citations. Professor Langer has authored more than 1,500 scientific papers and is the most cited engineer in history as well as one of the 10 most cited individuals in any field.[8] Professor Langer's research laboratory in the chemistry department at MIT is the largest biomedical engineering lab in the world with more than $10 million in annual grants and more than 100 researchers. He has also participated in the founding of more than 40 biotechnology companies including Moderna, best known for the COVID-19 vaccine. Professor Langer is an entrepreneurial faculty member who has both a highly decorated academic career and a successful business career. He has been able to take the learnings from his research in drug discovery and tissue engineering out of the lab and successfully bring them to the commercial marketplace. It is this combination of novel research, commercial application, and start-up success that illustrates the real impact the *innovation supply chain* can have.

The previous example and interviews are with technical leaders from MIT. But not all research needs to be technical to lead to a successful start-up. There are many examples of research in finance, business, and other areas that also fuel the *innovation supply chain*. There are also many other notable entrepreneurial faculty across the country such as the following:

- Daphne Koller from Stanford University is a co-founder of the online education platform Coursera.
- Dr. Rodney Brooks, former MIT professor and head of CSAIL founded iRobot, is the co-founder of ReThink Robotics and co-founder of Robust.AI.
- Dr. Regina Banks-Hall of Cleary University is founder and president of RBH Professional Development Institute, LLC.
- Peter Thiel from Stanford University is the co-founder of PayPal.
- Leslie Charm from Babson College founded Youngman & Charm consulting.
- Dr. Michael Camp from Ohio State University is a co-founder and co-fund manager at Ohio Gateway Tech Fund. He is also the founder and CEO of Prophetech Global and a founder and partner in BioVentures Group.
- Amar Bose of MIT founded the Bose Corporation.
- Henry Samueli from University of California Los Angeles founded Broadcom.
- Jason Corso from University of Michigan is a co-founder and chief science officer of Voxel51.
- Pat Hanrahan of Stanford co-founded Pixar Animations.
- Jennifer A. Doudna of the University of California Berkeley is the co-inventor of CRISPR technology and Caribou Biosciences.
- Luis von Ahn from Carnegie Mellon University started Duolingo and was the founder of re-CAPTCHA.
- Andrew Viterbi of the University of California San Diego co-founded Qualcomm.
- Scott Galloway of New York University is the founder of L2 Inc.

This list is not exhaustive. It's just a sample that serves to illustrate that faculty from many different departments and from many different areas of the United States have all founded successful start-ups and companies. The faculty become experts in their field, and that expertise can lead to novel research and successful business ventures. A 2020 study by Roche, Conti, and Rothaermel, published in the *Journal of Research Policy*, analyzed a novel dataset of 2,998 founders who created 1,723 innovative start-ups in biomedicine and found that 30% of those start-ups were founded by at least one professor.[9] Entrepreneurial faculty who have taken novel discoveries in their fields and turned them into successful commercial enterprises not only come from different backgrounds but the organizations they are affiliated with have different resources and support structures. They all have a drive to excel and push boundaries, and the work they do is not only impactful but game changing. These new ideas are the raw material of the *innovation supply chain*, and the entrepreneurial faculty members are the first step to put it in motion.

Innovation City USA

When most people think of innovation, start-ups, and the incredible economic impact of what that formula delivers, they can't help but think of Silicon Valley in California. But what led to that ecosystem developing there, in the Bay Area?

In 1925 Frederick Terman joined the Stanford engineering faculty. He stayed at Stanford because they matched his tenure offer from Carnegie Mellon (in another life, Pittsburgh may have become Silicon Valley). He was a researcher in radio engineering and made many contributions to the field. Some of his famous students were William Hewlett and David Packard (the founders of Hewlett Packard (HP)). Terman is credited with not only encouraging Hewlett and Packard to turn their research into HP but also spearheading the creation of Stanford Industrial Park (now Stanford Research Park) on some vacant land Stanford held. He courted technology companies as tenants, initially hoping the proximity to Stanford would help Stanford graduates find jobs. Hewlett-Packard, General Electric, Eastman

Kodak, and the Lockheed Corporation were just some of the tenants that came to lease the space.[10]

This is the perfect formula for innovation and economic impact. The research at Stanford led to new start-up companies, which partnered with the more established companies. That led to the need for more skilled talent, which was then also supplied by Stanford. The results are still being seen today.

Legal Departments, Intellectual Property, Sponsored Research (OSP/RAS), and Technology Licensing/Transfer Office (TLO/TTO)

One objective of this book is to illustrate many different forms of what innovation engagement partnerships could look like. The legal department is an important stakeholder and should be included in mapping out how you are thinking about an engagement. This holds true for both the academic community and industry.

Legal departments are often blamed for partnership opportunities being "torpedoed." However, that's a sad way to look at it because the legal department is there to help manage risk and make sure that both sides understand the parameters of the engagement and are comfortable with the financial structure, intellectual property provisions, risk, and any potential downsides. They help keep everything on the rails. However, not every legal department is familiar with what innovation engagement partnerships can/should look like and what risks/challenges come into play. Understanding your organization's nonstarters are important so as to not waste time building support for something Legal could never support.

One example from academia is publication rights in sponsored research. Publication rights are considered core to the mission in academia and will not be relinquished. But, that doesn't mean there can't be guidelines and processes built in as to how the publication is handled. If the sponsor has a right to review and ensure nothing confidential or identifiable is shared, it may alleviate some concerns.

Another topic frequently addressed is intellectual property. Industry typically wants to own any intellectual property developed with the reason that they are paying for the research so they should own the "product." But in most cases, the faculty group that the company chose to work with has been working in that area for years to build their expertise. If intellectual property does arise from a specific sponsored research engagement, it is likely the culmination of many years of work far beyond that one project. And, as I explained previously in the case of WiTrack from CSAIL, if the IP is given up by the university it will likely stop the research vein and any future developments that could arise. IP is definitely an important consideration but understanding the full array of licensing options can often address this effectively. Understanding the nuances of what's actually involved is important to discuss with the legal department. Up-front conversations can smooth out the contracting process.

Next, most research contracts between industry and academic institutions are often negotiated through an Office of Sponsored Programs (OSP) or Office of Research Administration Services (RAS), not always the Legal department. OSP/RAS are responsible for creating the agreements that will govern the research portion of an engagement partnership. They are important stakeholders! OSP/RAS handle not only agreements from industry sponsors but also research proposals and grant proposals with large foundations and governments. These units are well versed in contract management and help faculty with proposal preparation, budgeting, and compliance with the many conditions often found in federal and foundation grants. For industry-sponsored projects, OSP/RAS set up the project and manage the reporting, budgets, publication, milestone deliverables, audit, and all other aspects of research administration through the project's completion or close-out.

Once a sponsored research project is completed, the Technology Licensing Office (TLO) or Technology Transfer Office (TTO) may become involved if the research led to intellectual property. Most colleges and universities have some form of a TLO or TTO that aids in commercialization of discoveries through granting licenses on intellectual property assets and/or identifying potential applications and partners to bring those discoveries to market. The history of these departments is intertwined with science policy of the United States. In the 1940s, Vannavar Bush was the head of the United States Office of Scientific Research and Development (OSRD). The OSRD during World War II oversaw military R&D including the development of radar. Radar was developed in the "Rad Lab" at MIT, on the very site CSAIL now stands. Professor Bush was part of MIT's Department of Electrical Engineering and went on to become vice president and dean of MIT's School of Engineering. But in his role as head of OSRD and scientific advisor to President Roosevelt, Professor Bush advocated for an expansion of government support for science. His July 1945 report titled "Science, The Endless Frontier" laid out his vision and called for federal support of basic research and research related to the topics of national security, industry, and human health and welfare as well as the creation of the National Science Foundation.[11]

With the National Science Foundation, the federal government expanded its support of university research. Through the 1950s, research expenditures grew modestly. However, in 1957 the Soviet Union's launch of Sputnik "provoked national anxiety about a loss of U.S. technical superiority and led to immediate efforts to expand U.S. R&D, science and engineering education, and technology deployment. Within months, both the National Aeronautics and Space Administration (NASA) and the Advanced Research Projects Agency (ARPA) were established. NASA's core included the aeronautics programs of the National Advisory Committee on Aeronautics and some of the space activities of the Department of Defense (DOD); ARPA's purpose was to enable DOD to conduct advanced R&D to meet military needs and to ensure against future 'technological surprise'. Federal appropriations for R&D and for mathematics and science education in the NSF and other government agencies rose rapidly over the next decade, often at double-digit rates in real terms."[12]

The 1970s brought an energy crisis to the United States. The Department of Energy (DOE) was created and given the responsibility to fund energy-related R&D to address the issues that led to the energy crisis. Over the course of a few decades, additional new federal agencies were born and funding R&D in several areas beyond military research grew. However, in 1973 President Nixon abolished the President's Science Advisory Committee and the Office of Science and Technology. The responsibility for serving as science advisor to the president was given to the director of the NSF,[13] but in 1975 the NSF itself was reorganized into seven new directorates that fund science and engineering research: Biological Sciences; Computer and Information Science and Engineering; Education and Human Resources; Engineering; Geosciences; Mathematical and Physical Sciences; and Social, Behavioral, and Economic Sciences.[14]

The 1970s in the United States not only saw an energy crisis but also high inflation, labor issues, consumer angst, and Cold War tensions. An economic catalyst was needed and in 1980 the Bayh–Dole Act was enacted to ignite impact on inventions that were created with the $75 billion a year invested in government-sponsored R&D.[15] Before the Bayh–Dole Act, the government owned all the inventions created with federal funding. A nonexclusive license could be obtained by anyone who wanted to get one but that did little to spur economic activity. Very few inventions made it to the commercial market. With the enactment of Bayh–Dole, universities now owned the intellectual property developed from federal funded projects, which ignited the spark that would lead to an ecosystem of innovation and economic impact from university lab to industrial commercialization.

Overall, the TLO and TTO offices help to move university inventions out of the lab and into the marketplace. Technology transfer offices do generate some revenue through licensing, but most are covering costs at best. Universities don't create products and need commercial operators to be the conduit for economic impact. Universities have become more aware of the importance of intellectual property and though there may be an income stream for licensing, sharing knowledge is still a main motivation. If we are lucky enough to have another discovery along the lines of Gatorade, Vitamin-D milk, MRI technology (State of New York – Stonybrook), or the seat belt (University of Minnesota), the reward can be tremendous. Revenue generated, and overall economic gains, could benefit all the organizations in the *periodic table of innovation elements.*

To further explain the crucial role the TLO/TTO plays in the innovation engagement partnerships, I asked a colleague of mine who works in technology licensing/technology transfer to share his thoughts. Focus Feature 2.2 is contributed by Daniel Dardani who is the Director of Physical Sciences and Digital Innovation Licensing and Corporate Alliances in the Duke University Office for Translation and Commercialization.

Focus Feature 2.2 Technology Transfer for Commercial Impact

Technology Transfer: The Unsung Hero of University–Industry Innovation

By Daniel Dardani, CLP, director of Physical Sciences and Digital Innovation Licensing and Corporate Alliances, Duke University Office for Translation and Commercialization

When we think of our universities, images of cap-and-gown-clad scholars might come to mind, debating lofty ideas inside chalk-dusted lecture halls. But behind those ivy-covered walls, something arguably more impactful has been quietly unfolding–technology transfer. Technology transfer may be the most important development to come from universities in 50 years, and yet most folks in the public have never heard of it. Technology transfer, simply put, means the transfer of technology out of the ivory tower and into the public where it can serve society. For most, our growing reliance on university-borne innovations–like indispensable life-saving drugs and smartphones–demonstrates how mainstream tech transfer has become in spite of most people not knowing that it even exists!

Technology transfer is a process that starts in research labs, and to a certain degree before that, in the minds of many creative problem solvers all engaged in the academic research endeavor. Think of tech transfer as a conveyor belt, transporting important intellectual property (IP) out of the university and into the hands of companies, entrepreneurs, and, eventually, you. Companies are incentivized to participate as key financial stakeholders who stand to benefit greatly from successful outcomes. This unspoken partnership whereby companies are motivated to polish, propel, and amplify early-stage innovations, or technology "embryos," nursed by the universities, is the heart of tech transfer's resounding success. And the numbers speak for themselves. By some estimates, the economic impact of tech transfer has contributed $1.7 trillion to the U.S. economy over the last two decades and created 2.7 million jobs. That's not just a trickle-down effect, it's a tidal wave of innovation, jobs, and societal benefit.

The Bayh–Dole Act: Catalyst for the Innovation Boom
This law, passed by Congress in 1980, flipped the script for how federally funded research inventions were handled. Before Bayh–Dole, anything created with federal funding belonged to the government agencies that provided the grant money, and unfortunately, those innovations often went unused, trapped somewhere in between stagnation and bureaucratic limbo. The Bayh–Dole Act gave universities unprecedented freedom to own the inventions developed through federal funding, allowing them to control (a.k.a. patent and license these inventions to private companies) that IP's pathway to the marketplace.

In other words, it opened the floodgates for industry to now use academic research labs as an outlet for corporate R&D. Almost overnight, tech transfer offices (TTOs) sprang up at universities nationwide, or caused pre-existing ones like at MIT and Stanford to reorganize and serve as matchmakers between academia and industry. Hungry companies, eager to sample the fruits of university research, lined up to license technologies that could give them a competitive edge. A by-product phenomenon formed, as it also spawned a new wave of spin-out or homegrown start-up companies, often led by graduate students who took their lab work and ran

(continued)

(continued)
with it. Universities were now also tasked with assisting these new ventures to help launch, find funding, and disrupt long-standing status quo industries with leaner, meaner ideas and innovations. Corporate relations and industrial partnering offices launched within universities, or had to pivot at schools that already had established industrial liaison teams, to offer a new service model that enabled access to labs and researchers offered options to sponsor technologies that they could later license, and promoted larger, master-level agreements to create research centers or institutes focused along allied tech sectors. Very quickly, the traditional narrative of the university as a passive citadel of truth and epistemic knowledge was evolving into a new role as an active agent for job creation, as an engine for innovation and a driver of techno-entrepreneurship.

The Biotech Boom: An Early Tech Transfer Success Story
A prime example of tech transfer's transformative power, aside from changing the traditional role a university plays in society, is found when we look at the biotech industry. Back in the 1970s, biotech was a niche field. However, the success of Cohen–Boyer recombinant DNA patent license and the Chakrabarty decision at the Supreme Court of the United States among other things, ushered in a new age. Fast-forward to today, and biotech is a multibillion-dollar steamroller, thanks in part to university inventions moving into the marketplace and biotech corporations going all in on local and regional partnering close to campuses. In cities like San Diego, Boston, and in the Bay Area region, biotech companies erected labs and complexes within sight of local universities. Companies like Genentech and Amgen, both of which stemmed from university research, revolutionized the field, developing breakthrough therapies for conditions like cancer and rare diseases. And that's just one industry. Tech transfer touches nearly every field – from clean energy technologies to advanced materials to software algorithms and open-source

software. Nowadays there isn't much seen that doesn't have some roots in a university lab.

Why Industry Collaboration Is Key

Tech transfer wouldn't exist without strong partnerships between academia and industry. Universities often excel as hotspots for new ideas and groundbreaking discoveries. However, taking that invention from the mind of an ingenious student, from a lab notebook, or from a rudimentary business plan to a full-fledged product that you can buy at the store requires investment, scaling infrastructure, and business savvy, all of which are strengths of the corporate world. Industry partnerships and corporate alliance-building programs bridge this gap, bringing the professional investment dollars, market know-how, and commercial distribution channels to the table. One of the main roles a university's tech transfer office plays is to facilitate these relationships. First, by filing the IP that will serve as the contract asset of transfer. IP protects both sides by securing the innovation on behalf of the university and its inventors, and by de-risking the prospect of commercializing it by industry for about 20 years of its lifetime. Bringing new products and services to market based on early-stage academic discoveries is risky, and IP assuages that risk, letting the company recoup its investment, on top of profit, should it work out for the duration of the license agreement, which is often tied to the lifetime of the IP. Thus, companies get access to cutting-edge technology, and universities receive reasonable consideration in the form of licensing fees, royalties, and often, equity in the start-up. This money received by the university is distributed in part to the inventors, schools, departments, and labs, creating a harmonious cycle of reinvestment into more research and education sparking even more discoveries.

Start-Ups: The Main Engines of Tech Transfer

While all companies play a critical role in commercializing university technologies, the real stars of the tech transfer show are

(continued)

(continued)
often the start-ups. Start-ups by design are nimble, risk-taking businesses who often bet on a fresh idea. They can also pivot faster and remain patient longer while awaiting profit than established giants, who expect to see measurable impact each quarter. Universities benefit from having their faculty and students want to build start-ups based on their inventions. It's a guaranteed license for starters – no need to cold call companies in the hopes of finding a match. Second, the university prefers long-term relationships from its licensees, and who better to champion the IP for the long game than the group that conceived it and likely knows it better than anyone else? In fact, many universities, including Duke, provide resources to researchers interested in starting companies using university IP. Those resources may include incubators, accelerators, new venture programs, translational funding to help with mentorship, and even gap funding. More established start-up cultures, for example, at MIT, have robust ecosystems that support a variety of start-up activities. The Martin Trust Center for MIT Entrepreneurship and MIT's Venture Mentoring Service provide crucial education and guidance, while initiatives like STEX25 at MIT's Industrial Liaison Program connect start-ups with industry experts and potential partners emerging from academic research.

Forward Looking: The Future of Tech Transfer
Tech transfer continues to evolve as universities become more adept at navigating the commercialization landscape and transforming to meet the needs of business. With the rise of digital innovation and artificial intelligence, universities are entering new fields of discovery and entrepreneurship. At the same time, they're experimenting with novel business models, such as software licensing and open innovation, where collaboration and sharing are prioritized over traditional proprietary approaches. The convergence of machine learning and healthcare offers ample opportunity for clever new deals that leverage algorithms with engineering principles, and combine MedTech with patient records and health data.

These demands will forge new opportunities for TTOs to invent new license agreement models that accommodate these emerging technologies and to seek to build business engagements from healthcare providers to enterprise software companies, to data and compute conglomerates.

As we look toward the future, it's clear that technology transfer will continue to play a pivotal role in shaping the global innovation landscape, acting as the essential bridge to industry. Tech transfer is much more than a license transaction; it's a dynamic ecosystem of creation, risk-taking, and industry partnering. It empowers start-ups to disrupt and innovate, gives established companies the cutting-edge tools they need to thrive, and enables universities to have even greater societal impact.

When it all comes together, the university–industry collaboration helps ensure that brilliant ideas born in academic labs don't remain locked away in academic journals getting dusty sitting on library stacks or hidden online, but instead make their way into concrete and tangible products and services that improve lives, create jobs, and fuel economic growth. So, the next time you marvel at a high-definition flat screen TV, benefit from an MRI image, or simply look something up on Google, remember each of those started in a university lab, brought to life through the unsung hero of innovation – technology transfer.

> Daniel Dardani is a veteran technology transfer and IP executive with decades of experience in licensing and innovation strategy. As the Director of Physical Sciences and Digital Innovations Licensing and Corporate Alliances in both the Office for Translation & Commercialization (OTC) and the Office for External Partnerships (OEP) at Duke University, he oversees licensing and partnerships in engineering, MedTech, software, robotics, and AI. Before Duke, Daniel spent nearly twenty years at the MIT Technology Licensing Office as a technology licensing officer managing many technology
>
> *(continued)*

> *(continued)*
>
> transfer tasks in addition to handling a large and sophisticated portfolio of technologies including: computer and information technology, patented algorithms, copyrighted software, digital imaging, video games, machine learning/AI, data, and cyber security technologies. Dan is a Certified Licensing Professional, CLP™, and is on the Board of Directors of AUTM and on the Advisory Board for an IP Program at Cardozo Law School in NYC. He has degrees in physics and political science from the University of Rochester.

■ ■ ■

The TLO/TTO office is involved in licensing intellectual property, but much of what is developed still stays in the university database because universities are not very good at marketing. They are great at letting the world know of the discovery through well-worn channels of academic publication but are still learning the world of commercialization.

Some key examples of universities licensing IP that launched new companies and generated remarkable economic impact are GOOGLE (Larry Page and Sergey Brin as Stanford PhD students licensed the algorithm which would become Google) and QUALCOMM (CDMA – Code Division Multiple Access technology was licensed from UC San Diego by co-founder Irwin Jacobs). AUTM is the professional organization for people who work in technology transfer. The organization is dedicated to developing best practices for university technology transfer offices to work with industry to "ensure that inventions with high commercial potential reach the marketplace for the benefit of people everywhere."[16] Figure 2.3 shows the 2023 infographic from AUTM of academic technology transfer by the numbers.[17]

Aside from the work the TLO/TTO does to move innovations from the research labs to commercial enterprises, another important factor for innovation that must be addressed is the plethora of open-source software that is available from universities. A recent March

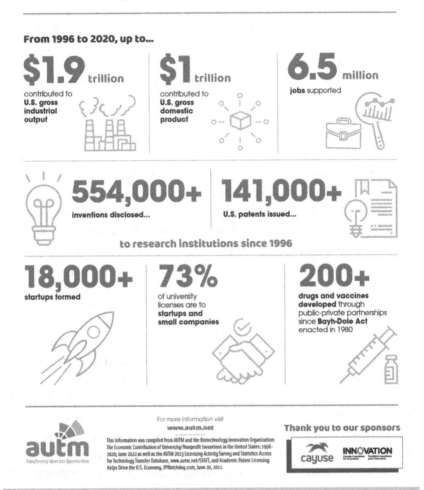

Figure 2.3 Infographic from AUTM illustrating academic technology transfer by the numbers 2023

2024 article by Rachel Layne published in Harvard Business school's *Working Knowledge* states "Many companies build their businesses on open-source software, code that would cost firms $8.8 trillion to create from scratch if it weren't freely available."[18] The article goes on to highlight the work of Harvard Business School Assistant Professor Frank Nagle who calls open-source software "the 9 trillion dollar resource companies take for granted."[19] We covered open-source code in Part 1 but access to the code and the people who created it (who know what it can really do) is an often overlooked ROI from innovation engagement partnerships.

If you faced a challenge you could not find a commercial solution for, did you consider open source? Most of what is available in open source is not commercial grade, but it may get you 60%, 70%, or even 80% there and save considerable time, money, and resources in solving your challenge. One of the most overlooked benefits in engagement partnerships is connecting around open-source capabilities. As Mike Stonebraker said, all of his companies have been built on open-source code. It can be extremely valuable, but it's not usually easy to discover by interested commercial entities. This is where connecting through an affiliate or alliance program can be beneficial. Those broad programs are familiar with the work being done in the labs and departments. Some even manage open-source code databases to make locating and sorting the code available easier for potential commercialization partners.

What starts as an idea becomes an invention that fuels the innovation economy as the World Economic Forum described it. The inventions become the intellectual property that is licensed, the start-ups that disrupt or create whole industries, and the products everyone wants. But it is the ideas and the initial nurturing support that molds the raw material into something usable. In this ecosystem, we can't mine the raw materials from the earth or snatch them from the air or sea. Instead, the raw materials we need come from the minds of students, faculty, researchers, and others.

The competitive advantage, product enhancement, game-changing new technology or the next new industry won't happen without investments in the raw materials. Government research grants and industry-sponsored research are certainly investments, but so are the investment of time and dedicated people to create, manage, and optimize new transformative innovation engagement partnerships. Everyone in the ecosystem has a role to play and keep the *innovation supply chain* fully functioning to deliver the impact and economic growth we all want.

Students as Stakeholders

Whether you are a company looking to hire talent, an organization looking for student participation or an academic institution involved in education and research, students are not just customers, they are stakeholders. If your engagement partnership envisions connecting with students, you will need to understand how that can be done successfully.

In some cases, it's a career fair. In other cases, internships or co-ops. Still others may have widely varying ways to make appropriate connections. One thing we've done in our lab to help recruiters understand how to best connect with CSAIL students is to host the recruiters from all our member companies for a special event just prior to the big undergraduate career fair of the fall. Most of them will be at MIT for the event and it is a great way for them to learn the nuances of connecting with graduate students in computer science and artificial intelligence. At this event, we invite students at different points in their educational journey to be on a panel to present to recruiters what works, and what doesn't. It's been viewed as being helpful from both the student perspective and the recruiter perspective. Recruiters learn *No, students do not want to be texted.* That feels too "in the friend zone." Emails are for professional correspondence (even if the students don't generally communicate via email). And recruiters learn that PhD students in the first few years are so focused on making progress on their PhD, they are not thinking about employment until at least year 3. But if your company has been around the lab, the students most likely have attended your events and are familiar with you. So, when you do look to recruit, you get a good response from the students in the lab.

Students can also be a critical part of an engagement program. In many disciplines, there is a pressing need for skilled talent. To achieve economic growth in a region, a skilled workforce is necessary. However, this doesn't always require bachelor's degrees or PhDs. The manufacturing space is a prime example.

According to a study by the National Manufacturers Association, manufacturing in the United States could need up to 3.8 million workers in the coming years.[20] Specifically, the study found the following:

- 65% of manufacturers polled said attracting and retaining talent is their primary business challenge.
- About 90% said they are forming at least one partnership to better attract and retain employees, and on average they have at least four such partnerships.
- Approximately 47% indicated that apprenticeships, work study programs, or internships at manufacturing companies would be the most effective way of increasing interest in the industry.

It's also not just a temporary challenge. Filling manufacturing jobs, which by their nature are not aligned with the GenZ preference for flexible work, requires forward-looking companies to think beyond higher education and bring the pipeline programs into K-12 classrooms. Faced with these challenges, Toyota's Dennis Dio Parker launched the FAME career pathway project (Federation for Advanced Manufacturing Education); see Focus Feature 2.3.

Focus Feature 2.3 Community College Impact in Partnering with Industry

FAME: Federation for Advanced Manufacturing Education
By Dennis Dio Parker, Toyota Motor Engineering & Manufacturing assistant manager and founder of FAME

Overview
FAME is a career pathway education program that was first visioned by Toyota in 2005 and launched in 2010 in Kentucky. Reaching

from the Pre-K-12 level to master's degrees, it creates a seamless and progressive STEM-oriented pathway that becomes a hop-on/hop-off, stackable track after high school graduation. Because the model as launched uses an in-depth but general curriculum, it's applicable beyond manufacturing and serves any company that uses technicians, allowing many types of companies (public utilities, food processors, pharmaceuticals, mining, distillers, and more) to join.

Originally targeted for implementation in eight locations where Toyota had manufacturing sites, due to the exceptional performance of the program today, it has more than 50 chapters (locations) in 17 states, participation by nearly 500 companies, and active engagement with more than 50 colleges and universities. It is growing rapidly and is starting its first international chapters. The occupational scope is also expanding. Because of FAME's highly flexible and transportable model, it can be used for other occupational sectors and new pathways are being developed to accommodate needs both within and beyond manufacturing. One of the most striking features of FAME is that it directly states a goal to produce global-best, entry-level workers and works to both benchmark programs internationally and continually strengthen the program to effectively meet this target. This makes it especially attractive to employers who wish to improve workplace business performance and to add an additional competitive tool to their operation.

Another unique feature is that the program was developed to both operate as a Lean-designed program and produce Lean-prepared graduates. This makes it further attractive to employers because it becomes a new source for acquiring Lean-educated graduates for their workforces. Because of the growth beyond Toyota's immediate footprint in the United States, the company partnered with The Manufacturing Institute, the workforce partner of the National Association of Manufacturers (the largest trade group in the nation), to assume leadership of FAME. While no

(continued)

(continued)

longer leading the program, Toyota maintains close involvement and continues to contribute to development of the program.

History of FAME

While FAME initially appears to be a program that started in 2010, it is actually the latest phase of a program that started in 1988 with Toyota at its Kentucky manufacturing site (today the largest in the world for Toyota). In that year Toyota launched a multiskilled technician training program and hired Dennis Dio Parker from the Navy nuclear submarine service, among others, to instruct it. Parker soon assumed leadership of the program and in the succeeding years drove four significant improvements, renaming the program each time to reflect the new version. In this sense, the base program has been in continuous operation since its original inception, though the program today looks far different from the first version. The transfer of the program to The Manufacturing Institute with its expanded resources and new leadership is the fifth phase.

What's the Problem?

Toyota is globally known as being a problem-solving company, and it was problem solving that generated the FAME program. Like many companies, Toyota struggled to adequately staff its skilled technician force. As previous efforts to solve the problem fell short, a new perspective began to develop. Part of this perspective was that even if Toyota was able to gain the numbers of technicians that it needed, there would still be core issues which would affect the performance of the Maintenance (what Toyota calls the skilled force) function. This was ultimately defined into three distinct problems:

1. **The NUMBERS:** There were not enough skilled technicians to be hired (at the higher competency level that Toyota needed) to fill job openings.

2. **The QUALITY:**
    a. New entry-level technicians, freshly graduated from their preparatory programs, were not work ready and for a number of reasons, many based on the soft skills.
    b. Programs in the United States for developing new technicians were, on the whole, not as effective as programs in other nations, especially those with industries that were competitive with Toyota. It created a talent competitive disadvantage: other companies in those nations with better programs gained new employees who were more work ready and could contribute more from the outset.
3. **The BUBBLE:** A significantly disproportionate number of technical workers were near the retirement range. While these workers were highly competent their time with the company was going to be short, and there was no effective way to replace them.

The FAME program was designed to simultaneously resolve all three of these problems. There were no preexisting programs with this broad vision and so the vision and the work to achieve this had to start from the ground up. Given that an entirely new vision was necessary, it's also significant that this work was done from outside the traditional education field; in other words, it was a private company that was generating a new vision involving a new kind of engagement by schools and colleges. With a pure focus on performance outcomes and the educational activity necessary to both achieve those and to sustain the system it led to an entirely new kind of program. Fifteen years after the launch of the program in 2010, there is still no known educational program that functions like FAME, nor that continues to achieve the outcomes which FAME does.

(continued)

(continued)

The FAME Chapter
FAME is based on the operation of local "chapters." It starts not with a school but with a group of employers which come together to operate as a unit, and which will then choose which college will best serve the needs of the FAME program. This working group is the "Federation" aspect of the program. This is the general explanatory illustration of the FAME chapter.

The FAME Career Pathway
Pre-K-12: Managed and deep engagement with local school systems that ultimately produced a greater number of STEM-interested students who will ultimately make decisions to pursue post-secondary STEM education and careers.

AMT Program: Advanced Manufacturing Technician, the original "gateway" program in FAME. It directly takes applications from high school graduates (and nontraditional applicants beyond graduation) and graduates them with an associate degree into direct employment with their sponsoring employers. Today, the "gateway" program is expanding beyond just technicians to meet needs in other occupational sectors.

FAME Extended Programs: Direct and seamless program continuations from AMT to bachelor's degrees and from those to master's degrees. Schools and programs are carefully chosen and coordinated to ensure that they accept a full transfer of credit from the associate degree and can provide advanced degrees without requiring the student to quit their full-time job with their FAME employer.

The FAME Curriculum
The FAME AMT Program produces a fully multiskilled technician who will provide the greatest flexibility for their employer.

What Makes FAME Different?
These are some of the features of FAME which principally contribute to the program's performance and/or which make it unique:

Pathway Scope
The program's reach with identified practices and engagement from Pre-K-12 to the master's level (and a vision for PhD), with defined connecting points and established partnerships, and the stackable programs and credentials at the adult level which set up the possibility of decades of continuing and work impactful education on a voluntary basis, all in one system is unprecedented.

Lean Program Design
The pathway is designed to operate by Lean principles and incorporates many Lean practices, including managing talent flow as a Lean Continuous Flow model, and setting the number of new students to be recruited each year according to a Pull System model, driven by employers.

Lean-Prepared Graduates
The AMT Program, the two-year associate degree level of the career pathway, includes five Lean courses for credit. This provides an employee from Day 1, who has more direct Lean education than the vast majority of company employees.

The Professional Behaviors
Many consider soft skills to be the rising workforce crisis of the time. FAME recognized this from the beginning and has implemented a highly structured and broad program for addressing it. The scope and depth remain unprecedented compared to other education programs at any level.

Comprehensive Design and Support for All Aspects of the Model
FAME brings together into a single working "engine" all of the key aspects of a fully successful and sustaining education model that produces talent at the highest level. Employers, students, schools at all levels, economic and workforce development, supporting organizations, and more are all included. The engagement of each is well defined, ready-to-go training for each role is provided,

(continued)

> *(continued)*
> documents and other important guides are developed into ready-to-go templates (e.g., bylaws for a FAME chapter, employer agreements). Higher-level strategy visions are developed to assist employers in integrating it into wider roles. Training is available all around, examples of which include student recruiting, employer recruiting, train-the-trainer, mentor training, and much more. Countless templates or direct products are ready to use, such as videos, templates for flyers, brochures, posters, and more.[21]
>
> *Denis Dio Parker is currently the Toyota Motor Engineering & Manufacturing assistant manager and founded the Federation of Advanced Manufacturing Education (FAME) while employed with Toyota Motors North America. He is a US Navy nuclear submarine veteran who joined Toyota in 1987 and grew the FAME program and specific learning tracks to the success it is today.*

■ ■ ■

What Dennis has been able to do with the FAME program is truly exceptional. It fills both an educational and employment need that boosts the local economic region. One thing every economic region is going to be facing soon is the reality of AI in the workplace. Are students getting enough training or experience with the tools while they are in school to be productive in the workforce? When new technologies disrupt, there is always a lag effect. However, engagement partnerships can also be used to address this problem so students are more AI workforce ready when they graduate.

Recently, I was at a conference speaking with a woman from a company who had had a few interns on her team this past summer. The interns were all smart, eager, and professional, but she expressed frustration that they knew so little about what her company actually did, and they were not as productive as they could have been. From an engagement partnership perspective, this could be addressed in a number of ways depending on the institutions engaged.

First, there is often an opportunity for companies to sponsor projects for student teams to work on both at the undergraduate and graduate level. If a group of students works on the type of problem your company faces and uses the skills they've learned in the classroom, you may have more productive interns the following summer. Students who have the skills now understand some of your company's challenges. If they come aboard as an intern, they will have perspective from working with company representatives on issues that actually matter to your company. Take the AI challenge; for example, a project where AI tools must be applied can prepare interns for a fruitful summer.

Curriculum is another potential area of engagement. Beyond just speaking in the classroom, some academic institutions actively engage industry in advising on curriculum. Curricula needs to keep pace with changes. If not, students will be ill prepared to be effective in the workforce. Kenneth R. Lutchen, Interim Provost and Chief Academic Officer of Boston University, is a proponent of industry being involved in shaping curricula. He sees the need for industry to work closer with academia in "Science, technology, engineering, and mathematics (STEM) fields, including data science, business and financial analytics, and machine learning. . . .. (because they) evolve quickly, as do the methods and practices used to study them (and) . . ..for the STEM disciplines – where graduates will be confronted on the job with fast-moving technologies – the problem is becoming acute."[22]

In his article "A New Model for Industry-Academic Partnerships," Lutchen calls for "the creation of sustainable partnerships with a consortium of companies from a variety of industries. Representatives from those participating companies serve on ongoing advisory boards charged with providing real-time input on the critical technological skills students will need in their careers."[23] Industry advisory boards of this nature exist at Arizona State's Polytechnic School, the University of California San Diego, Oregon State University, Purdue University, and Boston University. The win-win of this model is clear. To quote Lutchen: "Businesses benefit from a pipeline of well-prepared personnel, while higher ed institutions gain enviable reputations for providing them."[24]

Additionally, a practical example of engaging students in real-world work that helps set the student up for success, as well as gives the company valuable work product, is Orange Umbrella at the University of Miami School of Communications. Orange Umbrella is a student-run consulting organization that specializes in services such as design and branding, social media, public relations, photography, videography, and strategy. The students who participate in Orange Umbrella work with real clients on real business problems, while still in school. Students learn beyond the classroom, come to understand the nuances of dealing with clients, and gain not only practical experience but confidence. And all this translates into interns and employees who can be far more effective.

Recruiting talent can be challenging today. Students have so much going on – too many demands pulling them in 10 different directions. Here are some tips:

- If you come to campus to recruit, know your audience! Undergraduate and graduate students are different.
- Don't compete with yourself. Don't set up competing events by doing multiple things on campus at the same time. The message gets diluted, and students sign up for one event, but then the other event turns out to be closer to their class, so they just go to that one. Spreading too thin leads to low attendance, wasted food, and wasted efforts.
- If you come to campus for both undergraduate and graduate recruiting, talk with the engagement staff – understand how students at that university prefer to engage. One size does not fit all.

For companies looking to recruit, some things to think about:

- **Timing:** the university engagement team knows the students. Ask when is the best time to plan recruiting events. You don't want to come to campus only to compete with a student activity, mandatory student life programs, or something else that was not on your radar.

- **Know your audience:** A few years ago I was working with an enthusiastic recruiter who had lots of ideas and lots of energy. He had plans for a two-hour presentation, with lots of cookies, smack in the middle of the afternoon. He elaborated on how successful his model worked at all the schools he's been to. But remember each school is different. Classes fall at different times. Some are on semesters, other trimesters, and still other quarters. His plan had no one sign up so he was willing to listen. We changed the timing, format and talk structure. Ultimately his event drew about 40 students with some interested in working with the company.
- **Leverage university partners.** At MIT, graduate students are not likely to attend a general company presentation, but undergraduates may. The companies we work with at CSAIL are invited to give a technical talk and students engage around technical issues and interests. This may not be true for other universities, even technical ones. To plan the most successful student engagement, work with the university-based teams that engage with the students you are targeting. In many cases, there may be different organizations for undergraduate and graduate students.

These examples are representative of just a few situations to think about. This is where the structure of the engagement partnership is important. If the path is through an organization that does not directly deal with the students your organization is looking to connect with, you may not find the desired success in talent acquisition.

Student Entrepreneurs

Students have inventive, game-changing ideas and fresh perspectives. They are often the creative genius behind not only technology spin outs but also nonprofits and social-centered organizations. Beginning with famous tech names such as Meta/Facebook and Google, students have been the driving force behind many of the innovative new technologies and processes developed at universities. Much of this is due to increased offerings and support for entrepreneurial activities. At MIT we have dozens of players in the support ecosystem but foundational entrepreneurial skills are honed at the Martin Trust Center for MIT Entrepreneurship. Students from all over campus can take a wide variety of entrepreneurship classes, connect with other entrepreneurial students, use conference rooms for meetings, connect with advisors and entrepreneurs in residence, and compete in the capstone educational venture accelerator Delta V. This program helps students "hit escape velocity and launch into the real world."[25] How does it work? Over the summer, from June to early September, student teams working on their start-up idea come together on campus, or at MIT Delta V NYC. The teams refine their market strategy, focus on building the founding team, and simulate engagements (such as speaking to a board or pitching for funding) they will need to master to become a successful start-up. More on the Martin Trust Center and the role it plays in the section on "mapping your connection points."

Another interesting approach to instilling entrepreneurial skills in students can be illustrated by a class taught by Prof. Ramesh Raskar who leads the Camera Culture research group at MIT's Media Lab. Each year he teaches *Foundations of AI Ventures: Venture Studio*. This course looks at opportunities for AI innovations that can be spun into start-up companies in the areas of digital health, climate change, and mobility. CEOs, VCs, and academics provide mentorship to the student teams as they develop business plans which could receive seed funding depending on the judges' scores from demo day during the final class.[26]

Similarly, there is a class taught by Sloan Senior Lecturer Tod Hynes called *Climate & Energy Ventures*. Through hands-on practical experience, student teams create business plans for start-ups in the energy and climate space. This class combines unique perspectives of engineering, policy, and business students to look at MIT technologies and determine a path for commercialization. Over the last 10 years, this one course has spun out over 60 companies, many with significant market traction.

Instilling entrepreneurship skills in the next generation is a critical factor in keeping the *innovation supply chain* not just functioning but thriving. There are many different models for organizations in the academic sector to experiment with and many opportunities for those in the industry sector to play a key role in advising and supporting the innovations.

Some concrete examples of entrepreneurial student success include the stories of FedEx and Dropbox. First, FedEx started as a student project that became a billion-dollar world freight organization employing 400,000+ people. In 1962, Fred Smith was a student at Yale University. He wrote a term paper on his idea for freight delivery and received "an average grade."[27] That paper was the basis for what would later become Federal Express, better known as FedEx. Next, Dropbox started as an idea MIT student Drew Houston had on a long bus ride from Boston to New York City.[28] He had been planning to use his time on the trip to code. Then he realized that he had left his USB drive at home. Unable to do his work, he came up with the idea of a platform that would free its users from the need to use physical storage space. Dropbox has 18.22 million paying users, generated $2.5 billion in revenue in 2023, and employs 2,693 people.[29]

Catch-22: Seamless Student Floating and IP Confusion

The talent connection has long been a stalwart of academic–industry partnerships but recently there has been a thorny issue popping up that should be addressed. Often the "seamless" flow of students – usually graduate students – working on research at a university and working part time at a company in the same area of that research, has led to intellectual property challenges. The line between the students' research at the university, which would fall under university IP rules, and the student's work at the company, which would fall under the company's IP rules, has been blurred. If a student is working on a project that has promise to positively impact a company's processes or products there is generally the desire on both sides to work together. In the situation of an internship, it can be handled more clearly by the employment process at the company and internship policies of the university. For example, the employment agreement can require the student intern to acknowledge IP generated from the work at the company, belongs to the company. Where that work leverages a student's knowledge but does not use the actual code or research done at the university, the background IP can remain with the university and when the student returns in the fall, the student can continue the line of research and maintain IP ownership within the policies of the university.

When the student intern is employed part time at a company, while at the same time working on the research at the university, it can be a bit more complicated. To explore this, I interviewed Myron Kassaraba, vice president at MassVentures.

Conversation with Myron Kassaraba

1. Students are stakeholders in academic–industry engagement partnerships. One of the tangible benefits to both academia and industry is to have talented students work at companies on projects that align. What have been some of the challenges you've seen impacting students?

There can be challenges, particularly with internships, when students are pursuing their own research for their thesis or are involved in research being conducted in a university lab. Both the university and the company have policies regarding the ownership of intellectual property as well as rules about publication of research results. Sometimes, these can be in conflict and can cause problems that would be best to identify and avoid in advance. Since each institution has unique policies, it is important to inspect the nature of the work that will be asked of the student and if and how it relates to the company's projects they will be working on. A general rule-of-thumb is to "leave your university research at the university and the company research at the company." The majority of problems occur when there is mixing of the two.

2. Do these challenges arise mainly with undergraduate, graduate, PhD students? What is the employment arrangement that is the most challenging?

At most US universities, students that are in graduate research programs in labs pursuing a PhD or are hired as Post Docs are treated by the university as employees for the purposes of intellectual property (IP). This means they are assigning their rights to inventions to the institution. In most cases, undergraduates or students in graduate programs, like MBA, where they are paying for credits, own their own IP. A company hiring an intern will require that student to be subject to their employment agreement. If that is the case, as previously mentioned, it is important to maintain separation between the work being done during an internship and what is happening at the university before and after the internship. Academic–industry engagement can take other forms such as sponsored research agreements that go into much greater detail around IP ownership, publication approval, and potential commercialization of jointly owned inventions.

3. What student employment arrangements work well?

For any student working on research at their institution, it is most important to identify the scope of work or projects that they will be expected to work on during their internship at a company. This allows their PI (principal investigator/faculty advisor) and research administration groups to try to ensure that there isn't any overlap. One of the challenges is that many universities do not want to get in the middle of the student/employer relationship.

4. Can you share some examples and how they impacted the broader academic–industry innovation engagement partnership?

In one situation, a research grad student worked on a project at an employer and then brought some of that work back with them to the university (with permission). The student then developed some improvements independently while continuing to collaborate with the company on a publication that resulted in a patent filed by the company. This situation caused tension between the inventors, the university, and the company. It was eventually resolved amicably but reinforces two things, the first is bringing work back from the company to the university should be discouraged and secondly, if there is work that continues beyond the end of the internship, there should be an extension of the employment agreement with the student.

In another situation, an intern worked on an interesting project over the summer and the collaboration continued after the conclusion of the internship resulting in a joint publication. The company wanted to file a patent on inventions that were described in the publication – but because there was no collaboration agreement that extended beyond the term of employment, an agreement on joint-ownership could not be reached and a patent was not filed that could have benefited the student, the university, and the company. Another reminder that the internship needs to be viewed as having a clear scope of work with a beginning and an end. If there is activity that extends beyond the end of the internship term, that needs to be addressed between the company and the university.

5. How can faculty help address challenges and support the engagement partnership?

Students working on their own research or the research of their PI (principal investigator) should be made aware of the boundaries between work (software, inventions) owned by the university and that owned or claimed by the employer and the risk to them and the university if there is intermingling without the appropriate agreements. The student needs to be reminded to remember which hat they are wearing at what time since they are bound by different agreements when they are in the academic environment vs. their role as an employee of the company.

6. How can industry human resource departments help address the challenges and support the engagement partnership?

Those individuals at companies that are managing university relations and recruiting/on-boarding interns from an academic research institution should be cognizant of the fact that these issues with intellectual property exist. Care should be taken to identify any potential conflicts or concerns up-front since dealing with them after the fact can be complicated. The teams at the company should also be made aware of maintaining clear boundaries between the student's academic work and their contributions to the company's product and services.

7. Are there processes that could be put in place to help avoid these issues that can complicate partnerships?

The number one thing that can avoid complications is education of all parties involved in the partnership that these boundaries exist and that they should be managed in advance and not after-the-fact.

8. If there were a checklist to help address potential challenges up front, what are the top three things you would recommend be on the list?

1. Discuss the scope of any project or work expectations from a student involved in research at the university in advance.
2. Make it clear to all parties, the student, the university, and the employer that boundaries exist regarding IP ownership and should be respected.
3. Make sure that if there is activity that extends beyond the term of an intern's employment, even if it is just commenting on a publication, that there is an agreement that covers it.

9. Do you have any other thoughts or advice to share given your broad experience in this area?

Partnerships such as summer internship or co-op employment are extremely valuable for both the students and their institution and the company. When these engagements include students that are involved in research at their university, some simple precautions up-front can avoid messy and sometimes uncomfortable complications later.

Note that these comments are not meant to provide legal advice, and they represent the personal opinion of Mr. Myron Kassaraba and not that of previous employers.

Myron Kassaraba is a vice president at MassVentures where he leads initiatives focused on technology transfer and investments in academic spinouts. Myron's career in tech transfer began at MIT's Technology Licensing Office, where he managed a portfolio of AI, computing, and software technologies. Most recently, he was the Director of Commercialization at Northeastern University's Center for Research Innovation where he led the licensing team. He is active in AUTM. Myron holds a BS in political science from Northeastern University and has completed executive development programs at The Wharton School.

Everyone involved in building innovation engagement partnerships should be aware of the potential for issues to arise such as the ones described above. The best way to avoid potential conflicts is to educate faculty, students, and industry counterparts. Additionally, it is important to establish clear policies that help the engagement partnerships stay on solid footing and avoid pitfalls that can derail the relationship.

There is so much more that could be said about engaging student stakeholders, but it is beyond the scope of this book.

Corporate Business Units

Business units that participate in innovation engagement partnerships can be the CTO's office, R&D, engineering, marketing, innovation, strategy, human resources, university relations, and learning and development among others. Each business unit has specific goals and metrics. Innovation engagement partnerships often start by focusing on one unit's interaction with the academic sector. But, as the planning materials in Part 4 will illustrate, there is often more than just one area of alignment and viewing the connections more holistically can often yield significantly more ROI on both sides.

At the most basic level, learning and talent are foundational elements of innovation engagement partnerships. Companies not only need the educated students and professionals to stay competitive but also need to upskill the current workforce and often provide learning opportunities as a benefit. The departments of human resources, learning and development, and university relations are most often involved when talent is part of the plan. Academic organizations involved in educating the workforce and providing professional training may offer discounts on programs as part of the innovation engagement partnership. In CSAIL Alliances, we offer discounts not only for programs CSAIL produces but also for programs from MIT School of Engineering's Professional Education, MIT Office of Digital Learning, and even the Sloan School of Management's open enrollment executive programs. Some of the companies we work with do an excellent job of connecting the internal stakeholders and leverage the discounts codes to the extent that the savings actually pays for the Alliance's membership. Others, however, have not connected the dots and do not leverage the discounts as much as they could. In our engagement reports, we even point out the number of times the company email extension was used to register but did not use a code. It is a real dollar value ROI that is untapped.

An example of an innovation engagement partnership in the human resources/learning and development space is Georgia Tech's partnership with AT&T to develop its online Master of Science in Computer Science (OMS CS) program in 2014. It was not only the first-degree program from an accredited university that operated on an online platform for course delivery (the platform was provided by Udacity) but also the first of its kind developed in collaboration with a corporate partner. At the time it was first offered, students of the online master's program would pay $7,000 versus nearly $45,000 for on-campus students.

For AT&T specifically, more than 80 of the initial students were employed by the company. AT&T invested over $2 million to build the online program, which is open to students from across the globe, not just AT&T. The motivation was to make technical education more accessible and create a significant training option for its workforce. Bill Blase, senior executive vice president for human resources at AT&T, is quoted in a press release saying at AT&T "We need highly skilled software engineers, network engineers and data scientists. Through this program, we will enhance training for our current workforce and ensure a great pipeline for these roles and others going forward."[30]

Alternatively, corporate business units such as the Chief Technology Office, Engineering, and Research & Development may lead with innovation engagement partnerships grounded in research with specific faculty. Often, researchers from companies will connect with faculty at conferences and learn about areas of research at universities that are complementary to what they are working on. Relationships with faculty and students are beneficial to industry and can yield new approaches, new ways of thinking about a problem, and even gain a few steps ahead of competition by leveraging university created advancements through future-focused initiatives.

Working directly with faculty is a great way to connect deeply in a subject matter and stay at the cutting edge of developments in that field. However, a single faculty member is not likely to assist a company with talent acquisition, talent development, or even connections to other faculty who may be relevant to the company's challenges. For example, we recently welcomed a company to Alliances who had a years-long research relationship with one of the faculty members in our lab. The company decided they wanted to broaden the engagement with CSAIL and in our first meeting, we identified not only additional faculty who they previously were unaware of, but also novel ways to engage students they had never done before. Just one meeting equaled multiple new connection points for a win-win collaboration.

A corporate business unit that is often not thought of in engagement is the Marketing department. There can be some useful ways marketing can be leveraged for beneficial wins. On the corporate side, it may be possible to partner internally and have marketing support for a prize in a competition or to sponsor a conference. In both cases there is not only likely to be press coverage of the events, but also visibility to students/audience the organization may be interested in attracting. The marketing department may be able to partner with another business unit to achieve the overarching goals of the company.

Finally, most companies now have some form of an "innovation" department. Companies today need to stay vigilant to stay competitive. It is imperative that companies keep an eye on the rising disruptive start-ups with new technologies and invest in attracting and keeping top talent. Innovation has become a top priority. In 2023, nearly 80% of companies worldwide ranked innovation as a top-three priority.[31] But what is within the scope of these innovation departments and what do they look like?

The scope can vary quite a bit. I've met with innovation leaders focusing on learning and development pathways, start-up acquisition, corporate venture funding, transformation and innovation culture implementation among others. There does not seem to be a uniform definition of "innovation" within corporate innovation units. Some companies have a chief innovation officer (CINO) leading the innovation charge. According to Harvard Business Review, twenty years ago this position (CINO) was virtually unheard of, but by 2017, 29% of *Fortune* 500 companies had a senior innovation executive.[32] Other companies don't necessarily have a CINO and instead cluster innovation units in pockets within different departments. In this approach, different units across an organization have small teams that are responsible for innovation as it relates to that department's goals and objectives. This model takes innovation at "the ground level" and can lead to various units being part of an engagement plan. Moreover, if you google "university innovation department" you'll find a long list of innovation departments across a wide range of institutions with a focus on entrepreneurship, education, or tech transfer and commercialization.

In sum, innovation comes in many varieties and all are valid. The world is changing so quickly and competition is ever fiercer. There are multiple business units working on innovation and multiple academic units that can align well in fostering innovation. A Wellspring research report noted that as part of innovation efforts, 41% of corporate leaders are developing research partnerships with academia.[33] But there are other points of alignment too. The next section illustrates how to approach mapping connection points for an engagement partnership.

Step 4: Map Your Connection Points
What Is Your Innovation Strategy?

Exploring the innovation landscape in academia is just as multifaceted as the corporate approach. Many different units with different missions are involved in innovation. These departments often nurture the excitement of discovery into the commercialization of a company or product. There are many different structures, and each fills a need in the path to impact. But the key factor to success is the partnership of academia and industry to bring those discoveries to scale for positive economic impact!

At MIT, we have a large campus in the heart of Kendall Square in Cambridge Massachusetts. Kendall Square is known as "The most innovative square mile on the planet" (see Figure 2.4). Yes, it's in Cambridge, Massachusetts, not Silicon Valley

Figure 2.4 A photo of the marker "Most Innovative Square Mile on the Planet" Kendall square, Cambridge Massachusetts. Photo by Lori Glover.

But what makes this area so innovative? Kendall Square is a vibrant ecosystem with a variety of elements in the *periodic table of innovation elements*. It has many companies, colleges and universities, start-ups, venture capital firms, incubators and accelerators, law firms, hospitals and healthcare research, co-working spaces, maker spaces, local nonprofits supporting business, workforce development groups, independent research labs, and more. How did it start?

Up until the 1960s Kendall Square was an industrial center of factories producing soap, furniture, electronic equipment, rubber goods, ink, and even candy (NECCO wafers from the New England Candy Company). When one of those companies, the Lever soap company, decided to pull out of Cambridge, it was a problem for the city. Lever was the largest employer and had a big footprint in Cambridge. The mayor at the time went to MIT's president, John Killian, for help. In 1960, Killian announced that MIT would purchase the former Lever Brothers factory site and begin developing it into office buildings to facilitate collaboration with industry.[34] It was dubbed Technology Square. This was the first step in creating the rich academic–industry engagement partnership that would spawn the ecosystem of the most innovative square mile on the planet.

But as we all know, nothing happens in a vacuum, and considerable effort is needed to seed the ecosystem and keep it thriving. To fuel the innovation engagement partnerships, there are many resources for students, faculty, and community members to turn cutting-edge research into trailblazing new companies or revolutionary new products. The ecosystem supports these efforts and is critical to the economic development of the region. I want to highlight a few of the different organizations in this ecosystem because of their specific missions and how they play into innovation and alignment with engagement partnerships. These are just examples of what can be done to foster innovation and drive impact. Everyone has different ingredients to work with, but I hope in sharing some models, new ideas in partnership will spring up.

Commercialization of Academic Research: The Deshpande Center for Technological Innovation

The center was established in 2002 by a philanthropic gift from Gururaj "Desh" Deshpande and his wife, Jaishree. Its mission is to empower talented researchers to make a difference in the world by "developing innovative technologies in the lab and bringing them to the marketplace in the form of breakthrough products and new companies." The motto of the center is "from idea to impact" and to achieve this, the center awards research grants and other types of assistance to MIT faculty members whose work "shows the potential to benefit society, transform markets and industries, and improve the quality of life for people across the globe." Since its inception, the Deshpande Center has launched over 50 start-ups including some who have been acquired (Vertica was acquired by Hewlett Packard) and others who have gone public (Myomo Inc.). The companies from the Deshpande Center include 25 in healthcare and 11 in clean tech. They have raised more than $1.5 billion in capital and "are developing and delivering ground-breaking products and services that not only change people's lives today but have the long-term potential to transform key markets including energy, healthcare, materials, and information technology."[35]

This center is an example of how philanthropy can impact innovation. It was the philanthropic gift that got it started and though this book has not discussed philanthropy, in this case it was a gift that established something enabling real impact. The establishment of this center to get innovation out of the lab and into the marketplace nurtures the development of a technology to the commercial stage. See Focus Feature 2.4.

Focus Feature 2.4 Commercialization for Impact

Impact of Commercialization on Research and Researchers
By Rana K Gupta, executive director, Deshpande Center for Technological Innovation

The notion of impact now appears in every major research institution with an entrepreneurial and/or commercialization program.

One is challenged, however, to find a consistent definition of, and for, metrics for impact. Because impact is personal. How and why a given researcher views, and therefore attempts to create, impact is a function of each researcher's values and objectives. This focus feature paints a picture, based on my observations, of the impact commercialization can make on research and researchers. I'll (1) explain my experience in realizing the importance of impact to researchers; (2) offer a multi-faceted view of research commercialization impacts; and (3) explain the Deshpande Center's role at MIT in helping create impact by commercializing MIT technologies.

My introduction to the notion of impact started when I was an early-stage, technology VC over 20 years ago. I quickly realized many of the researchers coming to our office, upon learning what we (VCs) do, did not have an interest in the VC model. Loss of control and/or being sold (acquired or going public) was not of interest. That led me to start asking, "What is your objective?" Their answers and my subsequent conversations and observations in the following years as an investor, advisor, CEO, mentor, teacher, and Director, Faculty Entrepreneurship at Boston University (BU), and now Executive Director for the Deshpande Center led me to realize most researchers are interested in making an impact. That they were in our VC office meant they were already interested in commercialization. What they had not contemplated is why, until I asked, "What is your objective? What will make you happy?" Over the intervening years, the more I asked, the list and range of impact answers grew. This, in turn, expanded my notion of commercialization beyond (a VC's notion of) liquidity. The researcher's notion of impact is yet another variable for us to consider when working with that researcher to commercialize their idea. I'll summarize by saying their answers are the reverse of the classic movie cliché, "it's not personal, it's business." When engaging in technology commercialization and asked about impact, researchers' answers express an emotional, "it's not business, it's personal" sentiment.

(continued)

(continued)

Fed by countless conversations, below is a categorized list of impacts revealed to me over years of asking, "What's your objective?" Please also note, the impact objectives listed below are not mutually exclusive.

Financial

- Wealth creation (generational wealth)
- Another income stream
- Economic development

Product

- Utility in the market: innovation in the true sense: idea × value
- Societal

Research

- Symbiotic relationship: virtuous cycle, IP umbilical cord
- Commercial learning to improve grant performance
- Shipping millions
- Articles, interviews, and references (the likes of the) NYT and WSJ

Financial

Financial impact can take a few forms. Three are cited here. The first two refer to money made by the scientific founder(s) from a spin-out. One form of this may be wealth creation referring to the big score when a company is sold or goes public, and shareholders' personal wealth increases by such an amount that it makes a difference in their financial well-being. A second I've heard is, "I'd like a second income to augment my professor salary." Third, societal impact in the form of jobs and economic development can be an impact objective. As aptly quoted by one such scientific founder, Alfred Crosby at Umass Amherst who, when learning that his (ten-year-old) company had to shut down said, *"I am proud of the economic benefit we gave to our employees and their families for those years. I consider that a success."*

Product
This is, by far, the most answered and overwhelmingly desired impact objective I've heard in the generalized form, "I just want to see it out there." As Doug Holmes, a professor at Boston University eloquently said about his idea, *"I think this has utility and I want to find the applications that will use what I've invented."* While this may sound as their focus is reduced to a product and therefore specific, it is most often the opposite. Researchers strive for major societal impacts with their ideas. Via commercialization they have a vision their idea can solve a big problem, one that will help millions.

Research
Most of what the media highlights are the above two impacts: financial and product. This section addresses the value to researchers and their research. The very process of advancing an idea to product has an educational impact often sought after (and often learned after-the-fact) by researchers. Many times researchers have said, "I want to learn how companies think, how ideas become products, how it can improve my research." It's already impactful when they recognize it's a new skill set to take their idea in its current form (a technology) and transform it into a product. Others that have begun to understand the challenges of commercialization realize the markets (applications) where they thought they'd bring value were not interested. Then there is the realization that one cannot call it innovative until it's in use and adopted (innovation = invention x value). Just learning the process is impactful. Post-launch, I've witnessed two manifestations of symbiosis. The first is exemplified by a quote from my interview with Sangeetha Bhatia, a professor at MIT. She referred to the "virtuous cycle." The full quote is as follows: *"As I advanced*

(continued)

(continued)

my research, I found that the impact of my lab discoveries would hit a limit. The technology was difficult to scale without a dedicated team and collaborations with pharma became mired in long institutional negotiations. Instead, with a company established, I could easily route potential users to the company to purchase kits directly. Further, as we made more discoveries in the lab in the platform, we became an innovation engine for the company developing new applications. Therefore, once we had a tool in the market, it actually helped enhance the impact of my research and gave us new ideas. Some people think commercialization and research are an either/or. I believe it's a virtuous cycle." This is a dynamic relationship between the start-up and the professor's lab.

The second example of symbiosis is what one may call the IP umbilical cord. Think of the researcher's work as feeding the licensee its Gen2 and Gen3 products as the researcher learns more about market needs. A researcher's ongoing work can feed new inventions and data to a spin-out or third-party licensee to enhance or strengthen the original idea. It's important to note in these symbiotic scenarios, the PI is taking an active role in commercialization.

On grant writing, multiple researchers that engaged in commercialization seek a causal relationship with grant acceptance. As the government increasingly requests ideas that can have commercial value, those PIs that have experienced firsthand their technology's transition to product gain insights into:

- How products are commercialized, for example, de-risking the tech to make the product
- How market needs are identified
- The distinction between a technology and a product
- The value of customer feedback

Anecdotally, researchers see the impact commercialization can have on subsequent grant success.

Here's my favorite commercialization impact statement designed to challenge conventional notions of its value to a researcher. In a recent interview, former MIT professor, Joel Dawson, offered a superb, expansive description of impact from commercialization perhaps not evident to many researchers, as he states. The quote is as follows: *"One of the lessons I learned is, if having an impact with your technology is your dream, the surest way to make that impact is to commercialize it. As researchers we are taught that papers and conferences (where we explain the details) is how we'll make the impact. But if you're shipping millions of dollars-worth of your product, people will know it works and at first that is more important than knowing how it works. If it makes money, people will license it, buy it, copy it. The detailed understanding of your technology will come much later, very slowly ... and among far fewer people than you think."*

The last research impact from commercialization I'll note is recognition of the scientific founder in the media in the form of articles, interviews, citations, and conference invitations. Academics that have succeeded in commercializing breakthrough technologies become key opinion leaders, recognized by peers, and are sought after for their insights and ongoing research on the topic.

The Deshpande Center for Technological Innovation (DCTI)
The Deshpande Center's mission as stated by our founder, Gururaj Deshpande, is *"helping faculty and students move their technologies to market, where their ideas can make the world a better place for all."* We are interested in three impact metrics: educational, societal, and financial. Professor Dawson's quote is an example of educating a Deshpande Center participant about the impact of commercialization. Second, we look for technologies with the potential to

(continued)

(continued)
make a transformative impact on society. Three examples of technologies that have achieved this mission-driven impact are:

- **Myomo:** Kailas Narendran, Co-Founder of MyOmo quotes: *"The vision for the technology was to rehabilitate, non-invasively, people who had suffered neurological damage from a brain injury. That was not heard of at the time."*
- **Gradiant:** Anurag Bajpayee, CEO and Co-Founder quotes: *"Gradiant redefines industrial possibilities, growth doesn't have to be environmentally disruptive – we are treating and recycling some of the most contaminated waters in the world. To make a dent in the state of water on this planet, we need to take on these difficult challenges... Since the industrial revolution, we have only been taking from nature, by doing what we do, we can turn the clock back and give nature water back."*
- **Akselos:** First ever "digital twin" model leveraging scientific machine learning for $B energy assets (e.g., oil & gas, wind turbines), contributing to the International Energy Agency's (IEA) net zero by 2050 scenario.

And because our teams are either creating spinouts or licensing to third parties, we track financial impact. As of 2024, $21M granted has resulted in:

- >$1.1B in disclosed value from acquisitions and IPOs
- 12 acquisitions (5 under NDA) and 3 IPOs
- 1 unicorn in wastewater treatment (only one in the water industry)
- J&J acquired therapeutic (bladder cancer): projected $5B product p.a. (one of the acquisitions under NDA!)

Conclusion
The above is a quick summary of several impacts resulting from research commercialization. The objectives behind these vary from financial to societal, and from product or research to reputation. It is for these reasons this is personal.

Rana K Gupta is the Executive Director of the MIT Deshpande Center for Technological Innovation. Previously, he served as Director of Faculty Entrepreneurship at Boston University (BU) and Managing Director of BU's Business Innovation Center. In addition to his work at BU, Rana served as CEO of cancer diagnostics company and Yale University spinout HistoRx, founder and CEO of mechanical adhesive technology company and UMass Amherst spinout Felsuma, LLC, and was a Managing Director at Navigator Technology Ventures, an early-stage technology venture capital firm spun out of Draper Laboratory

Rana received his bachelor's degree in mathematics from Earlham College, a master's in operations research from Stanford University, and an MBA from NYU's Stern School of Business.

■ ■ ■

Entrepreneurship Education and Support: The Martin Trust Center for MIT Entrepreneurship

Entrepreneurial education is a foundational building block of many innovation engagement partnerships and virtually every innovation ecosystem. Students as well as businesses need entrepreneurial creativity to think outside the box, explore new business models, and drive economic growth. Entrepreneurship is not just for technology fields. According to the *U.S. News and World Report* for 2025, some of the best undergraduate entrepreneurship programs in the country include Babson College, MIT, University of Michigan-Ann Arbor, University of California – Berkeley and Indiana University – Bloomington.[36] This mix of public and private institutions each has a different perspective on entrepreneurship but each is also successful at producing results.

At MIT we have the Martin Trust Center. The center is dedicated to teaching students' innovation-driven entrepreneurship through courses, programs, facilities, and mentorship. Students can take courses, receive mentorship, and participate in programs to help them turn ideas into companies and products. The center offers 60+ entrepreneurship and innovation courses across campus, a dedicated education and innovation (E&I) track for MBAs, and online courses for self-learners at MIT or people around the globe.

Bill Aulet has led the Martin Trust Center for more than 15 years. He is passionate about entrepreneurial education and has often told me "Entrepreneurship can be taught. There is a systematic approach for building innovative products and companies. And it can scale." His teachings not only apply to undergraduate and graduate students but also companies who want to become more entrepreneurial. His latest book *Disciplined Entrepreneurship*[37] takes materials from years of his teaching entrepreneurship and organizes them into a useful framework. In a recent article he states, "Great ideas regarding entrepreneurship come out of Silicon Valley. After all, it is one of the key centers of innovation-driven entrepreneurship, however, the product is often specific to that context. The entrepreneurial process should be studied. You can learn from anyone, but it should not be thought of as unassailable or the only way."[38]

Similarly, innovation engagement partnerships and innovation ecosystems don't all follow the same process in construction or connection points. It is not one size fits all and whether you are from academia, industry, or other organizations in the *periodic table of innovation elements*, how you build partnerships will depend on what you have to work with, strategic vision, support, and people.

Successful innovation engagement partnerships can have many different forms.

Start-Up Mentoring and Advice: Venture Mentoring Service (VMS)

New entrepreneurs need help. VMS supports innovation and entrepreneurial activity throughout the MIT community. This free service matches prospective and experienced entrepreneurs with skilled volunteer mentors using a team approach. Groups of three to four mentors work with the entrepreneur(s) to provide practical, day-to-day professional advice and coaching. This is not only valuable mentoring but also networking. Companies can volunteer to be a mentor which is not only very valuable to the start-ups spinning out of the university but also gives the companies insight into the start-up ecosystem at the Institute.

Legal Help: The Boston University (BU) Law Clinic

In this book we have already looked at some challenges with intellectual property, but there are so many other issues new entrepreneurs need to address. From corporate structure to founding team roles, legal help is a necessity. Many students who want to start companies do not have money to work with specialized law firms. They often don't even know what questions to ask. The Boston University Law clinic plays an important role in the greater Kendall innovation ecosystem. The clinic is a free and confidential legal service for students at MIT and BU who seek legal assistance related to their research, advocacy, and creative projects. BU law students work under faculty supervision from BU's law school. The clinic has three main practice groups: Intellectual Property & Media Privacy, Security & Health, and Venture & Finance.[39] Proper legal frameworks help start-ups succeed in commercialization and make collaborating with industry easier.

Co-working Space and Connections: The Cambridge Innovation Center (CIC) and Venture Cafe

The CIC is now a global leader in building and running innovation communities. When it started in 1999 it was a place for its founder, Tim Rowe, and his friends to collaborate on their businesses. The CIC now has nine campuses across three continents and is home to thousands of entrepreneurs and organizations of all sizes, work styles, and industries.[40] It's more than just co-working space. The CIC houses over 650 companies in Cambridge alone, including start-ups, accelerators, and global pharmaceutical companies. Many companies who want to tap into the innovation ecosystem of Kendall Square will start by establishing a toe hold at the CIC. It puts them in the heart of everything with neighbors from start-ups to boutique law firms to global trade organizations.

To foster the "running innovation communities" as part of their mission, the CIC started the Venture Cafe in 2010. The event calendar is full of opportunities to learn and connect by bringing together entrepreneurs, investors, academics, companies, students, and the community. The events provide options for organizations in the ecosystem to connect and create new innovation engagement partnerships.

Community Nonprofit Support Organizations: MassBio, the Kendall Square Association, and Massachusetts Technology Leadership Council

Nonprofit industry associations also play a vital role in the innovation ecosystem. There are many different organizations that are part of the innovation ecosystem, but I will highlight three of them here. First, MassBio is an organization that supports the life sciences cluster in the state. It provides resources to over 1,700 member organizations at all stages of the biopharma lifecycle. The organization actively promotes business partnerships, educational, and networking opportunities. It is funded through the dues of its members. MassBio specifically "creates unique opportunities for meaningful connections with key opinion leaders and subject matter experts on a diverse set of topics including academic–industry collaborations, start-ups, partnering, and capital."[41] It is a sector-specific organization that connects academia, industry, and others around a deep understanding of the needs of that industry.

Next, the Kendall Square Association (KSA) was formed back in 2009. It came about because community leaders from academia, industry, research, biotech, healthcare, creative centers, and more recognized a need to provide a forum for people involved in the Kendall Square innovation ecosystem to exchange ideas on how to improve, promote, and protect the region so many call home. KSA not only provides community events such as live music, free fitness classes, and farmers markets but also tackles issues that affect everyone such as transportation. For industry engagement, KSA offers professional meet-ups that enable people from across Kendall to connect and work collaboratively with their counterparts in similar roles at other Kendall Square companies.[42]

Finally, Massachusetts Technology Leadership Council (MTLC) is the largest technology association in the region. MTLC is "dedicated to convening leaders with diverse perspectives to solve[43] pressing global challenges and boosting economic growth in the area." Through MTCL, the organizations in the ecosystem come together and focus on the economic growth of the region. It is a membership-based organization that catalyzes connections for start-ups, brings academia and industry together, and through their programs and initiatives cultivate essential relationships among executives that "help unlock new avenues for growth."[44]

Accelerators, Incubators, and The Engine

As with any innovation hub there are accelerators and incubators for start-ups. But one thing that is different is the MIT Engine. The Engine is an accelerator in form, but its mission is to focus on "tough tech." "*Tough tech* is transformational technology that solves the world's most important challenges through the convergence of breakthrough science, engineering, and leadership."[45] It is for technologies that take time to mature and involve complicated systems in climate, health, etc. The Engine provides its companies with access to specialized infrastructure including labs, equipment, tools, and workspace. It is an important part of the ecosystem that moves "transformative technologies from idea to impact." The Engine is not exclusive to MIT and houses start-ups from all over the world.

Corporate Venture Arms, Venture Capital Firms, and MIT's E14

Many companies have venture arms and invest in start-ups. There are also many venture capital firms that play an essential role in funding the start-ups that spin out of academia. This capital is a crucial element that enables the start-ups to grow. At MIT we also have the E14 Fund. E14 was born out of a pilot experiment at MIT's Media Lab. Back in 2013, the MIT Media Lab launched an experiment that tested different models of financial and nonfinancial support for MIT start-ups. This experiment was successful and in 2017 the first fund was created. There was a second fund in 2020 and now a third fund in 2023. The E14's average funding is between $500,000 and $1 million.[46] E14 invests only in MIT start-ups and unlike traditional venture capital, E14 gives a large percentage of the profits back to MIT which can go back to funding research and, hopefully, producing even more transformative tech and start-up companies. Funding for research is the single most important factor in the ability of an innovation ecosystem to deliver impact and economic growth. The E14 fund also offers programs to help students understand the venture world better and how to think about things like "going to market." Their VC fellowship program provides current MIT students an opportunity to learn from the partners of E14, as well as build connections in the start-up ecosystem.

All of these organizations involve academic and corporate partners. They come together in an innovation ecosystem to deliver positive tangible impact where there is a win for all involved. The impact can be measured in the start-up companies created, jobs generated, innovations in existing industry, workforce upskilling, increased productivity, new education pathways, increased customers, gains for industry, and overall economic growth. Innovation engagement partnerships are a catalyst for the *innovation supply chain* and the models can be deployed effectively across the county.

> "*MIT alumni have launched 30,200 active companies, employing roughly 4.6 million people, and generating roughly $1.9 trillion in annual revenues.*"[47]

Foundational Framework The previous examples exist in different forms in many areas of the country. I used Kendall Square to illustrate the functions of these organizations because it is what I am most familiar with. Think of your local area. What organizations exist that serve similar functions?

Knowing how your needs connect to a potential partner's needs is the foundation of an engagement framework. The academic sector and the corporate sector both have personnel distributed across multiple units. The units, especially in large organizations, may not be communicating internally. This lack of communication can lead to disjointed, transactional interactions that don't produce the impact and positive ROI of a longer-term strategic engagement partnership. Often in industry, this happens because different units have different budgets and there are restrictions of what budgets can be used for. But remember, funding is only one part of a successful engagement partnership. Funding for a research project may come from the research unit but human resources may benefit from talent connections and the innovation arm from plugging into start-ups. Similarly, at universities there may be many different departments involved. Typically, the career center won't know much about how to connect with research. Structuring connection points also involves building your team that is responsible for innovation engagement partnerships and identifying stakeholders they need to work with.

Let's start mapping.

In terms of visualizations, figuring the right connection point to begin an engagement partnership can be tricky. From the outside, no one knows the exact mission of a specific corporate department except that company. See Figure 2.5.

Figure 2.5 Illustrates the difficulty many academic and nonprofit organizations face in determining how to start an innovation engagement partnership with industry

It's not easy to navigate companies. Therefore, companies who do want to engage with the academic sector should participate in the many events industry support groups and community nonprofits offer to help foster connections.

Similarly, universities can be extremely difficult to navigate. The most common thing I hear from companies is frustration over how to connect with the right people. At MIT we have 48 (that I know of) different organizations that collaborate with industry in some form; some are discipline specific, others work with undergraduates or graduates, some work only with large multinational companies, others work with small companies and start-ups, some are education focused, others research focused. See Figure 2.6.

Depending on the category of the need, connecting the dots will look different for each desired partnership. And it may be that for a particular set of institutions there is only 1 connection point that

Figure 2.6 Illustrates some of the many departments at MIT who work with industry. Each one has a different focus, faculty, research, connections, etc. When mapping a comprehensive engagement plan, understanding not only the paths at an academic institution, but also the connection points within the broader ecosystem can be valuable

Part 2 Step 4: Map Your Connection Points

fills the need. For example, a company wants to partner with a local university for talent but perhaps that university does not focus on the discipline needed by that company's R&D unit. There are many universities, research labs, and nonprofits in the ecosystem that have niche specialities. For example, turfgrass management. This speciality is the practice of caring for grasses, groundcover, and plants for installments in recreational areas, green spaces, and golf courses. For a niche speciality such as this, there is a short list of universities, and their corresponding ecosystems, that can address innovations most effectively because they have all the elements to do so. Connecting around niche areas can be an effective approach for both the academic and commercial sectors. In Part 4 there are worksheets to help align approaches to engagement partnerships and evaluate the right partners for the stated needs.

From a high level, mapping the need to the respective units in both the academic and industry sectors could follow this chart:

For example, you are in industry and the need is talent. You could connect with undergraduate, graduate, professional associations, workforce development organizations, professional training centers, etc. Or, you are in the academic sector and you need community support/philanthropy so you would map to corporate philanthropy offices.

Industry Sector	Need Expressed	Academic Sector
R&D, Engineering, CTO, innovation, etc.	Technology advances	Individual research groups, industry engagement units, research lab, incubators, accelerators, technology collaboratives
Human resources/university relations	Talent acquisition undergraduate, graduate, professional	Undergraduate career development center, undergraduate department centers, workforce development agencies, retraining organizations, specialized certificate granting professional organizations, career centers, lab centers

Industry Sector	Need Expressed	Academic Sector
Learning & Development	Workforce education/ upskilling	Executive education (business schools), professional education, domain-specific departments, centers, institutes, professional associations, professional training centers and providers, workforce development centers
Corporate philanthropy	Community support/ philanthropy	Resource development, philanthropic partnerships, nonprofit centers, community organizations, technology councils
Innovation department, innovation teams, venture arm	Start-ups	Entrepreneurship centers, individual academic departments, start-up support programs, labs, centers, institutes, incubators, accelerators, start-up communities, co-working spaces
Business units	Business process improvement	Business school units, faculty, centers, institutes, professional associations
Business units, legal department	Technology transfer	Technology transfer office, Technology Licensing office, legal department
Engineering, R&D	Outsourced engineering	Outsourced engineering centers, maker spaces, foundries

When mapping connection points, another question I often hear is "Do we have to be located near campus?" to make connections and leverage the ecosystem. If organizations are located within the same geographical region, there can be close and frequent collaborations with the entire ecosystem. Think back to the section on Kendall Square. Proximity is beneficial for everyone. If distance reduces the relationship to transactional matters and information is not shared broadly, the distance can become a challenge.[48] However, if there are specific connection points and the teams work well together to share information, proximity does not have to be a challenge. We will look more closely at building effective teams in Part 3. Since the pandemic we have all become accustomed to virtual connections. Meeting virtually, holding virtual events, and posting content online to share are all ways to bridge the distance gap and keep the communication flowing. Ultimately, *it is communication that matters, not miles*.

Step 5: Understand Possible Paths of Engagement

In this step we will look a little closer at what is actually involved in the different paths of engagement. Some are simple, others more complex. Some require a small investment of time or money while others require a significant investment and infrastructure. Different institutions utilize different models, and the engagement paths apply to both the academic sector and the industrial sector.

Some common models include the following:

- Membership
- Consortia
- Fellowships
- Grant awards
- Sponsored research
- Advisory boards
- Curriculum/strategic advisor roles
- In-residence positions
- Joint research centers
- Consulting

- Internship/sabbatical
- Professional programs
- Start-up/innovation programs
- Capstones/projects
- Philanthropy
- Pipeline programs
- Visiting researchers/fellows
- Partnering for economic development and societal impact

Below is additional information on the various paths and level of engagement (time, money, etc.). On a scale of I to III, with (I) being generally less expensive and lower time commitment (though there is always the opportunity to spend more time growing the relationship) and (III) being the most involved in terms of time commitment, funding and scope, each potential path is explained in more detail.

Membership (Engagement Level: I)

Many organizations use the membership model to connect with supporters and their community. This is the model many nonprofits use and is also a model common in academic engagement. One of the most common forms of a membership program for academia is an affiliate program. They can be associated with a specific department, a lab, center, a college within a university or an institute. Academic affiliate programs vary in the membership benefits afforded but generally all provide the ability for members to attend annual meetings, receive copies of newsletters/reports, recruit students, and make faculty connections. Some affiliate programs also have tangible benefits such as professional education discounts or complimentary conference passes. They are a "low barrier to entry" to become better acquainted with the organization and help identify key connections for a broader engagement partnership.

There are also professional associations in the innovation ecosystem that utilize the membership model. Generally, unlike most university-connected affiliate programs, professional associations allow individual memberships. This can enable an individual exploring connections to access the ecosystem. Additionally, organizations like InnoLead[49] are focused squarely on the innovation ecosystem and use membership to connect the tools they create, such as downloadable templates and reports on innovation to the companies in the ecosystem. They also hold conferences to share best practices for people working in strategy, R&D, new ventures, design, technology, or innovation.

Generally, affiliate programs are open to business of all sizes. Depending on the structure and purpose of the program, government agencies, nonprofits, and foundations may also be members. Affiliate programs therefore also offer broader opportunities to make additional connections in the innovation ecosystem.

Consortia (Engagement Level: II–III)

Consortia are formed when a group of organizations come together around a topic and work collectively to address it. Consortia can have goals around research, technology, policy, or economic development that advance mutual goals. In a consortia, every member has the same benefits and generally pays the same amount for those benefits. In terms of research and technology development, it can be cost-efficient. The cost of the research funding is spread among several companies that would all benefit from the resulting technology(ies). Often they are precompetitive in nature addressing disruptive new technologies that can be applied in several different industry sectors. Among the members, each could benefit from the technology development but use it in different ways.

Alternatively, consortia can be a group of companies in a sector who work together, and all want to see certain challenges in the space addressed. For example, a consortium for embedded systems may focus on advances in that specific space but may have members from consumer electronics, automotive/transportation, telecommunications, aerospace, and even agriculture. Solutions and new technologies that are developed apply to the topic (embedded systems in this example), but each member may adapt it for their specific use case or in a use case that applies to the group.

Some consortia address needs that are common to diverse groups such as workforce issues. For example, recently "Cisco and a group of eight leading companies including Accenture, Eightfold, Google, IBM, Indeed, Intel, Microsoft and SAP, as well as six advisors, announced the launch of the AI-Enabled Information and Communication Technology (ICT) Workforce Consortium focused on upskilling and reskilling roles most likely to be impacted by AI. The Consortium is catalyzed by the work of the US-EU Trade and Technology Council's (TTC) Talent for Growth Task Force, with the goal of exploring AI's impact on ICT job roles, enabling workers to find and access relevant training programs, and connecting businesses to skilled and job-ready workers. Working as a private sector collaborative, the consortium is evaluating how AI is changing the jobs and skills workers need to be successful. The first phase of work will culminate in a report with actionable insights for business leaders and workers. Further details will be shared in the coming months. Findings will be intended to offer practical insights and recommendations to employers that seek ways to reskill and upskill their workers in preparation for AI-enabled environments."[50]

In a consortia format, the organizing unit acts as the convener bringing together various interested parties. A consortium that pulls together multiple companies and several universities to address a topic not only with research but also education, pipeline development, in-kind resources, knowledge building, and key transfers to the private sector is a transformational industry–academic endeavor. Foundations and other nonprofits may also participate as well as governmental entities in some configurations. An example is illustrated by the C3.ai Digital Transformation Institute which, in 2020, brought together a combination of industry as well as public and private universities to address AI Innovation. Members include C3.ai, the Microsoft Corporation, the University of Illinois at Urbana-Champaign, the University of California Berkeley, Princeton University, the University of Chicago, Massachusetts Institute of Technology, and Carnegie Mellon University. The consortium funds research, supports education, and produces reports and scientific papers that build the greater body of knowledge for societal good. One of the biggest intangible benefits of consortia is the community they build. Learning from one another, challenging what has been to discover something new and pushing innovation in a field can advance an entire sector. A consortium of this scale requires significant financial commitments and a complex structure to deliver on all the various components.[51]

Another example of a successful consortia model is The Food and Nutrition Innovation Institute at Tufts University. As part of the Friedman School of Nutrition Science and Policy, the institute works with companies and nonprofits in the food science, nutrition, and food tech spaces. Their mission is to use an innovation ecosystem approach to build the infrastructure for an economy that sits at the intersection of nutrition and foodtech.[52]

Though this book does not cover the various models of government involvement in engagement partnerships, it is important to note the National Science Foundation government sponsored Industry–University Cooperative Research Centers (IUCRCs) serve a vital role in the innovation supply chain as well. IUCRCs can leverage government funding. The main goals of IUCRCs are as follows:

- Conduct high-impact research to meet shared industrial needs in companies of all sizes
- Enhance U.S. global leadership in driving innovative technology development
- Identify, mentor, and develop a diverse high-tech, exceptionally skilled workforce

"The IUCRC program provides a structure for academic researchers to conduct fundamental, precompetitive research of shared interest to industry and government organizations.[53]" IUCRCs are funded through the National Science Foundation (NSF), which provides "funding to support Center administrative costs and a governance framework to manage membership, operations, and evaluation. Each IUCRC is expected to grow over time and be independently sustainable by the end of the award period."[54] In terms of impact and ROI, IUCRCs can demonstrate that "every year, more than 2,000 students engage in industrially relevant research at centers nationwide, giving them on the job training for a career in the private sector. About 30% of these student researchers are hired by the member companies."[55]

Though this book is United States focused, some countries, such as those in the European Union (EU), favor engagement through consortia and this model is actually required for all collaborative projects under Horizon Europe (the EU's €95.5 billion (US$110.57 billion) research and innovation funding scheme for 2021–27 formerly known as Horizon 2020).[56]

Fellowships (Engagement Level: I–II)

Fellowships are an engagement path that can be offered by both the academic sector and the industrial sector. In the academic sector, fellowships are common with graduate or undergraduate students. A company may choose to offer a fellowship in a specific field of study that aligns with their interests and often can name the fellowship such as "The XYZ company fellowship in data science." Fellowships can provide strong connections to the students who receive them and the faculty/researcher whose group the student is in, as well as serve to spread brand awareness on campus if it is named. Additionally, fellowships are usually treated as gifts and may be tax-deductible to the company (check with your tax advisor). Fellowships typically cover the student's costs and a small living stipend. An example would be the Two Sigma PhD fellowship program which provides the recipient with a one-time $10,000 award and $75,000 per year, for two consecutive Academic years, to cover tuition, fees, and a stipend for living expenses. This program is open to all doctoral students in STEM fields.[57]

Alternatively, fellowships are also offered in industry to faculty, researchers, creative talent and more. For faculty, these fellowships are often aligned with a sabbatical, but other professionals can also be eligible for fellowships. One example is the Bosch Research Industry Sabbatical program. In this program, participants work on specific industry cases within Bosch's research environment with state-of-the-art technologies and tools. The program can run from two months to one year. During this time participants are employed by Bosch Research and receive a salary, but their university contract is paused.[58] This type of program can be extremely useful in infusing creativity and new approaches to company problems as well as providing an impactful framework for the faculty.

Finally, there is the in-residence model. This can be an entrepreneur in residence at a university, entrepreneurship center, incubator, accelerator, etc. In this structure, a successful entrepreneur is brought in to work with the community within the host organization. The model can also be flipped where an academic sector organization offers fellowships to industry professionals for a set time period where honorary affiliation is granted to someone to join the organization as a collaborator and work alongside advising and sharing perspective with the organization's employees. This is a useful way to build bridges and form connection points.

Grant Awards (Engagement Level: I–II)

Grant awards are an engagement path that are usually offered as part of an industry plan to engage external researchers, other talented professionals, and university faculty. In this engagement path, the company typically establishes a formal program with challenge problems, eligibility criteria, and clear awards in both monetary amount and duration. These are beneficial for the company because, for a set funding amount, the company receives hundreds of proposals with novel ideas on addressing the problems that are a challenge to the company. In evaluating the proposals, the company gains insights in ways to approach the problem with novel ideas and then can make awards on the proposals that seem to align for the most promise. It also connects the company to many faculty across many different institutions and in an emerging field. This engagement path can help the company play an integral role in the research community. Some examples of corporate grant programs to highlight include:

> **NVIDA faculty grants:** These awards are for full-time faculty members at accredited academic institutions that award research degrees to PhD students. The project must use NVIDIA technology for the innovation.[59]

Amazon research awards for academics and nonprofits: This program offers unrestricted funds and AWS Promotional Credits to support research at academic institutions and nonprofit organizations in areas that align Amazon's mission to advance "customer-obsessed science."[60]

Sony Research Awards: The awards fund cutting-edge academic research and help build a collaborative relationship between faculty and Sony researchers. Awards of up to $150,000 USD per year for each accepted proposal aim to support pioneering research that could drive new technologies, industries, and the future.[61]

Lilly Research Awards (Eli Lilly Co.): The Lilly Research Award Program (LRAP) emphasizes collaboration between Lilly scientists and external researchers. Instead of an outright grant to an external researcher, LRAP provides Lilly scientists working on basic and applied research projects with an avenue to partner with global external researchers to collaboratively advance research projects. Research proposals are prepared jointly by a Lilly scientist sponsoring the project and an external investigator.[62]

Adobe Data Science Research Awards: Each year Adobe funds North American college or university faculty researchers to promote the understanding and use of data science in the area of marketing with grants of up to $50,000.[63]

3M nontenured faculty awards: Each year for the past 30 years 3M has run a program to provide grants to early career faculty to foster new ideas in their own areas of interest as well as an opportunity to come to 3M and interact with company researchers. "For 3M researchers, it is an additional opportunity to stay in touch with the creative ideas that are stimulating some of the nation's brightest young scientists."[64]

Roblox Creator Fund: An award such as the Roblox Creator award is open to all creators, not just faculty. This program is for creators and developers who want to "build the next generation of experiences on Roblox" and awards start at $500,000 per project.[65]

Part 2 Step 5: Understand Possible Paths of Engagement

Sponsored Research (Engagement Level: II–III Depending on Scope of the Sponsored Research Engagement)

Sponsored research is a typical path for industry to work with universities, independent labs, and research centers when there is a specific problem and scope unique to a company. We discussed the mechanics of sponsored research and intellectual property issues in the previous chapters but in terms of choosing sponsored research as an engagement path, what are its unique aspects?

There are actually several. First, sponsored research has a specific scope of work crafted and agreed upon by the researcher and the company. For the company, this generally means the scope aligns with a specific problem they need solved. If the research is successful, the intellectual property that arises from the research may be licensed by the sponsor company. But even if the research does not yield IP, it may still provide valuable insights into what did not work and why. That information can be just as valuable as IP in eliminating wasteful and nonproductive research paths.

Second, a company sponsor becomes very familiar with the faculty researcher and the students in their group. Students who work on the company-specific challenge may be interested in continuing the line of work at the company after graduation. This engagement path, therefore, can serve both the goals of addressing a challenging need and attracting talent that can continue to address challenges in the space beyond a single research project.

Third, if the work is performed by researchers at the company and in the university or research center, there is often the opportunity to co-author scientific papers. Co-authorship can be beneficial to both academia and industry researchers. Where industry researchers alone have significantly declined in number of publications over the past several years, co-authorship with academic and research centers has increased.

In an article on the shifting corporate–academic relationship, a Nature Index post reported that "The number of partnerships between a corporate and an academic or government institution has more than doubled in the five years since 2012, when the index began tracking high-quality research. From an initial 12,672 pairings, the connections have grown to 25,962 in 2016, half of which were in the life sciences".[66]

This Nature article went on to share data on the trending behavior of corporations when it comes to research. According to Robert Tijssen at Leiden University, Netherlands[67,68] corporations have been cutting back on their research spending and scientific output for several decades and instead are either outsourcing discovery research or carrying it out more with external partners.[69] For the *innovation supply chain*, this shift is noteworthy. Overall, corporations contribute to a minor 2% of high-quality research tracked by the Nature Index. On current trends, their contribution could further diminish.[70] If companies are doing less of the innovative research on their own and instead partnering with academic and other research organizations, how is that shift being translated to support in these initiatives? Everyone wants the new technologies and start-ups but without solid support at the research level, the end products can't happen. Sponsored research is a key pathway to supporting this research. See Figure 2.7.

Advisory Boards (Engagement Level: I)

Advisory boards are an extremely useful yet often under-utilized engagement path for both the academic sector and the industrial sector. In the academic sector, industry advisory boards can provide valuable insight to the challenges companies are seeing, corporate community goals as well as provide valuable information regarding the industry trends and skills needed by employees. Alternatively, with many technological advances happening so quickly, many companies have enacted Science Advisory Boards which bring in professionals from the academic sector to inform the company on the latest developments and help the company roadmap their innovation strategy.

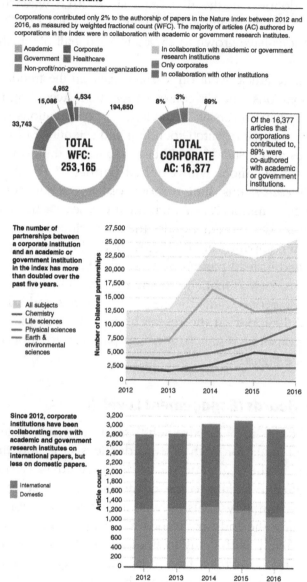

Figure 2.7 Illustrates corporate contributions to scientific publications published by discipline between 2012 and 2016. Of the 16,377 papers corporations contributed to, 89% were co-authored with academic or government institutions.

Curriculum/Strategic Advisor Roles (Engagement Level: I)

This path is one used by the academic sector to better understand and meet industry needs. Industry advisors who assist academic departments with building curriculum help ensure students are work-ready when they graduate. Industry experts are incredibly valuable in this role. Working together, industry and academia can help ensure future talent has the skills needed to succeed and keep innovation thriving. In the entrepreneurial area, industry experts are critical to help students understand real challenges. Students can be creative with solutions, but understanding what the problems are, and being trained with the skills to address the problems, is important. Engaging industry in curriculum design underscores the partnership and the value of the expertise industry brings. One conclusion that can be drawn from a survey of the literature is that the university–industry collaboration has proved to be a crucial element in the innovation and economic development of regions and countries worldwide.[71] Though funding is often a component of engagement partnerships, time and expertise are also crucial components.

Joint Research Centers (Engagement Level: III)

Joint research centers are just that – joint. A company and an academic institution, sometimes involving a government entity, build a new center to work together on specific topics. This may include research, education, talent, and more. Oftentimes this involves an on-campus presence of a company or joint endeavor in a research park. For example, at Purdue University there is The Joint Transportation Research Program. That program facilitates collaboration among the Indiana Department of Transportation, higher education institutions and industry "to implement innovations that result in continuous improvement in the planning, design, construction, operation, management and economic efficiency of the Indiana transportation infrastructure."[72] Centers can be involved and often include a significant investment of resources.

Consulting (Engagement Level: I)

Similar to other paths mentioned, consulting can be a path offered by both the academic sector and the industrial sector. For entrepreneurial faculty, starting a consulting practice where they work for companies in a consulting capacity is attractive. Most faculty appointments provide for the equivalent of one day per week consulting privileges. For industry looking to connect with faculty expertise on a specific project for a limited time frame, hiring an academic consultant may be the path forward.

In his October 2022 article in *Science*, Prof. Stephen Cheung of Brock University in Ontario Canada states "one of the fundamental realities of university life is that – lip service from the administration notwithstanding – the primary criteria for career advancement are grants from traditional funding sources and published basic research. In contrast, industrial collaborations and applied research are given little if any consideration or appreciation, despite the fact that there are probably at least as many funding opportunities in industrial and applied research as there are through traditional avenues."[73] Consequently, some faculty who want to engage with industry and innovate use the consulting path.

Similarly, academic institutions may seek out expertise of industry and look to consulting as the connection path as part of an engagement partnership.

Student Internships/Co-ops/Faculty or Professional Sabbaticals (Engagement Level: I)

Summer internship pipeline programs are used by many organizations in the innovation ecosystem. Internships enable organizations to create a talent pipeline with bright minds. Internships are usually offered in the summer which is most conducive to the academic calendar. Similarly, co-op programs provide experience for students but usually for a longer time than a summer break.

Faculty can also spend a sabbatical at a company – and conversely, industry professionals can spend time as a fellow or visiting researcher at a university. First, faculty sabbaticals in industry can be attractive. They provide the faculty member the opportunity to see the impact first-hand. Additionally, some faculty feel an industry sabbatical is essential in order to experience for themselves the types of jobs their students are likely to take at graduation and throughout their careers.[74] Alternatively, industry members can look to spend up to a year at a university as a Visiting Industry Researcher or Visiting Scientist. These are different from industry fellowships in that they are actual appointments, not honorary. The individual remains employed by their company but pauses their activity to work at the university. At CSAIL, my department manages the Visiting Industry Researcher Program. This program welcomes qualified industry researchers to the lab to embed in one of our research groups and work side-by-side with faculty researchers and students on projects. Visiting Industry Researchers (VIRs) need to meet MIT requirements for the appointment (a combination of education and work experience) and interview with the faculty researcher who leads the group they wish to join. A VIR comes to the lab as a member of the MIT community and can participate in all campus activities and benefits such as the library and recreation programs. This engagement model is sought-after for the shared learning and understanding gained by the VIR that can be brought back to their company. Often a VIR comes to the lab "attached" to a company's sponsored research project but it does not have to be that way. VIRs can also come to the lab and work on ongoing projects that are government funded.

The benefit to the innovation engagement partnership and *innovation supply chain* from the immersion experiences is that they provide each party a perspective they would not have otherwise obtained. With the deeper perspective, the organizations involved can align more efficiently, and move the ground breaking research out of the lab to commercial scale for positive economic impact.

Degree Programs/Micro-credentials/Professional Programs/Executive Education/Custom Programs (Engagement Level: I)

Universities, professional associations, skill building organizations, and edtech companies all provide professional and executive learning programs. In the case of innovation engagement partnerships, this path is one of the best places to start. Recently, Honeywell CEO Vimal Kapur remarked "There is always a trend which makes your skills obsolete, every five years."[75] This fast pace of skills becoming obsolete has led to new approaches in micro-credentials. Certificate programs, graduate/master's certificates, and now "MicroMasters" are being used to gain specific skill upgrades needed to stay competitive and fuel innovation. Some MicroMasters programs are offered through online Massive Online Open Courseware (MOOC) company EdX (now part of 2U). These programs are a series of graduate level courses that provide deep learning in a specific career field and are recognized by employers for their job relevance. In MOOC tradition, they are open to everyone. You do not need a specific degree as a prerequisite or a specific grade point average. There are no admissions tests. The MicroMasters programs are offered in a wide range of disciplines. The programs typically range from 3 to 8 graduate level courses and cost between $1,000 and $4,000 for the entire program.[76] Students completing the program successfully may then apply to the university offering credit for the MicroMasters certificate and, if accepted, can pursue an accelerated and less expensive Master's Degree.

Some great examples of MicroMasters programs are MIT's Principles of Manufacturing which include 8 graduate level courses to be completed over 18 months at a cost of $1,260 for the complete program. Purdue offers Quantum Technology: Computing and Sensing. This program consists of 3 courses and can be completed in just eight months for a cost of $4,275.[77] Quantum is a rapidly accelerating field, and quick upskilling can be extremely beneficial as companies chart their innovation roadmap. In both cases, there is the option to continue for a master's degree at the university if admitted.

Many leading companies create long-term innovation engagement partnerships in talent acquisition and development. Having a tuition benefit as part of employee benefits is one element but some companies partner to enable large groups of employees to receive upskilling either through publicly offered executive/professional education or custom programs developed specifically to address that company's roadmap delivering the skills they need their employees to have.

Ongoing long-term partnerships for continuous upskilling impact the innovation ecosystem by injecting the latest teachings and newest advancements into the commercial center frequently. The sprinkling of new ideas ignites continuous creativity and keeps the *Innovation Supply Chain* humming. The world is changing faster than ever before. To stay on top of those changes and keep innovating, you can't put off learning. Don't fall into the trap of being "too busy to be successful."

Start-Up/Innovation Programs (Engagement Level: I–III)

This path can encompass a variety of connection points. Start-up connection points can be as simple as guest lecturing in an entrepreneurial class, becoming a mentor in a start-up advisory service, supporting a commercialization center, backing start-up competitions with prize support, participating in formal programs like Delta V or Mass Challenge, or venture funding.

If start-up connections and becoming part of the innovation ecosystem are part of your goals, mapping out the available options that align with your needs and capabilities is the first step. Depending on the intensity of the effort and scope of engagement, this path can be simple or extremely complex.

Capstone Projects/MBA Projects (Engagement Level: I)

The NEET/Aurora Flight Sciences focus feature illustrated how both academia and industry can benefit from capstone projects in engineering. But what options are there outside of engineering?

To start, let's look at action learning and the MBA student. At MIT Sloan School of Management there are several ways for industry to connect with MBA students. For example, the Generative AI Lab (GenAI-Lab) pairs student teams with cutting-edge projects involving generative AI technologies. Companies can submit ideas for projects and, if selected, have the MBA students work on solving the problem. The focus of the projects is on strategic implementation and practical application, emphasizing how generative AI can drive innovation and solve complex business problems.[78]

Another interdisciplinary example is Worcester Polytechnic Institute's (WPI) Interactive Qualifying Project (IQP). WPI is a leader in project-based learning and the IQP is designed to provide students with the experience of working in interdisciplinary teams to solve a problem or need that lies at the intersection of science and society. Science, engineering, and business students come together on interdisciplinary teams and "immerse themselves in problems of societal importance – problems that matter to people and communities."[79] It is a degree requirement and all students, no matter their major, must participate in order to graduate.

Philanthropy (Engagement Level: I–III)

Previously the example of MIT's Deshpande Center illustrated the impact a significant gift can have on the innovation ecosystem. But not all gifts have to be large to be impactful. Some of the challenges most faculty face is supporting students. A shift in funding can mean a gap opens that jeopardizes an appointment. Gifts to faculty can help them smooth out funding and avoid gaps, as well as purchase equipment or other materials necessary for their research.

Philanthropic giving can also create scholarships, endow professorships, help construct needed facilities, or fund specific programming to help students with extracurricular activities such as robotics competitions. There are also transformational gifts that enable academic and nonprofit organizations to go all in and make exponential impact possible.

For any nonprofit, gifts are an essential part of funding. Small general gifts can help operations and basic programming. Larger gifts can be used to create impactful programs. MassChallenge is an example of a nonprofit dedicated to helping start-ups and the innovation ecosystem. It connects entrepreneurs with other organizations to "create sustainable change and disrupt the status quo."[80] It is a 501(c)(3) nonprofit and has offices not just in Massachusetts but in other states and other countries.

With gifts, it is usually a simple monetary transaction that does not require time from the donor. However, if the donor is interested in seeing how the gift is being used for impact, the donor is often invited to talks, lunches with the team, or included on paper and report distribution channels etc.

Next-Generation Pipeline Programs (Engagement Level: I)

There are groups in the innovation ecosystem who have their eye on how to keep the talent pipeline full. The programs that focus on this future talent concern are often referred to as Pipeline or K-12 programs. It is important to note, that in many places around the country the math taken in middle school will determine which majors may be open to a student when they look to college. Consequently, if not enough middle school students take the necessary math classes, the colleges and universities won't have enough students in high demand majors such as computer science, data science, and engineering. That then leads to a lack of graduates in those disciplines for companies to employ which can hurt industry competitiveness and success. We really are all in this together so finding ways to work together is crucial.

One of my favorite Pipeline/K-12 programs I have been involved with is the Engineering Ambassadors program.[81] This program was started in 2009 by Penn State (but other institutions joined later) initially to encourage more women to get interested in engineering. An executive from Pratt & Whitney (now part of Raytheon) put significant support behind the program to address the "leak" in the pipe. The pool of graduates may have some diversity, but the data showed as individuals advance in their careers to management, there is "leakage" of women and under-represented groups. One way to approach this was to address it in the middle schools so students had an opportunity to take the math they would need to major in engineering in college – basically broaden the pool even more. Next, the aim was to provide role models who could share their excitement and enthusiasm for the profession so middle school students would consider an engineering path. The program was application based open to students in STEM, and selected "ambassadors" received extensive communication and presentation training. The ambassadors would then present in middle schools throughout the academic year sharing their stories as well as a fun hands-on activity reflective of STEM challenges. The following summer, each ambassador had an internship with a sponsor company and brought all their new skills, as well as academic knowledge, to their job. Many ambassadors received job offers from the companies they interned with. This program is a great example of ensuring the pipeline grows while providing work-relevant training to interns who become valued employees.

Economic Development and Societal Impact (Engagement Level: II–III)

Individual programs on local economic development may emerge as partnerships among universities, nonprofits, state/local economic development agencies and companies. This is also an area where the federal government is active and supportive. One example is the federal Build to Scale (B2S) program that awards up to $5 million to cities, states or nonprofits, higher education institutions, research parks, economic development entities, etc. who are backed by a city or state. The core goals of the program focus on spawning innovation for positive economic development and specifically: (1) enable high-growth technology entrepreneurship and foster inclusive access to proven entrepreneurship support models; and (2) increase access to capital in communities where risk capital is in short supply by providing operational support for early-stage investment funds, networks, and training programs that focus on both traditional and hybrid equity-based financing.[82] Industry partnerships are important to the success of these programs as they become the customer of the start-ups and employ the trained personnel.

Technology Development/Engineering Centers, Maker Spaces (Engagement Level: I)

Maker spaces (also known as fablabs or hackerspaces) may be associated with a university and provide students, as well as the broader innovation community, access to tools and equipment to make an idea a physical reality. The maker movement is hands-on learning where there is no cost to trying out and failing. Maker spaces enable anyone to take an idea and make a physical product. It's experimentation (that raw material of the *innovation supply chain*). A recent *Forbes* article noted "Every day, new ideas are coming to fruition in these community workshops, where thinkers and tinkerers can go to create things that might otherwise never see the light of day, thanks to the shared resources offered there."[83]

In the United States, the maker movement really took hold in the mid-2000s and now maker spaces can be found in many universities across the country.[84] The spaces often contain the same equipment industry uses so companies can leverage makerspaces not only for design, prototyping and discovery but also talent acquisition.

> *The next frontier for university technology transfer will likely be in the transformation of data-rich sectors using artificial intelligence (AI) and machine learning technologies. One area largely accumulating data is the healthcare sector. Medical knowledge is doubling every 73 days, yet we are barely scratching the surface of utilizing this data.*[85]
> *IpWatchdog 2020*

Licensing Technology/Open-Source Code (Engagement Level: I)

In the previous sections both technology licensing and open-source were covered. However, this is such an important part of the *innovation supply chain*, I want to share a few more points. In universities, the TLO/TTO is usually a rather small department and does not have a large budget. It is not possible to patent every invention disclosed. Also, though Bayh–Dole places IP ownership of federally funded research with universities, it does not allow any of that funding to be spent on filing patents or patent protection. "In 2018, universities spent over $425 million in patent-related legal expenses. . . Patents are expensive and there are never enough funds to file for patents on all of the inventions that warrant protection. As a result, more than 95% of foreign rights are never protected, and less than 30% of patents are ever converted to a full patent from the provisional filing."[86] This goes to the heart of innovation and economic impact in the United States. We are an innovation economy and to keep competitive and our country's economy growing, industry and academic organizations need to be strategic in building long-term win-win innovation engagement partnerships.

Taking the chart from the previous chapter, let's add the engagement vehicles to each side for a better picture on how to plan paths of engagement.

From a high level, mapping the need to the respective units could follow this chart:

Engagement Vehicle-Industry	Industry Sector	NEED-Connect the Dots	Academic Sector	Engagement Vehicle-Academia
Research challenges, technology roadmaps, strategy plans	R&D, Engineering, CTO, etc.	Technology advances	Individual research groups, industry engagement units, research lab, incubators, accelerators, technology collaboratives	Sponsored research, Consortia/Initiative membership
Internships, co-ops, capstone or project sponsorship	Human resources/university relations	Talent acquisition undergraduate	Undergraduate career development center, undergraduate department centers, workforce development agencies, retraining organizations, specialized certificate granting professional organizations, career centers, lab centers	Tech talks, PhD events, lunch & learn, job posting, reverse research "fairs," sponsored research career fairs, undergraduate skill development, professional skill development, career change services

(continued)

(continued)

Engagement Vehicle-Industry	Industry Sector	NEED-Connect the Dots	Academic Sector	Engagement Vehicle-Academia
Training/upskilling benefit	Learning & Development	Workforce education/upskilling	Executive education (business schools), professional education, domain-specific departments, centers, institutes, professional associations, professional training centers and providers, workforce development centers	Degree programs, graduate degree programs, professional/executive programs, MicroMasters, certificates, CEUs, professional credentialing, alternative credentialing
Community partnerships, inspire giving culture, employee volunteerism, brand visibility	Corporate philanthropy	Community support/philanthropy	Resource development, philanthropic partnerships, nonprofit centers, community organizations, technology councils	Student programming, K-12 pipeline programs, faculty gifts, student fellowships, guest lecture in classes, naming of conference rooms or buildings

168

Innovation Alchemy

New technology or processes to enhance products/processes, launch new ones, test viability of new technology	Innovation department, innovation teams, venture arm	Start-ups	Entrepreneurship centers, individual academic departments, start-up support programs, labs, centers, institutes, incubators, accelerators, start-up communities, co-working spaces	Start-up connection programs, start-up ecosystem participation
Participate in projects, internships, employee fellowships or visiting university appointments	Business units	Business process improvement	Business school units, faculty, centers, institutes, professional associations	MBA projects, internships, consulting, faculty sabbaticals
License technology, leverage open source, connect with start-ups	Business units, legal department	Technology transfer	Technology transfer office, Technology Licensing office, legal department	Exclusive or nonexclusive license, open-source licenses, engage start-ups, acquire start-ups
Specific SOW	Engineering, R&D	Outsourced engineering	Outsourced engineering centers, maker spaces, foundries	Work-for-hire

(continued)

There are many different structures for engagement. A company's research department can connect with an individual researcher, the company university relations team can engage career offices and departments on student employment, and individuals (often alumni) participate in classrooms as guest speakers or serve on advisory boards. There are also connections built around the sponsorship of a capstone project, or a faculty member may consult for a company. In the research sphere, there could be a master level research agreement involving multiple research departments or an individual sponsored research project with only one research group. Broader engagement, which may include multiple different connections points across several objectives, within a formal program such as consortia participation and affiliate program/corporate affiliate partnership participation can be a particularly useful starting point. This book is not meant to list every possible form of engagement but instead call attention to a few models and help you think through the questions on alignment, ROI, and implementation.

Now, let's look at creating engagement plans.

Key Takeaways from Part 2

1. Clear objectives and strategic alignment from the start are essential for success.
2. Acknowledge constraints. We all have them.
3. TLO/TTO can be a useful partner.
4. When recruiting, know your audience. What works well in one organization does not necessarily work well in others.
5. Understand the level of effort needed to make the partnership successful and plan accordingly.
6. Communications matters, not miles.

Part 3

Step 6: Create Your Plan

Step 7: Build Your Team for Success

Step 8: Execute the Plan

Step 9: Track Your Successes/Learn from Mistakes

Step 10: Innovate

Step 6: Create Your Plan

> *Universities provide the earliest look at where the next big idea will come from. Companies who are aligned with early-stage research see advanced signals of what's going to be the next big opportunity, and they get a head start on competition.*
>
> — *Mark Sedam, UNH*[1]

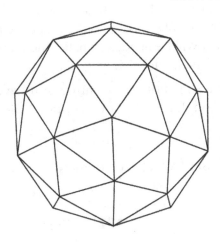

For every singular objective, think in terms of facets. There are many ancillary activities that align with, and amplify, the objective. The most effective innovation engagement partnerships take advantage of that amplification. To start, the academic and industry sectors obviously need to connect. However, that simple first step is often not so simple. How do you make the right connections? Most organizations (both academic and corporate) do not have one easy-access "front door" to help. In the research realm, many industry researchers attend the same conferences as academic researchers, and connections can be made there. In other cases, human resource offices and university relations teams often connect through academic career centers. Perhaps even the innovation arms of companies connect with the entrepreneurship centers at universities or incubators, accelerators, and start-up sandboxes in a region. Academic research labs and nonprofits in the innovation ecosystem also want to make connections. The goal may be to test a new technology, acquire real data to work with, or follow a myriad of other engagement paths that don't necessarily neatly fit in one of the established paths. Therefore, it's often not crystal clear how to start from either side.

Before you start creating your plan, whether from the academic or industry sector, you will need to answer these three questions:

- What is the goal (or goals) of the innovation engagement partnership?
- What engagement level are you comfortable with? Remember in Part 2 that Levels I, II, and III are grouped in terms of resource intensity. That can be time, people, money, equipment, etc. Be clear on what will be needed to make the engagement partnership successful and achieve its goals.
- Who are the stakeholders? Confirm you have the support of critical stakeholders. Without support, the best-laid plans will fail.

Let's take a closer look at each of these.

Objectives, Goals, and Alignment

When examining the full spectrum of organizations in the *periodic table of innovation elements*, a few "primary bonds" are clear. Most engagement partnerships start with one, or more, of these five objectives:

- Talent acquisition/students
- Talent development/professional education
- Research/R&D
- New technology/start-ups
- Just connecting – staying in each other's orbit to keep an eye on things

NOTE: There is also philanthropy, but that often arises out of connections through one or more of these and is not typically a stand-alone objective.

Rarely, if ever, is the path to collaboration laid out clearly, well-lit with directional signs, and no speed bumps or detours. Instead, for both industry and academic sectors, the people who build the engagement partnerships are often spread across different units, different departments, and have different goals and metrics. Communication among the units involved is important not only to ensure alignment but also recognize ROI appropriately and adjust if needed. However, such communication is often a challenge.

Many companies I have worked with express frustration over not having visibility into the whole engagement picture. If the benefits of collaboration are not shared broadly through an organization, how can you really measure ROI or realize tangible benefits? One of the biggest mistakes I see companies make is not sharing information about the engagement partnerships widely within their organizations. Impactful and successful engagement programs that are truly viewed as mutually beneficial have five things in common:

- Clear alignment on purpose
- Understanding of what each side brings to the table

- Clear communication channels both with each other and internally within their respective organizations
- Understanding of the ROI, both tangible and intangible
- Commitment to the relationship (purely transactional one-off engagements do not lead to innovation or economic impact)

At MIT CSAIL, our Alliances department is our "front door" for industry engagement with our lab. We have a "For Industry" tab on the CSAIL home page that links directly to the Alliances page.

CSAIL Alliances built out a separate website because the industry audience has a different focus than prospective students or the academic research community served by the main site. We are one lab of the dozens of labs and centers at MIT that engage with industry. So the first step in alignment is determining *which* academic disciplines are going to be involved. For a company that wants to engage in computer science and artificial intelligence, CSAIL is the place to start. However, if it's quantum, then you would want to connect with the Center for Quantum Engineering. Conversely, if it's business, it may be the Center for Information Systems Research (CISR) or undergraduate talent in MIT's Career Advising and Professional Development (CAPD). Most academic organizations are similarly organized with technical research being separate from business research and both separate from undergraduate career services. The first step is identifying that clear purpose of the engagement partnership you want to build.

Aside from finding the right path and connections within the academic sector, companies need to think about strategic goals and communicate that to the academic team. Often the motivating factors for initiating the innovation engagement partnership change over time. That is why strong communication is key and established check-ins are utilized to keep evaluating the alignment. For this, you need a team focused on ensuring success. Remember, successful innovation engagement partnerships are not transactional. There is a great deal of effort that goes into building strong, multifaceted relationships that deliver value and impact for years. To keep them producing and delivering, you will also need to continue to innovate and explore new areas.

For academic institutions seeking connections with industry partners, the same is true. Are you looking to help students find jobs or obtain research collaborations for faculty researchers, data shares, and connections to learners who may be interested in executive or professional education? Similarly, there is not one front door for innovation engagement partnerships at companies either. How do you start connecting? An important step is to bridge the silos at your own institution. In a recent Starship[2] meeting, participants from Sloan had identified some companies the MBA students were interested in working for but who had never participated in any of the MBA-focused engagement programs. Once they shared this challenge in Starship, I and others in the group were able to help them by sharing the connections we had at the company. The more we all work together to achieve win-win engagement partnerships, the more impact and economic benefit we will have.

Also, innovation engagement partnerships do not have to start out as large endeavors. They can be a small engagement that puts in place a solid foundation (remember communication, culture, and relationships) upon which additional valuable connections can grow. Partners are chosen for different reasons – maybe there is one set of partners for student talent/opportunities and another for research and yet another for start-ups. In any event, each collaboration should have a long-term view. It would be wonderful if every meeting resulted in the perfect connection and all parties came away with exactly what they were looking for, but that is not reality.

Initial Planning Structure for Engagement Partnerships:

1. Start with a clear objective.
2. Plan the timeline. What will the initial phase of the engagement partnership encompass? Make sure it's long enough to see results.
3. Identify who will be involved from both sides.
4. Determine how you are going to define *and* measure success.
5. Establish reasonable and actionable milestones (more about that in Part 4).

6. If milestones are met and the plan is to grow the engagement partnership, move onto the next step. If not, take the time to revisit why the milestones are not being met and invest in fixing the foundation! You cannot build a long-term strategic partnership if the foundation is not solid.

Secret Sauce Recipe for Success

I've shared Figure 3.1 in many talks I have given on the subject of innovation engagement partnerships. The "shared vision" refers to the alignment of goals. "Strong communication" should involve clear and frequently connections, not simply yearly check-ins. And don't assume anything. If something isn't clear on alignment, communicate and resolve it. Next, your team should include "catalyzers" – those "boundary spanners" who can identify opportunities, understand alignment, and ultimately (moving to the fourth quadrant) build strong personal relationships with trust and understanding. All together it is a "virtuous

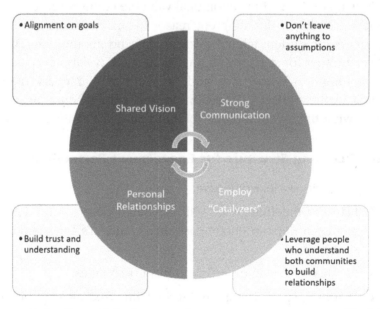

Figure 3.1 Essential elements for engagement success. "Building Partnerships with Industry" deck by Lori Glover

circle" and the formula to build strong innovation-oriented collaborations and partnerships that will drive positive impact for the institutions involved and the broader ecosystem.

Starting with initial objectives, you should also consider all the ancillary connection points that could impact or amplify the success of the stated goal. For example, if you are from industry looking to connect on talent, consider Figure 3.2.

Connecting through a career center is one connection point, but there are others that could make achievement of the stated goal

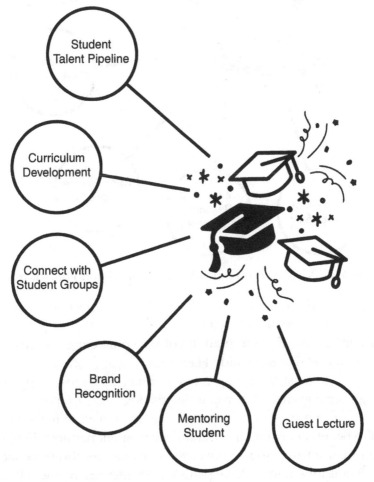

Figure 3.2 Visualization of possible connection points for talent

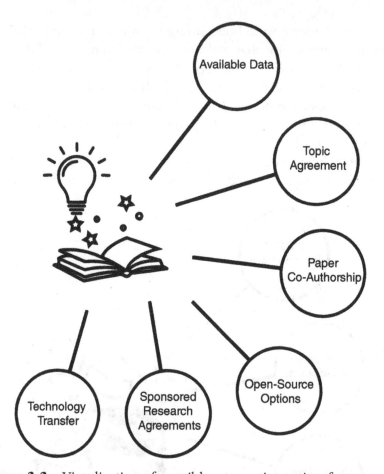

Figure 3.3 Visualization of possible connection points for research

easier and more impactful. Consider all the connection points that will enhance the stated objective.

Additionally, if your plan involves connecting on research, considerations should include Figure 3.3.

Often, innovation engagement partnerships grow organically. Though organic growth is wonderful, relying solely on personal contacts can result in siloed programs that are not very inclusive and hard to penetrate. For an innovation engagement partnership to truly have broad impact, spur innovative solutions, and bring economic benefit, it is important to have plans for broader reach. The following are some examples to consider.

Research Focus

A multifaceted engagement between Takeda Pharmaceutical Co. and the MIT School of Engineering can illustrate several ways an engagement partnership can be valuable to the partners and boost innovation. This program was launched in 2020, right before the pandemic. Initially, the focus was to explore AI capabilities. In the four years that have transpired, AI has exploded, whole new technological capabilities have come into being. Researchers such as Dr. Jim Glass from CSAIL expressed enthusiasm for the engagement partnership because it was "a chance to branch out and make an impact . . . and the idea of collaborating with people who were experts in areas where I'm not . . . was very appealing." In just four years, the research program yielded a catalog of 16 new research papers, 20+ projects, multiple discoveries, and even a patent for a system that could improve the manufacturing of small-molecule medicines.[3] Connecting Takeda's expertise in biopharmaceuticals with MIT's expertise in Artificial intelligence and machine learning fueled the *innovation supply chain* and resulted in new actionable knowledge and technologies. When each stakeholder recognizes and appreciates the value and expertise the other brings to the collaboration, solid relationships are built and the work being done can yield positive results for both as well as boost the economy.

> *Over the past few decades, a whopping 11,000 companies were started at universities, and the success rate of university start-ups is high. Universities are pushing boundaries and leading science—and industry wants to get in on the ground level.*
>
> — *Venturewell*[4]

Broad Exposure and Engagement

Another example of a multifaceted successful engagement, though on a smaller scale, is CSAIL's engagement with Ocado Group plc. As a member of CSAIL Alliances Affiliates, Ocado has broad access to the lab with visibility into research, talent acquisition, talent development, new technology development, start-ups, and more. Ocado joined CSAIL

Alliances in 2016 to help their R&D team identify and explore research and new technologies that could improve efficiency and their ability to scale. They were particularly interested in connecting with leading researchers working on automation. They made several deep connections in this area with researchers whose domain expertise is aligned with their challenges. However, they also were exposed to other areas that were relevant but not necessarily within their initial scope. By 2017, Professor Wojciech Matusik and co-founder Javier Ramos had developed a custom optical coherence tomography (OCT) scanner that could visualize materials at the width of a human hair. This technology was also 100 times faster than anything commercially available at the time. Using this technology, they developed a prototype that was the foundation for the launch of Inkbit – a completely novel additive manufacturing system. Inkbit CEO Davide Marini shares, "Instead of going for the traditional venture capital funding strategy, I chose to raise money from corporations and strategic investors because they gave us an understanding of the market and they could potentially become our customers." It was perfect alignment for Ocado who saw the opportunity and invested. For Ocado, Inkbit's proprietary 3D vision system enabled "transformational advances."[5] Ultimately the engagement partnership initiated not only a thriving business relationship but also an exciting use case for the technology. If not for the broader lens, this innovation connection would not have happened.

Keep the gradient.

— *Prof. Daniela Rus*

Ocado continues to be a thriving member of CSAIL Alliances. Perpetual benefit and positive impact set up innovation engagement partnerships for continued success. But how do you chart a sustainable engagement? As you create your plan, along with the factors mentioned previously, remember all ROI is not necessarily tangible or monetary. Additionally, reaching beyond personal connections opens up more opportunities for value to be created and innovations to ignite. But most important for continued success is to make stewardship of the engagement partnership someone's job!

Overall, there are many benefits to both academia and industry in creating innovation engagement partnerships. Figure 3.4 shows slides I've used in several talks to sum up the top benefits consistently identified by academic and commercial organizations involved in innovation-based collaborations.

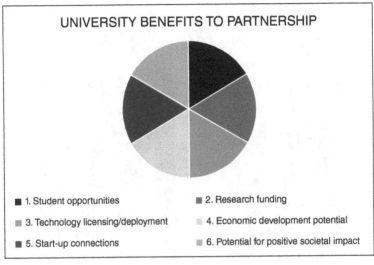

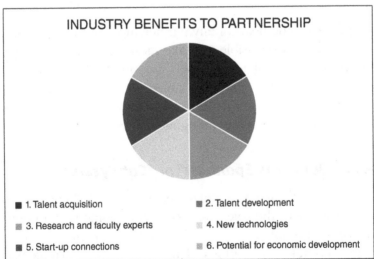

Figure 3.4 Top areas of benefits for universities and industry engaged in innovation partnerships

Step 7: Build Your Team for Success

People are at the heart of any partnership. Scoping the tasks and staffing the team responsible to make these innovation engagement partnerships successful is extremely important. Thinking back on different interviews and talks I've given on this subject, what most people want to know is "what do I need for the team to be successful?" The following are a few thoughts I can share.

Look for "Boundary Spanners" or "Catalyzers"

You do not need a team of PhDs. Instead, think of what the functional necessities of the roles are. You want people who understand the academic disciplines they will interface with *and* who understand the business applications of those disciplines. Think back to Natasha's Boundary Spanners who have an eye for alignment, enjoy building collaborations, and are willing to learn what they don't know.

Industry and academia are very different worlds. Anyone who works in this space needs to not only understand that but also understand how to build the bridges that traverse the divide. I often say my role is a "matchmaker and translator." Asking the questions to find the right alignment is important.

The single most important characteristic for the team involved in building innovation engagement partnerships is the ability to work successfully across all levels of the organization and various disciplines/departments to build coalitions.

Focus on Efficiency

You do not need an army. A few talented folks can build amazing collaborations. In industry, some companies are structured where innovation engagement partnerships are viewed from across the organization and research, innovation, talent acquisition, talent development, and other departments involved see the "big picture" for engagement. However, in many companies the departments are silos. A few people who understand how to share information and build value across the organization are necessary to really see impact. Connect with people who understand BOTH industry and academia's role in the *innovation supply chain*.

Accountability and Ownership: If It's Important to the Strategy, Make It Someone's Job

Stewardship of the innovation engagement partnership should be someone's job. If it's not, it's just one more thing on an already full plate and the time, money, and effort put into creating the plan will be wasted. This applies to both industry and academia. I have seen situations where the retirement of the primary person who built the engagement partnership and nurtured its success quickly turns to failure when a new person is handed something they know nothing about, and doesn't see the point in figuring it out, because it is not tied to their metrics. Additionally, there are cases where a faculty member is put in charge of an engagement when they are already over committed and, aside from the slice of research that is applicable to their group, they have no bandwidth to help with anything outside that scope.

Build a Network

Invest the time to make multiple connections to support the innovation engagement partnership. No matter what organizations in the *periodic table of innovation elements* are involved, get to know multiple people in those organizations. Awareness is the first step in having the innovation engagements take hold. In today's job market, people move on. If your main contact that you've invested all your time with leaves, what happens to the engagement partnership? For my team, we look to build relationships across seven main connection areas: principle point of contact (our POC/champion), CTO's office/engineering, R&D, innovation, HR for talent acquisition and L&D for talent development, innovation to connect with start-ups, and billing/procurement for payment. With multiple connections, the value of the collaboration impacts multiple departments. This can help broaden engagement and impact. For academic programs, the industry departments can vary depending on what connection points you manage. For industry, think about what you want to accomplish and foster those connection points. In some cases, as with CSAIL Alliances, we can help with research, talent acquisition, talent development, start-ups, conferences, etc. – but with a computer science and artificial intelligence focus. Map out the connections points you need to make to ensure success of your engagement plan.

Increase Visibility and Accessibility

Help out the team by lighting the path. One of the biggest points of frustration from the organizations in the innovation ecosystem is lack of transparency in how to make connections. Everyone has a website. Make sure your website has information on how to connect! For academic institutions, put it on your website that you are interested in working with industry. For industry, make it easy to find the programs you put in place to foster collaborations and who should be contacted if you want to have broader discussions. If a decision is made to commit to a collaboration at a very senior level but no one who is responsible for making that collaboration successful has been brought into any of the formation discussions, that is not a recipe for success.

Division of Labor

No one person can do it all. Understanding the various necessary tasks and allocating them among the team is also an important factor to consider. Remember, a team can consist of one functional unit or individuals brought together to work on the innovation engagement partnership. Throughout this book I have referenced the different elements involved and there is never one-size-fits-all to make collaborations work. However, there are a few key principles that are consistent:

- Someone must create the structure and ignite the partnership. This person is the one who gets the parties to the table.
- Stewarding (and ideally growing) the innovation engagement partnership is an additional job.
- Promoting and monitoring the collaboration is important. Tell your story. Success can spawn new ideas and keep the *innovation supply chain* moving. And to tell that story you need data.

No matter how you structure the team, these three tasks must be accounted for.

Team Structure: Hunters and Farmers

When you think of the team responsible for innovation engagement partnerships, it can take several forms. The team may comprise a specific unit, a cohort of peers from different departments, or loosely distributed personnel across the organization. Regardless of the structure, there are people who are responsible for setting the strategy, initiating contacts, and securing the parties for the partnership. This part is clear no matter what organizations from the *periodic table of innovation elements* are involved. We can call these people the "hunters."

Hunters play a critical role because without them no engagement partnership would get off the ground. Farmers are the team members who manage the day-to-day engagement. They help make connection points, build trust, and ensure alignment. However, it is next to impossible for one person to be both the "hunter" and the "farmer" in an innovation engagement partnership unless they are really responsible for only a small number of the partners. In a well-planned roadmap thinking about possible expansion and who the stakeholders would be will save time and frustration. The roadmap for the innovation engagement partnership can be shared with the "team" and serve as a reference point for anyone who becomes involved, so even if people change roles or jobs, the initial work put into mapping the plan will continue to assist the "farmers" as the innovation engagement partnership matures.

Step 8: Execute the Plan

Now that you have created a well-structured plan for an innovation engagement partnership, you need a clear execution strategy. Where should you start?

An excerpt from an article by Jeffrey Bardzell puts a bright light on the problem: "Recently, a colleague of mine from industry expressed some of the challenges she faced when reaching out to a university seeking collaboration, a proposed collaboration that she was able to fund. In spite of doing her homework and offering funding, her efforts generated little interest. Meanwhile, I have been struggling for years to improve the level of industry participation in my academic unit, even though leadership, faculty, staff, and students all want it."[6] If both parties, broadly, want to collaborate, why is it so hard to get started?

In some situations, old philosophies and outdated thinking still persist. For academics, there is a perception among some that collaborating with industry, or spending time in industry, is damaging to an academic career.[7] Conversely, for some in industry the perception of the "ivory tower" and "impractical theory" still exists. That thinking does not take into account all the changes the past two decades have brought with the explosion of start-ups spinning out, the sharing of code in the open-source community, and the very real desire for many faculty to see their work have a positive impact on society. Old ways of thinking must change if we are to work together to achieve the innovation and growth everyone not only wants but the country needs. Now, to execute the plan, a few things have to be lined up first. No matter which organizations are involved, open channels for collaboration need to be identified. Going back to building the team, who is going to be responsible for promoting opportunities?

Setting the Plan in Motion

In innovation engagement partnerships, catalysts tend to be industry researchers, industry leadership, academic deans, HR/LD departments, individual faculty, lab directors, administrative units, executive directors, VC partners, etc. If you have invested the time, you have a clear focus on what your partnership will focus on. After aligning the topics and departments involved, engage the stakeholders. This step works best when your networks are leveraged.

Action Items for Academic Organizations

1. Leverage your external network: For faculty or researchers, if you want to approach ABC company about a new research consortium on a cutting-edge topic, think about your network. Who do you know at ABC company you could start the conversation with? Something along the lines of an "informational interview" with your contact can go a long way in determining who the right people are to approach, the company's appetite for industry/academic engagement, and overall the company culture when it comes to collaborations.

In terms of identifying who at ABC company could help you, think about your former students, former colleagues, university alumni, or industry researchers in your field who present at your conferences. Starting with a personal relationship can help you gather additional information to strengthen the proposal. Your contact may then be able to provide you a "warm intro" to the decision-maker and pave the way for the conversation.

2. Lean into your internal network: If you don't have someone immediately in your network, leverage other units in your organization who may have the right connections. In universities there may be a unit similar to CSAIL Alliances that works with corporate engagement, employer relations, department advisory boards, etc. Invest in the organizations that support innovation in your region to make connections. Let them know you are willing to be a speaker or serve on a panel. The first step in executing any plan is to simply let potential collaborators know you are willing to work with them.

3. Know your audience: For academics, if it's a company you are reaching out to, understand that the fact that you "can" do something revolutionary with your latest project is fantastic. However, why should industry care? And more importantly, why should that specific company care? How does this new capability you are hoping to refine with ABC company's collaboration benefit ABC company? Unless it is a philanthropic gift, companies need to show why money, time, or effort is being spent on that activity. Make sure the value proposition to the company is clear.

4. Old-fashioned "lead generation" and "marketing": Harness the power of your website, social media, and other platforms to let potential collaborators know what you are doing and that you are open to exploring innovation engagement partnerships. For faculty, you may consider having an "academic" website and an "industry engagement" website. The achievements you need for tenure and academic promotions rarely, if ever, speak to what industry is looking for in collaborators. The effort does not have to be onerous. One thing we do in CSAIL Alliances is video "spotlights" of our faculty and students to showcase the work they are doing and how it may impact industry.

They are short spots, less than 15 minutes. In terms of effort, they do not require extensive preparation or PowerPoint presentation. Just answering some questions, sharing some papers, and giving us access to video demos you've already completed. We do all the editing and polish the final product that appears on our website (https://cap.csail.mit.edu). We often ask the faculty or student featured to share the post on their social media so there is amplification of the asset. The more exposure, the more people learn that person and topic are interested in collaborating.

From the industry/commercial side, many of the nonprofits in the innovation space have membership programs and are very good at lighting a clear path. However, research labs, and especially universities, can be much more opaque. Now that you have put the effort into scoping your innovation engagement partnership and you know where you want to start, how do you find the door(s) in?

Action Items for Industry

1. Find the way "in": Doors, front porches, windows. . .connecting is about people, and the best way to find the right people to work with on an innovation engagement partnership is to get involved in the ecosystem. Many of the colleges and universities in the United States are decentralized. Faculty are usually independent, decide on their own research agenda and manage their own groups. An individual faculty member may choose to join a department's industry engagement programs, or may not. Clarity on the goals of your engagement plan will help you identify the right connections to make. There may be paths that lead to career services, professional education, entrepreneurship center, an individual researcher, a group of researchers, or even a university-wide program involving multiple departments. This is where the scope of your plan, and how you will measure success, comes in. For example, if you are a VC firm, you may start with the entrepreneurship center. Through that connection you may realize there is a specific lab working on the topic you are interested in, and they have several start-ups. Conversely, if you are ABC company, you may know of a specific researcher from conference presentations but also want career services and entrepreneurship/start-ups to be involved in your plan. You may choose to connect through one "door" or several.

When you look at the broader ecosystem, many nonprofits and community organizations exist to help make connections. There are also meet-ups, commercial conferences, and community events. Getting involved in organizations that foster engagement partnerships for innovation is an easy way to begin to make connections both locally and more broadly.

2. Leverage your network: Cold calling faculty is not usually a good way to spend your time. Similar to the faculty/research approach, personal connections are a wonderful start. If you know someone at the institution you want to engage, you can start with them to understand how to navigate the units you need involved in the innovation engagement partnership plan you have created. If you don't know someone, the website of the organization should give you contact information and if not, most administrators in this space are on LinkedIn and work in "corporate engagement," "strategic alliances," "outreach," "external relations," "corporate relations," "member support," or something similar.

Also, whenever possible, attend ecosystem events that showcase the work of different researchers or professionals in the space. Make the effort to go in person when there is the opportunity. Making a connection with the speakers, participating in roundtable discussions, or even having a quick conversation once the talk has finished makes an impression. People are then much more likely to respond to emails, phone calls, or LinkedIn requests when they remember the in-person connection. This makes the process of executing the plan that much easier.

3. Keep objectives top of mind: But most importantly, what are the objectives of your plan? For instance, if you are looking for a faculty consultant for a short-term project, that is very different from looking for a solution to an industry challenge through sponsored research or industry consortium. The connections need to align with the objective.

4. **Leverage broad connections:** Old-fashioned *lead generation* and *marketing* can be used here as well. "Lead generation" admittingly is a little different in this situation. Programs such as researcher awards, seed grants for novel idea exploration, faculty + student team awards, community innovation grants, and prize competitions in regional accelerators are all ways for the industry sector to yield a great amount of "leads" with a low lift. Researcher award programs may bring in dozens if not hundreds of proposals. The proposals will give you a good idea of the types of projects researchers are working on and what organizations may be doing the work that aligns best with your interests. Similarly, engaging in "call-oriented" industry consortia is also an excellent and extremely cost efficient way to identify not only researchers, faculty, and students working in your area of interest but also to access early research results and utilize prototyped tools to develop ways to address challenges that are in your plan's scope.

Heeding the Call: Two Models for Industry Consortia?

There are two models I can highlight to illustrate how this type of industry consortia can work. First, as mentioned previously, in CSAIL Alliances we have "initiatives." The industry consortia built around a common theme. A small number of companies (generally 8–12) join the consortia, and each contributes the same amount of funding and receives the same benefits. Each company has a seat on the executive board and engages in dialogue with researchers on the challenges they see for which there is no current commercial solution. Collaboratively the board (member companies, faculty leads, and lab administration) create "problem statements." These are challenges that, if solved, would be very useful to industry as well as advance the research field. Those problem statements are broad challenges and not specific to any one company but cover a problem each company is dealing with in some way. Think more along the lines of "how the AI arrived at X – more explainable AI in finance applications," not "company Z needs an algorithm that does A." Every company is interested in the overarching topic and when those problem statements go to the entire lab – all 130+ researchers – the companies can review all the proposals from all the different discipline perspectives on how that researcher would approach the problem. From this one call, the companies could connect with 20–30 research groups. Once the review of the proposals is complete, the companies rank them in order of interest. Typically, 5–10 proposals are funded each year. The companies then see 5–10 projects funded and results presented at the annual meeting. In some cases, the projects yield actionable information immediately such as SCRAM, which had been mentioned earlier. In other cases, they yield the data needed for the researcher to apply for a larger government-funded grant. However, in some cases, there may not be sufficient findings in just one year of the project. But, in every case the companies involved have leveraged that one financial commitment to connect on multiple research projects, faculty relationships, student relationships, and even start-up relationships across 5–10 groups, which could be as much as 100 people! Plus, all initiative members receive all the benefits of general CSAIL Alliances Affiliate, which includes student engagement, professional courses, start-up connections, conferences, speaking opportunities, lab visits, and so much more. It's a formula for amplification:

$$\text{Investment} \times \text{engagement} = \text{innovation}^3$$

Alternatively, there are consortia models that are built around novel tool development. An example of this is Machine Learning for Pharmaceutical Development and Syntheses (MLPDS). This is an industry consortium led by Prof. Regina Barzilay at MIT CSAIL and is specifically focused on the use of machine learning in pharmaceuticals. The companies involved are all pharma companies, but the topic is not new molecule or compound creation. It is the development of machine learning tools to help the pharma industry. For this reason, even fierce competitors can join the consortium. Nothing proprietary is shared with the researchers or other members of the consortium. Instead, the researchers build tools that each member then can use as they see fit. The algorithms created are developed and validated on public data. The member companies can then apply those algorithms to their individual proprietary data. Tool development and knowledge transfer happens through one-on-one meetings, teleconferences, GitLab software repositories, and consortium face-to-face meetings.

Executing the Plan, Spurring Innovation, and Yielding Tangible Positive Impact

In addition to making the right connections to get the conversations started, remember culture and reward systems. Time and ideas are the currency of academia, and industry has to justify expenditures and demonstrate value from those expenditures. Academia often takes the "long view," and research does take time. However, industry cannot support projects forever. Companies are not just funding sources. They have to be profitable to stay in business and, in the case of publicly traded companies, have shareholders to report to. They need to see benefits.

Along with sponsored research, other engagement programs should also look at contracts to put a framework to the innovation engagement partnership. Contracts can spell out the level of engagement to expect as well as identify the value map. There should be an agreement spelling out what is provided and what is received. Good contracts make good partners.

Competition

Next, in executing your plan, consider competition. Both internal and external competition can impact the success of your plan's execution. Time is finite. No one can do everything. Competition comes in several forms.

- **Time and attention:** Given any work day, there is only so much time that can be dedicated to tasks and, as is generally the case with human nature, we tend to do the things we like first. For innovation engagement partnerships, the ones that get attention and make progress in advancing innovations are those that:

    a. are well aligned with both the problem and expertise
    b. include necessary stakeholders to build the framework
    c. account for constraints
    d. have dedicated personnel working to make it successful
    e. measure for success

    For some faculty, connecting with industry is just not the way they want to work. If a faculty member with this outlook is put in charge of managing an innovation engagement partnership, it is not likely to be successful. That faculty member will spend their time on things they consider important to their career. Additionally, in practical terms, if Professor A is widely considered to be an expert in X, that person cannot take endless meetings to have general discussions. If Professor A took every meeting when would they have time for research, teaching, advising, and all the other requirements of an academic career? Time is valuable. When you get the chance for the meeting, use it efficiently.

    Conversely, for a faculty member who has been trying for months to get the attention of a corporate VP to connect on a possible collaboration, if the faculty member spends the meeting deeply explaining the technical elegance of their solution but leaves the VP dazed and not understanding any relevance to their company's needs, the alignment is missed. Again, time is valuable, and when you get the chance for the meeting, use it efficiently.

- **Funding and resources:** Similar to time, no organization has unlimited funds or resources. Competition for where those funds and resources will be spent is important to consider when executing your engagement plan. This is where value and alignment take the front seat. The importance of engagement and how it will benefit the parties and move everyone forward must be clear.

- **Positioning:** Navigating competition from other departments in your organization, or industry sector, can be a challenge. For industry, it could be your competition looking to engage the leading researchers in a field at the same organization as you. How do you get the attention of the researcher and put your plan in place? Alternatively, with universities generally being decentralized, other units may emerge who also want to work with the same companies you do. How do you make the case that ABC company should work with you? It's all about alignment. If your unit, company, research lab, or nonprofit offers the best alignment, that is where the best chance of success lies. In terms of internal competition, Aristotle's wisdom still rings true: "The whole is greater than the sum of its parts." Where ever possible, turn competition into cooperation and use the broader connections to map a comprehensive innovation engagement partnership plan.

- **Personnel and space:** I was recently asked by an early career faculty member "why doesn't every department have an organization like CSAIL Alliances to help faculty connect with industry." Well, as previously outlined, time, funding, and resources are not unlimited. For academic sector organizations looking to establish offices to engage industry, there is initial investment in personnel and space. Some of these offices do generate revenue, which is certainly appealing to many institutions, but others do not. Some are more service-oriented acting as a resource for faculty and students. Looking at the institution as a whole, and the units already in place, it may make sense to augment what is already in there, or evaluate a new approach and create a new innovation engagement partnership to achieve new objectives.

The United States is consistently at the top of the charts for innovation, talent, and industry growth. U.S. universities make up 50% of the *world's* top 50 universities and have the most Nobel Laureates of any country. This incredible combination of academic, industry, start-up, and supporting organizations keeps the United States consistently at the top of the charts for creating these game changing new companies (see Figure 3.5).[8]

From the writings of Vannevar Bush to the Bayh–Dole Act, the structure to fuel the *innovation supply chain* has been laid. Now we need to leverage it more efficiently to accelerate innovation even

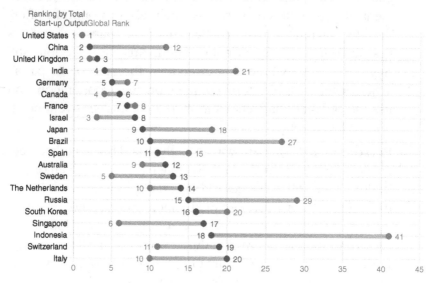

Figure 3.5 Global countries ranking in start-up output

more as technology advances with rapid speed. The jobs of the future cannot even be imagined today. To keep our economy thriving and continually advancing, we need multifaceted innovation engagement partnerships to look beyond a just present need and align for long-term strategic growth.

The mechanics of the *innovation supply chain* have shifted. The major science agencies are nearing a 25-year low for their funding levels, as a share of U.S. gross domestic product.[9] Industry is taking a larger role in this *innovation supply chain*, but, where government and academia are "from a similar cloth," supporting and enhancing increased industry involvement takes some planning for success. We all want the same thing – growth. This book is to help those in this ecosystem be creative, understand needs, frame return on investment (ROI) and chart paths to create innovation engagement programs. With some *Innovation Alchemy*, the *innovation supply chain* will not only stay fueled, but thrive. Industry and government support of research stabilize the "raw materials/ideas" supply. Industry not only levels out sharp peaks and valleys associated with government funding but also levels out time constraints in that not all companies' fiscal year aligns with the September 30 fiscal close of the government and can offer additional options through the year. To have successful innovation engagement partnerships that benefit all the parties involved, you need to know where the successes are, and what may need to change, to support future growth.

Step 9: Track Successes and Learn from Mistakes

No one is perfect; that's why pencils have erasers.
—*Wolfgang Riebe*

Everyone makes mistakes, and even the best-laid plans can overlook a critical component or misread a crucial stakeholder whose support is needed. For innovation engagement partnerships to be successful, the team managing the engagement needs to track success, quantify connection points if possible, as well as track the mistakes.

The only way to improve is to acknowledge what isn't working and strategize new approaches to accomplish the goal.

Here are six common mistakes to avoid:

MISTAKE 1: PRIORITIZING MARQUEE NAMES

There are more than 266 research universities in the United States and more than 5,300 colleges and universities. Also, according to the Census Bureau's Statistics of U.S. Businesses (SUSB) there are 33.2 million businesses, including small businesses, large corporations, and start-ups. Acquisition of high-profile logos is fabulous, but the *innovation supply chain* is not restricted to a few elite universities and tech companies. Don't artificially restrict your partnership goals. If you do, you may not see the success you desire.

MISTAKE 2: LACK OF COORDINATION

The right hand does not know what the left hand is doing. If multiple departments from the same organization reach out to explore engagement partnerships, it looks not only uncoordinated but sends a clear signal on the lack of communication among departments in the organization.

MISTAKE 3: NOT CAPTURING DATA

Data is everywhere. Everyone expects data to back up what you are claiming. Do not overlook the importance of capturing engagement data from every connection point possible.

MISTAKE 4: OVERLOOKING THE SMALL WINS

Recognize and celebrate the small wins. The innovation engagement partnership is a long-term project and small wins along the way should be celebrated. This recognition keeps the teams charged with stewardship energized and helps everyone involved feel part of something bigger. Plus, small wins add up. Success can be celebrated in steps.

MISTAKE 5: NEGLECTING SUSTAINABILITY

Make enough key connections on both sides of the partnership so that if one person leaves, the whole project does not fall apart. Innovation engagement partnerships are a team sport. They should involve as many of the stakeholders as possible, and not just in the initial formation. Keep stakeholders and team members informed and connected. If the engagement partnership is built solely on a personal connection, it is not likely to continue past the tenure of the individuals involved in creating it and therefore may not have the long-term impact desired.

MISTAKE 6: LACK OF ACCOUNTABILITY

Make it someone's job. In some cases, our POC's whole job is just managing the MIT relationships across campus. Those individuals are very plugged in and know what is happening on several fronts. In other cases, there has been a re-organization with the partner and a new person has been handed stewardship of the program without any understanding of its strategic significance, and it flounders.

Both the success and mistakes should be tracked and visited on a yearly basis. We use a customized version of Salesforce as our CRM to track engagements in CSAIL Alliances. Every year we prepare Engagement Reports for our member companies that show where connections are happening, what tangible and intangible benefits are derived, and then share suggestions for increased value in the coming year. An example of this is in Part 4. Having the reports, good communication, and positive relationships with your counterparts in industry or academia help keep the innovation engagement partnership on solid footing. When the foundation is strong, there is the opportunity to expand the relationship, increase start-up development, expand talent readiness, and create economic benefit for the whole region.

Step 10: Innovate

Innovation engagement partnerships are not static. The pace of change has never been faster. Consequently, fostering innovation and working to get novel advancements out of the labs and into the marketplace is a dynamic endeavor. Creativity, flexibility, and vision are all required to succeed. There will be new models, new policy, and new players in the *innovation supply chain* every year.

Staying informed, brainstorming new ideas, and expanding your network are essential to keeping engagement partnerships effective. In the introduction I mentioned several organizations to consider to help you build your community, continue to innovate, and grow your innovation engagement partnerships for impact.

UIIN, UIDP, NACRO, and ATUM are your people (see Focus Feature 3.1)! That is your community. Connections in all areas, both from industry and academia, can be found there. Plus, that is where you can continue to learn and find new opportunities for partnerships. These organizations offer conferences, workshops, courses, reports, and so much more. To keep your innovation engagement partnerships thriving, you too need to innovate, and these organizations can help.

Focus Feature 3.1 The Value of Professional Connections Through the Network of Academic Corporate Relations Officers (NACRO)

NACRO: Connect, Learn, and Innovate
By Joseph Huang, executive director at Stanford and co-president of NACRO

The Network of Academic Corporate Relations Officers (NACRO) is a professional society dedicated to the career development of university-based or research-intensive institution-based corporate relations officers. We believe in a vision of holistic corporate relations, in which the university or research intensive institution (like research hospitals) offers multiple ways for a corporation to engage with the institution, such as philanthropy, research, capstones, recruiting, and research parks. Corporate clients progress from transactional relationships that feature only one type of interaction to becoming strategic partners that engage in multiple channels.

NACRO has 500 members across Mexico, the United States, and Canada. We have an annual meeting in the summer, along with virtual content delivered around the year. Currently there are five regional meetups that subdivide NACRO membership into smaller geographical regions. These regions have regular meetings that make the entry into NACRO even easier, as members can share concerns specific to their region and meet their geographic peers.

The organization is nearly all volunteer run, with some tasks done by an association management company. NACRO is unique in that its leadership comprises two co-presidents and two co-vice presidents. Each committee also comprises a committee chair and a chair-elect. There is a solo member-at-large who does special projects. The board of directors for NACRO consists of the co-presidents, co-vice presidents, committee chairs, committee chair-elects, and the member-at-large. Each committee also has several subcommittees that complete specific groups of tasks to help the professional society run.

This means members can join the professional society and participate very quickly in committee work. Members learn leadership skills by leading committees, grow in public speaking by teaching content in the webinars and an in-person annual conference, and enlarge their network by meeting other people who do the same type of work across different institutions.

Joseph Huang is the executive director of Strategic Research Initiatives for Stanford University's Computer Science Department and co-president of NACRO. Joseph has extensive experience building research partnerships in both industry and academia. He received his bachelor's degree in chemical engineering from the University of California, Berkeley, and his PhD in chemical engineering from Stanford University.

■ ■ ■

NACRO participation is mostly academic/nonprofit. The benefits for academic corporate relations officers are not only connections with other professionals in the field but also career development opportunities for training through webinars, conferences, bootcamps, and executive education. There are also whitepapers and studies published that can be useful. NACRO also conducts member surveys that can help you understand what other institutions are doing, what is working, and where the challenges are.

UIIN is the University–Industry Innovation Network. This organization is based in Amsterdam and mainly has members from across Europe as well as Australia and Africa. Academic, industry, and nonprofit groups participate. This organization also provides training and workshops. In addition, it creates in-depth research reports relevant to academic–industry partnerships focusing on innovation and has a consulting arm that can customize programs for your organization.

UIDP is the University–Industry Demonstration Partnership organization. It is based in South Carolina and mainly focuses on North America. The organization hosts many regional conferences and events in addition to webinars, workshops, and its large annual conference. There are many resources for members who are from both the academic and industry sectors. UIDP also offers specialized sessions on topics such as contracting as well as its own initiatives.

ATUM is the professional organization focused on tech transfer. It has more than 3,000 members who come from more than 800 universities, research centers, hospitals, businesses, and government organizations around the globe. The organization offers webinars, on-demand courses, professional development courses, professional certifications, a training library, and more. ATUM publishes surveys and research too. Some of the charts in this book are from ATUM.

> **Key Takeaways from PART 3**
>
> 1. For every partnership planning strategy, there must be an execution strategy.
> 2. Data speaks! Track data wherever you can and learn from it.
> 3. Keep learning and innovating.

Part 4

Toolkit

Additional Resources

Toolkit

The following pages contain a collection of tip sheets, worksheets, and sample documents to help you think about a framework for your innovation engagement partnership. These are just some I have created over the years for talks, workshops, and my own process in building programs. There are additional materials available at www.innovationalchemy.net.

Best Practices

    Tip Sheet #1A: Tips for the Industry Sector

    Tip Sheet #1B: Tips for the Academic Sector

Readiness Quiz

    Benchmark Online Quiz: Readiness Quiz

Assessment Worksheets

    Worksheet #1: Ingredients Worksheet

    Worksheet #2: Alignment Worksheet

    Worksheet #3: Identifying ROI Worksheet

Worksheet #4: Innovation Engagement Program Development Worksheet

Worksheet #5: Alignment Worksheet for Industry Looking to Connect with a College or University

Worksheet #6: How to Measure ROI Worksheet: MERIT Chart to Evaluate Gains from Engagement

Worksheet #7: Mapping Connection Points and Assigning Value

Function-Oriented Checklists and Templates

IP Checklist for Student Internships

Sample Engagement Reports

Case Studies

Building CSAIL Alliances

Best Practices

The following charts reinforce best practices to aid the success of innovation engagement partnerships. No matter your organization's place in the *periodic table of innovation elements*, these best practices not only help lay the foundation for solid engagements but also help them grow and flourish.

For those in the industry sector (companies, innovation centers, venture capital, etc.), the following tips are good to keep in mind.

TIP SHEET #1A

Tips for the Industry Sector

1. Make innovation engagement partnerships someone's job. Someone needs to have responsibility for not only managing the partnership but extracting value for the organization.

Tips for the Industry Sector

2. Connect on multiple points. Make sure all the stakeholders in your plan are connected (business unit, CTO, HR, L&D, CEO, innovation/strategy, etc.). Internally let them know about the innovation engagement partnership. Externally, help the organizations in the innovation engagement partnership connect so information can easily be shared.

3. Share information broadly. Utilize internal message boards, Slack channels, and other internal communications to share information and benefits (such as course discount codes).

4. Attend orientation/onboarding sessions with all the stakeholders from your plan. Everyone who can derive benefit from the innovation engagement partnership should be in that meeting and have an opportunity to ask questions and determine best alignment.

5. Go to meetings in person whenever possible. Nothing is a substitute for being able to ask questions and engage in dialogue one-on-one. Use these opportunities to build your network and expand your innovation engagement partnerships.

6. Brand recognition. Don't forget to leverage opportunities to build brand awareness. The students, faculty, and other organizations in the ecosystem can be your future employees, customers, and partners. If you want a pipeline of activity, make sure you get your brand visible.

7. The academic sector is very different from the corporate sector – follow policies and be a good partner.

8. Work within the framework. Companies have varying fiscal years, but almost every academic institution follows the same September to June academic year in the United States. Starting something in June is likely to get off to a slow start.

(continued)

(continued)

Tips for the Industry Sector

9. Keep the longer view. A good innovation engagement plan will have short-term wins as well as progress toward longer-term goals. It should not be transactional.

10. Communicate with all internal stakeholders, and gather data on where the innovation partnership is making an impact.

11. Make sure there is a succession plan. If the innovation engagement partnership is part of your strategy, make sure it is in good hands if you take another role or leave the company.

Alternatively, there are similar points to keep in mind as you look to build innovation engagement partnerships from the academic sector. Whether you are a college/university, independent research center, nonprofit, healthcare organization, economic development unit, etc., the following tips to keep in mind help you engage constructively with the industry sector as you build innovation engagement partnerships.

TIP SHEET #1B

Tips for the Academic Sector

1. Make innovation engagement partnerships someone's job. Someone needs to have responsibility for not only managing the partnership but extracting value for the organization.

Tips for the Academic Sector

2. Secure support from multiple connection points. There will generally be one main person in your industry partner's organization responsible for managing the innovation engagement partnership but make sure to connect with all the stakeholders who can benefit from the goals of the plan.
3. Make information easy to find for partners. Share information and create content that shows how the partners can engage. Support your champions!
4. Hold onboarding sessions with every partner. In this session review goals, alignment, benefits, etc. Make it easy to find information and connect with the person responsible for working with that partner.
5. Have meetings, workshops, recruiting events, or other connection events in a variety of formats to enable widespread participation among partner employees.
6. Leverage your website to include information about ways to partner. Make sure you can "light the path" as brightly as you can on how to connect.
7. Be creative. Just because it's never been before doesn't mean it can't be done. Follow policies, but explore what is possible.
8. Communication is key. Innovation engagement partnerships take time to develop a rhythm, so communicate frequently to let partners know things are happening. Even if there is no "deliverable" to report on, keep people informed.
9. An innovation engagement partnership should not be transactional, but you should celebrate the short-term wins. Every win is data for ROI.

(continued)

> *(continued)*
>
> **Tips for the Academic Sector**
>
> 10. Data! data, data. Everything you do should be quantified as much as possible. What events were attended? How many people came to the tech talk? How many company codes were used for discounts?
> 11. Over time relationships evolve, so be sure to listen to the partner. Sometimes that means there are other connections points for the partner on campus. Overall you want the partner aligned for the long term.

Benchmark Online Quiz: Readiness Quiz

This quiz is a way to self-assess your readiness to either start your innovation engagement partnership or take it to the next level. Copy the following code, go to www.innovationalchemy.net, and click Readiness Quiz. Enter the following code and answer each question on a scale of 1–5, with 1 being least and 5 being most. When you complete the quiz, you will have a "readiness number" that indicates where you are in the journey of building innovation engagement partnerships for your organization, and you will have recommendations that refer you to specific areas of the book, worksheets, and supplemental materials that can be helpful specifically for you.

CODE: IAV12025

> *Building and strengthening the connections between business and academic institutions are critical to sustaining innovation, resilience, and growth.*
> — *Ben Mazur, managing director of Ignitec*

Assessment Worksheets

WORKSHEET #1: Ingredients Worksheet

What do you have to work with? What can you offer a potential partner? Start with checking off items on the left then build your own ingredients list on the right.

Sample ingredient: start-up connections	Check if you have the ingredient	Your additional unique ingredients
Talent		
Research capabilities		
New technologies		
Business insights		
Funding		
Equipment		
Start-up connections		
Datasets		
Educational programs		
Training programs		
Materials		
Conferences/workshops		
Advisory boards		
Program development		
Brand visibility		
Speaking opportunities		

©lglover

WORKSHEET #2: Alignment Worksheet

Use this worksheet to work through how you would approach an innovation engagement partnership. Focus on needs and alignment. Put yourself in your potential partner's shoes. Think of alignment from their perspective first and then go back and fill in how you can meet those needs.

Industry Sector	Academic Sector
Ex. need: Skilled workforce	Ex. alignment: Students
Ex. alignment: Vast datasets	Ex. need: Large dataset

<u>Your alignment chart</u>

©lglover

WORKSHEET #3: Identifying ROI Worksheet

Return on investment (ROI) is important for all parties in an innovation engagement partnership. Everyone has invested resources, and it is important there be a way to identify successes. In Part 1, we looked at identifying both tangible and intangible ROI. In this worksheet, look to identify not only tangible and intangible ROI of an engagement but also whether that ROI is likely to be immediately recognized, or the benefit will be seen at some future point. For example, for professional education, if the innovation engagement program offers a course discount, that course discount is both tangible and immediate in the savings. But there is also the additional tangible benefit of conferring needed skills to the organization's employees, though that will not be recognized until a later date when the course is complete. The ROI here also includes intangible factors such as employee goodwill (immediate) and potentially even increased employee retention (future).

Thinking of the innovation engagement partnership you are planning, map the tangible/intangible benefits and whether they are realized immediately or at a future date. So if the benefit you are mapping to ROI is both tangible and immediate, it would be in the upper-right box. But if it is intangible and future, it would be in the lower left box, etc. This will help you build your framework for assessing your program.

Intangible	Tangible	
		Now/Immediate
		Future

©lglover

WORKSHEET #4: Innovation Engagement Program Development Worksheet

Use this worksheet to align your plan for how an innovation engagement partnership fits within your organization. This worksheet can help organize thoughts in framing the program. There are so many great ideas, but with innovation engagement partnerships, staying focused and building a solid foundation are keys to success.

What is your organization's overall mission?	
What is your unit's mission within the organization?	
How will an innovation engagement partnership align with the missions?	
What are your organization's key strengths?	
What is your value proposition to the partnership?	
What are your key asks from the partnership?	
How can an innovation engagement partnership support/enhance your organization's goals?	
Are there competing interests internally? If so, how will they be addressed?	

How much time from internal stakeholders will be required to make the innovation engagement partnership successful? How will you address time allocations? How will the stake holders benefit?	
What customer/stakeholder needs will the innovation engagement partnership address?	
What will be deliverables? tangible/intangible benefits anticipated?	
Financial structure: will the new innovation engagement partnership be supported? How? Can it be made sustainable?	
Brainstorm your organization's "assets" that will be valuable to a partner in the innovation engagement partnership.	
Brainstorm needs of your potential partner(s) you envision you can address in the innovation engagement partnership.	

©lglover

WORKSHEET #5: Alignment Worksheet for Industry Looking to Connect with a College or University

For Industry looking to connect with academic partners, planning an innovation engagement partnership can contain many elements from the ecosystem. Look at all the possible connection points here and list potential partners across the first row. Which partners can be brought into the plan to address the goals you have set?

What the potential partner is looking for	Potential Partner:	Potential Partner:	Potential Partner:	Potential Partner:
Advanced learning- professional, executive, or employee training				
Career fairs				
Campus interviews				
Use of space				
On campus tech talks/info sessions/ PhD roundtables				
Direct email job announcements				
Resume books				
Connections to student groups/ sponsor student group meetings				

What the potential partner is looking for	Potential Partner: _____	Potential Partner: _____	Potential Partner: _____	Potential Partner: _____
Job postings				
Equipment/specialized services				
Host stakeholder dinners/lunches/breakfasts to bring network together				
Foster faculty connections				
Marketing: building brand awareness				
Sponsor research				
Explore technology licensing opportunities				
Community impact				
Philanthropic engagement				
Maker spaces				
Start-up connections				
Advisory roles				
Co-developments				

(continued)

(continued)

What the potential partner is looking for	Potential Partner: ____	Potential Partner: ____	Potential Partner: ____	Potential Partner: ____
Investment opportunities: start-ups				
Acquisitions: start-ups				
Attend events/networking opportunities				
Data share				
Speak at student groups events				
Speak in classes as guest speakers				
Provide class projects				
Student mentoring				
Join affiliate program				
Guest judges/moderators				
Start-up pitch presentation judge				
Sponsored coursework				
Hackathons or design challenge				

What the potential partner is looking for	Potential Partner: ___	Potential Partner: ___	Potential Partner: ___	Potential Partner: ___
Sponsor student club events				
Competition prize money/equipment				
Idea-a-thon using products				
PhD and postdoc tea/coffee				
Reverse poster session				
Lunch-and-learn with university alum				
Mentor opportunities				
Targeted diversity events				
Project assistance				
Offer internships, co-ops				
Micro-internships over a school break				
Volunteer for student resume reviews				

(continued)

(continued)

What the potential partner is looking for	Potential Partner: ___	Potential Partner: ___	Potential Partner: ___	Potential Partner: ___
Mock interviews: coach students on how to interview for jobs				
Connect with social impact programs that align with company values				
Host faculty sabbaticals/visiting researchers				
Student fellowships				
Visiting researcher at university				
Joint papers				
Executive engagement on campus				
Targeted philanthropy				
Faculty fellowships				
Serve on advisory boards				
Connect with accelerator				

What the potential partner is looking for	Potential Partner: _____	Potential Partner: _____	Potential Partner: _____	Potential Partner: _____
Connect with incubator				
Participate in proof of concept				
Design competitions				
Use of specialized equipment				
Center for outsourced engineering				
Joint publication academic papers				
Joint publication white papers				
Co-invention				
Capstone sponsorship				
Open-source technology connections				
Licensing intellectual property				
Connect with faculty consultants				
Brand recognition				
other				

©lglover

WORKSHEET #6: How to Measure ROI Worksheet: MERIT Chart to Evaluate Gains from Engagement

Use this MERIT chart to evaluate gains from the innovation engagement partnership.

Does your plan have MERIT?

M	**M**easure. Collect data on every facet of the engagement.	What can be measured? Access to data?
E	**E**xposure. What other opportunities has this engagement brought you?	Ancillary benefits? What benefits have surfaced not initially thought of? List them-tangible and intangible
R	**R**each. How broadly has your organization benefited from this engagement?	Who in your organization has benefited? What departments? How broadly are benefits distributed?
I	**I**mpact. What impact is this engagement delivering?	What concrete impact have you seen from the engagement? New insights? Cost reduction? Talent?
T	**T**angible and Intangible. Measure in monetary terms as well as broader terms that have yielded benefits.	What are the tangible and intangible benefits directly from the objective set out in this engagement?

©lglover

WORKSHEET #7: Mapping Connection Points and Assigning Value

How do you want to connect? Think of all the possible points of connection (refer to worksheet #5). Select a connection point, assign a value level, make sure it aligns with the overall innovation engagement plan, and state how you would evaluate success.

CONNECTION POINT	VALUE SCALE 1 – interesting 2 – important 3 – very important	ALIGNMENT How does the connect point help you achieve your overarching goal?	SUCCESS How to do measure success for each?
Ex. Start-ups	3	Plan is to engage with start-ups to scout new technology	Investment or partnership in new tech that addresses problem X
Ex. Develop faculty relationships	2	To stay connected to the cutting edge of the field	Faculty advisor talks and co-authorship of white papers

©lglover

Function-Oriented Checklists and Templates
IP Checklist for Student Internships

This IP Checklist for Student Internships can be used by both the company providing the internship and the faculty member advising the student. The issue with IP in student internships typically arises in research areas with graduate students, but it is a good idea to be aware of these issues in all engagements.

Questions to ask and why:

Question	Y/N	Example/Explanation
Is the student being offered an internship as an employee or contractor?		If the student is an employee that typically means IP generated belongs to the employer unless there is an alternate agreement. If it is a contract position the opposite is generally true without specific agreement. How the student is hired can impact how IP is treated.
Is the student signing an NDA, confidentiality agreement, IPIA (Inventions and Proprietary Information Agreement), none, all or something else?		Generally, NDA and confidentiality agreements are not sufficient to cover IP issues. If an employer asks for an IPIA or an IP assignment agreement, they will be signing over their IP rights to the employer for IP developed during their internship.
Will the student be working at the internship in the same area as their field of study?		If the work is research in the same area as the student's field of study, there should be special care given to scope and clear understanding of what work is being done at the university vs. the company.

Question	Y/N	Example/Explanation
Is the internship for a specific start date and end date?		The specific start and end date should be adhered to. If not, IP issues can arise. For example, a student is allowed to finish up a project for a few weeks back at school after summer break using university equipment. The student makes a significant enhancement to the project the company wants to use. Now there is an IP issue that could have been avoided.
Will the internship be exclusively at the company location using company equipment?		This keeps boundaries clean. If work is only done on company equipment at company location it will tend not to cross university IP rules.
Will the student have access to proprietary information?		Students may not understand what proprietary information is and should be counseled to be informed. Companies should always label and make clear any proprietary information shared.
Has the student been made aware of the care needed to be exercised with proprietary information?		Access to proprietary information may be necessary for the student to complete the internship but the student should understand that information cannot be used for their research. It's not just to keep confidential from other companies. It can't be used for any other purpose than the company project.

(continued)

(continued)

Question	Y/N	Example/Explanation
Will the student be expected or allowed to continue the work for the company while at the university?		This issue arises with part time employment situations. Keep company work at company and university work at university to avoid IP issues.
Has the student been made aware of the university IP policy?		Students should sit down with their advisor and review the university's IP policy and understand how it will impact them.
Has the student been made aware of the company IP policy?		Students should be made aware of the company IP policy and understand how it will impact them.
Has a scope of work for the student been provided? Either by the company or by the student.		Important for faculty/administrative services to review the scope to ensure no overlap of IP issues and avoid a potential issue.
If the internship is to continue past the initial end date, has a new agreement (employment or contractor) been signed?		If not IP issues could arise. If a new employment term is starting, new agreements reflecting the new term should be signed.
Has the student been asked to sign a noncompetition agreement?		Noncompetition agreements can impact a student's future employment abilities. In many states their enforcement is limited but in some it could have a detrimental effect for the student. Students should be made aware of what a noncomp is and what effect it could have.

©lglover

None of the above is intended to be construed as legal advice. This document is only to raise awareness of potential issues. If you have questions, seek out your legal advisor.

Best practices: keep boundaries clear. What is for university purposes stays at the university, and what is for company purposes stays at the company.

Sample Engagement Reports

Engagement Report [mon/yr] –[mon/yr]

Engagement Highlights

- Summary of successful engagement activities
- Everything on the list here should be elsewhere on the report

Employees can register for the CSAIL Alliances website to get the latest CSAIL news, resources, and more:https://cap.csail.mit.edu/user/register

A message from the Managing Director of MIT CSAIL Alliances

The report below is a high-level summary of your company's activity with CSAIL over the past year. It aims to identify the main areas of engagement, though there may be relationships with individual researchers or students that we are unaware of, and therefore, not reflected in this report. Industry involvement and perspective is very important to our research. We truly appreciate your engagement with the CSAIL community and your support of the research lab.

Lori Glover
Managing Director, CSAIL Alliances

Research and Technology Access

- Should include lab visits, participation in events and annual meeting, comp passes provided to premier events, access to regular research updates, etc.

For questions or more information, contact: [CRC name, title, and email address]

cap.csail.mit.edu
@CSAIL_Alliances
@mit-csail

227

Part 4   Sample Engagement Reports

Start-up and Broader Connections

- Access to start-ups, start-up events, website, other MIT-affiliated events (e.g., EmTech), etc.

Student Engagement

- Any job postings made, new hires, as well as engagement with MIT career fair, CSAIL Alliances student book, tech talks, etc.

Professional Development and Courses

- Info about courses taken; reminders on discount codes available, etc.

Sponsorships

- Info about sponsored research + visiting industry researcher opportunities; also, any gift funding or student fellowships supported

Upcoming Engagement Opportunities

- Call out specific programs and/or refer to web link with all upcoming CSAIL events:

CSAIL Alliances Engagement Report

Case Studies

1. Interdisciplinary industry–university collaboration: Lessons from an operations improvement project. A. Balakrishnan, S. Brown, D. Dunlap, R. Pahl, Interfaces, 1995, pubsonline.informs.org

A six-month Leaders-for-Manufacturing student internship at the Alcoa extrusion and tube plant in Lafayette, Indiana, identified a promising operations improvement opportunity in tube manufacturing and led to a two-year collaboration between Alcoa and faculty members from the schools of engineering and management at MIT to develop integrated process planning models. Project participants included production managers, supervisors, and planners at the plant, process engineers from the Alcoa Technical Center, and faculty and students in engineering, operations research, and management. The project demonstrated that the plant could reduce tube drawing effort by more than 20% by using decision support tools and improving the planning processes. It also generated techniques to diagnose problems, new performance metrics, and software for short-term and medium-term process planning, persuaded plant managers to take a systems view of process planning, led to undergraduate and graduate thesis research, provided examples for classroom use, and highlighted the enablers and challenges in conducting industry–university projects, particularly those dealing with supply-chain integration.

Source: Anantaram Balakrishnan et al., 1995, https://www.jstor.org/stable/25062051, last accessed on 19 February 2025 / INFORMS

A list of case studies from CSAIL Alliances illustrating how different companies from start-ups to industry giants – connect with academia for positive impact and growth can be found on the CSAIL Alliances website at Audrey Woods, https://cap.csail.mit.edu/sites/default/files/2023-10/Cisco%20Case%20Study.pdf, last accessed on 19 February 2025 / Cisco Systems, Inc.

Building CSAIL Alliances
The Story of CSAIL Alliances

Over the past few decades many universities have launched programs for "corporate engagement." On the industry side, University Relations teams worked hard to identify schools producing the graduates they needed, and R&D divisions embraced "Open

Innovation" (Chesbourough 2003). The Bayh–Dole Act of 1980, which gave universities the rights to own inventions developed with federal funds, galvanized commercialization of university research changing the R&D landscape, spawning a new breed of entrepreneurial scientist and enabling university spin-off companies. Some of those companies have grown into global brands such as Google, iRobot, and FedEx.

MIT was a pioneer in identifying ways to work with industry. Its motto *mens et manus*, mind and hand in Latin, naturally lends itself to industry collaborations. Back in 1948 (77 years ago!) MIT created its Industrial Liaison Program where interested companies "join" for introductions and access to the expertise and resources of MIT: research, education, talent, new technologies, and more. During the decades following, new, more focused programs in a variety of departments also developed.

At MIT's Computer Science and Artificial Intelligence Lab (CSAIL) in 2008, Prof. Victor Zue, CSAIL director at the time, brought together a few companies to connect to the lab in a new way. The companies in this group learned about research from across the lab. They met students, developed relationships with researchers, and learned of start-ups coming out of the lab. This original group of companies became CSAIL's "Industrial Affiliates Program." The program was small but important. In 2012, Prof. Daniela Rus became the director of CSAIL. She had a vision for stronger industry connections, and when the opportunity arose to restructure the program, I was hired to build it.

Over the following 10 years, CSAIL's Industry Affiliate Program evolved to become CSAIL Alliances, the second largest and most successful industry engagement program at MIT (the MIT Industrial Liaison Program (ILP) remains the largest). CSAIL Alliances is focused on connecting the research, technology, students, faculty researchers, professional programs, and start-ups of CSAIL to industry and other organizations interested in building innovation-focused partnerships that bring the research and new technologies out of the lab and into the marketplace.

Here is the story:

Back in 2013, the landscape looked like this:

- Aside from CSAIL, there were several other industry engagement programs already at MIT.
- The CSAIL faculty had multiple appointments in different labs/centers.
- The organic growth of start-ups was amazing, but there was no information on what groups they came from.
- There were no clear paths of engagement for industry at CSAIL beyond a basic "affiliate" program.
- The companies engaged in different ways in different places without a "report card," for lack of a better term, on what was working, what wasn't, and why.

The summer of 2013 was all about information gathering:

1. What were CSAIL faculty willing to do? Without faculty support, no engagement program at the lab level would be successful.
2. What were the needs of the lab this program was to address?
3. How would CSAIL's new program fit within the MIT ecosystem (compliment, not compete) and work with others who were already established? What were the internal and external constraints?
4. Obtain thorough understanding of the research areas, interests, and "wins" of CSAIL.
5. What did companies want from CSAIL? And what was it worth? How to reach them? And how to continue the dialogue?
6. What was the CSAIL culture, and how do we carefully curate outreach to industry with deference to the culture from the website to "marketing" to social media channels?
7. Who are the actual stakeholders in this?

8. What resources will be necessary to put a plan to build the program in place? How to structure it to make it sustainable?
9. How do we determine a clear vision of how the program would be formed from foundation through year 3 in an initial strategic plan? And then build 3–5 years strategic plans in the following years to stay on course, measure growth, and achieve deliverables (both to the lab and to the companies who worked with us)? We needed to know what is working, what is not, and how to fix it.
10. Staffing decisions: How was this going to be structured? Build it all? Leverage? Partner?

The numbered questions above refer to steps 1-7 in the book. Once the relevant information was gathered, a plan was created. Next, it was time to execute that plan (step 8), track successes as well as mistakes (step 9) and continually innovate (step 10).

By September, I had my answers and set the structural foundation of what would become "CSAIL Global Strategic Alliances" in place. To understand what ingredients were used and how they all came together, let's examine each of the items in more detail.

First, why did CSAIL want an industry engagement program in the first place? In this case, the needs of the lab were clear. CSAIL needed the following:

- Clearer pathways for industry and other organizations to connect with the lab (we are very large and unless you knew a faculty member, it was very hard to find out how to "break in").
- CSAIL's mission is to invent the future of computing and improve the lives of people around the world through computation. To do this, we needed broader connections with industry to drive impact
- CSAIL needed discretionary funding to support faculty research "start-up" packages (money, equipment, and services a new faculty hire receives when they join the lab), equipment needs,

student group support and more as these things cannot be supported with federal funding. Additionally, federal funding itself has been going down in volume for years, and the lab needed new ways to collaborate and fund the research that was developing disruptive new technologies.

Second, what was the faculty willing to support? The faculty – their research, students, start-ups, etc. – were critical to any program that would be built. However, the faculty were so busy teaching, doing research, serving on committees, working on spinouts, etc., that they had little, if any, bandwidth to take on new responsibilities with a new innovation engagement program. Time is a resource the faculty had very little of. Understanding how I could help achieve the larger goals and help the faulty directly was important. Identifying how I could help them preserve this resource was a key success factor for the program. Consequently, CSAIL Alliances takes many initial industry meetings for faculty. We help determine if there is a fit in terms of topic alignment, timeline, engagement structure, funding, faculty/student schedules, etc. This is a huge help to faculty because the meetings they do take at Alliances' request have all the alignment factors addressed. It's also a benefit to companies because they know when they meet with the faculty member, it will be with a researcher who is aligned with the specific issues they are interested in exploring. Factors that could have required multiple time consuming meetings on both sides have been addressed already. This makes the meetings for both parties much more efficient.

Third, there was the question of "fit": for Alliances itself. Like most organizations, MIT has many different units. I needed to understand what the other industry-facing programs were doing and what potential industry partners wanted from CSAIL specifically. Over the summer of 2013, I interviewed every one of our current industry partners and reached out to many of my contacts in my network. With the list of industry "wants" in hand, I came to understand one size did not fit all with regard to how companies were looking to engage with the lab. This led to the development of a structure that not only had multiple paths for engagement but also multiple paths for growth as the innovation partnership matured. Each program has a different set of benefits. For example, initiatives focus on a specific research topic, and the research is informed by the executive board, on which every member company supporting that initiative sits. This path provides for a connection around research as well as all the benefits of Alliances Affiliate. But the Student Engagement program connects only with students in the lab – not the research. A company can choose the path to engage, but as the relationship matures, different paths can be explored. It is a holistic approach that provides avenues for growth and does not silo connections.

Additionally, in that exercise I learned what other campus groups were doing and navigated how CSAIL could put together a complimentary set of offerings that addressed companies specifically interested in what the lab offered: AI and computer science. At this point many people would say "But didn't you run into opposition from the other groups on campus?" I am a firm believer in cooperation, not competition, internally. To illustrate how I handled this, I can share the example of Cybersecurity@CSAIL and IC3 at MIT Sloan School of Management (Now CAMS). Both Sloan and CSAIL were launching cybersecurity initiatives. Sloan focused more on the business challenges of cybersecurity and CSAIL dove deeper into technology improvements. There was an opportunity here! Companies who are interested in cyber want both business approaches and new technologies. So instead of approaching the same companies with competing proposals, I worked with IC3 leadership to create a reciprocity program with Cybersecurity@CSAIL. It was about "making a bigger pie." Companies that joined IC3 could come to our technical workshops, conferences, and initiative meetings, and Cybersecurity@CSAIL members could join IC3 events. It was a win for the internal units as we brought the work from both areas to connect with industry and for the companies it was an even bigger win – they doubled their connection points for research, talent, start-ups, and more. Everyone benefited.

Finally, now that I had a good idea of what companies wanted, what my key stakeholders were willing to do, and where CSAIL could fit in the industry connection landscape at MIT, I needed to figure out how to let companies know we wanted to partner. I did not have a large team, nor the budget to create one. The first person I needed to hire was a marketing person. Just being at MIT does not mean companies are banging at the door. I did all the "business development" and partner management, but I needed help telling our story and sharing our value proposition for connecting with CSAIL. Here is where another very important factor came into play. As I said several times in the book, know your audience. The faculty researchers and students of CSAIL are as much our audience as the companies we partner with. I like to say at CSAIL "we are the quiet guys. Deep technical knowledge but reserved and thoughtful." Consequently, any marketing we did needed to align with how the lab conducted itself.

We built a website to share content and handle incoming messages. I gave a lot of talks. Together this created many opportunities. I follow the "plant a thousand seeds" philosophy. And with continual planting there is continual harvest. The more companies that came to connect with us, the more we learned from them about other ways they wanted to engage. Creating value for them and for our faculty and students was the core objective.

As we grew, we strategically addressed the tasks necessary to continue to provide the strong level of service to our stakeholders. However, there were also constraints that had to be acknowledged. If we had only 120 faculty researchers, it is not realistic that we would grow to 500 companies. The companies would not be able to meaningfully engage and the faculty would be stressed with time commitments beyond their capabilities. Over the years the lab grew significantly, and we grew along with it. Today we are only a team of 12, and every person has multiple roles. We work together as a team to ensure the goals of the program are met for all. Working closely with our industry partners is essential. In Alliances, our client relations coordinators (CRCs) are "boots on the ground" in the lab and work proactively to keep their assigned companies up-to-date and engaged on what is most important to those companies. The CRCs know their companies' needs and will connect them with people, papers, new technologies, start-ups, educational programs, etc. that align to help their companies achieve their goals.

Building Alliances was one thing, but making sure we delivered on our goals was another. Every year the goals and outcomes were measured against the strategic plan. Within the first year of CSAIL

Alliances, we started yearly engagement reports. These reports are an extremely useful tool because they highlight both tangible and intangible elements of the engagement. We track data throughout the year: how many events/workshops/conferences was the client company invited to versus how many people from that company attended, did the company use the discounts codes for executive education programs, did they post jobs, did they engage in tech talks or attend monthly "Byte Bites" (research talks with snacks) to meet students and faculty, did they take advantage of the 30+ benefits of being a CSAIL Alliances member? When all the data is assembled, we can see how engaged a company is, track the successes, clearly establish tangible benefits (for example, how much money was saved on executive education using discount codes) and use the report to make sure the alignment is correct.

Over the years, CSAIL Alliances has grown from 1 to 11 different engagement paths to connect companies with MIT CSAIL. I worked with the ingredients I had to build programs that made sense for the topics, people and structure of CSAIL. Others, in both academia and industry, will have a different set of ingredients and create programs that can look very different but still may be very successful and deliver ROI – both tangible and intangible.

Finally, when building CSAIL Alliances, we tried not to put "a square peg in a round hole." There are things we can do and things we just cannot do. Companies come in all sizes and are focused on different things. Understanding this, and recognizing budgeting processes, is important. At CSAIL we have engagement programs ranging from free with minimal time commitment, to multi-million dollar engagements where our researchers spend time working at the company facilities and the company researchers spend time working at CSAIL. In between there are programs for student engagement, general lab connections, research-focused initiatives, SNAPSHOT programs, professional education, visiting industry researchers, SPARK start-ups, and so much more. It took 10+ years to build, and it works for CSAIL. My advice is to start small, and build on the wins.

One last item. None of this could have been possible without the support of lab leadership. The support of Prof. Daniela Rus, Director of MIT CSAIL, was critical to the success of CSAIL Alliances. She asked the hard questions, provided valuable insights and supported me as I built the program. Strong support from leadership cannot be underestimated in setting a program on a solid foundation and positioned for success.

When industry and academia come together for innovation engagement, we all win.

Conclusion

Academic–industry partnerships are not a new concept. Today, though, change is happening faster than ever before and there are significant shifts in the country's economic framework. To keep our "innovation economy" thriving we need to foster collaborations to bring the innovations out of the labs into the commercial marketplace. Where the academic sector is the genesis of new tools, methods, and technologies, commercial partners are critical in bringing those innovations to products and services that will drive economic expansion, job creation, and benefit people around the world. Both creativity and strategic execution are needed to be successful.

I hope this book serves as a useful primer to spark ideas and illustrate some connection pathways. There is no "one-size-fits-all." The examples and materials are to help you think about how to craft impactful innovation engagement partnerships for your organization. Research, talent, new technologies, start-ups, professional education, and maker spaces are just some of the possible connections points. The unique resources you can bring to the table will shape your plan. Industry and academia working together can yield tremendous benefits and bring new advances to the world. Every organization in the *periodic table of innovation elements* can play a role in the *innovation supply chain* with some *Innovation Alchemy*.

Additional Resources

You can find more resources at www.innovationalchemy.net.

- University Industry Innovation Network (UIIN): https://www.uiin.org

- University Industry Demonstration Partnership (UIDP): https://uidp.org
- National Association of Corporate Relations Officers (NACRO): https://www.nacrocon.org
- National Association of Colleges and Employers (NACE): https://www.naceweb.org
- University Professional and Continuing Education Association (UPCEAA): https://upcea.edu
- Association of University Technology Managers (AUTM): https://autm.net
- American Association of Engineering Education College and Industry Partnership Division (ASEE CIPD): https://cip.asee.org
- "Why Companies and Universities Should Forge Long-Term Collaborations" by Kenneth R. Lutchen, Harvard Business Review, 2018
- "Best-Practices for Industry-University Collaboration" by Julio A. Pertuze, Edward S. Calder, Edward M. Greitzer and William A. Lucas, MIT Sloan Management Review, 2010

You can find some sample sponsored research agreement templates at the following locations:

Washington University St. Louis: https://research.wustl.edu/sponsored-research-agreement-template

Florida Atlantic University: https://www.fau.edu/research-admin/docs/forms/sponsored-programs/sponsored-research-agreement-template-version-6-5-23.pdf

Penn State: https://www.research.psu.edu/Sponsored_Research_Agreement_-_Default

University of Texas system: https://www.utsystem.edu/documents/docs/general-counsel-documents/2009/sponsored-research-agreements

Notes

Introduction

1. https://www.nafsa.org/ie-magazine/2024/9/11/combating-enrollment-cliff#:~:text=The%20so%2Dcalled%20%E2%80%9Cenrollment%20cliff,opportunity%E2%80%94especially%20for%20international%20education.

Part 1

1. https://www.eda.gov/sites/default/files/files/tools/research-reports/The_Innovative_and_Entrepreneurial_University_Report.pdf
2. https://news.wisc.edu/the-person-behind-the-building
3. https://research.ufl.edu/publications/explore/v08n1/gatorade.html
4. https://www.library.hbs.edu/working-knowledge/why-great-ideas-get-stuck-in-universities
5. https://obamawhitehouse.archives.gov/sites/default/files/uploads/InnovationStrategy.pdf
6. https://venturewell.org/industry-and-university-collaboration
7. https://www.uc.edu/news/articles/2023/03/pg-uc-celebrate-partnership-that-accelerates-innovation.html
8. Kanter, Moss. "Collaborative Advantage: The Art of Alliances," 1994.
9. https://www.bpinetwork.org/grow-from-the-right-intro-infographic
10. https://hbr.org/2022/07/what-makes-innovation-partnerships-succeed
11. https://www.bls.gov/opub/ted/2024/median-tenure-with-current-employer-was-3-9-years-in-january-2024.htm
12. https://www.nokia.com/thought-leadership/podcasts/the-power-of-open-innovation/?did=D00000004859&gad=1&gclid=Cj0KCQjw1rqkBhCTARIsAAHz7K2RnufVqw0P5EshRlplfS5f3br7GNNFdgfIEDXdAPSxmkYeRA3RivEaAoF-EALw_wcB

13. https://en.wikipedia.org/wiki/Open-source-software_movement
14. https://www.mend.io/wp-content/media/2022/01/MEND-The-Complete-Guide-for-open-source-Licenses-2022.pdf
15. https://en.wikipedia.org/wiki/Open_source
16. https://www.gatesnotes.com/The-Year-Ahead-2024
17. http://www.cdio.org/about
18. For papers, see the following:
    Lavi, Rea, Bagiati, Aikaterini, Long, Gregory L, Salek, Mehdi, M and Mitra, Amitava 'Babi'. The Impact of an Interdisciplinary Experiential Learning Program on Undergraduate STEM Students' Career Readiness. 131st American Society for Engineering Education (ASEE) Annual Conference, Portland, OR, June 23–26, 2024. https://peer.asee.org/46397
    K. May, "From Industry to Academia: Aurora Employees Support MIT's NEET Experiential Learning Program," March 2023.
    E. Crawley, A. E. Hosoi, G. Long, T. Kassis, W. Dickson, A. Mitra. "Moving Forward with the New Engineering Education Transformation (NEET) program at MIT-Building community, developing projects, and connecting with industry." 126th American Society for Engineering Education (ASEE) Annual Conference, Tampa, Florida (2019). https://peer.asee.org/authors/39545
19. https://engineering.tamu.edu/student-life/project-showcase/Capstones.html
20. https://www.cmu.edu/tepper/recruiting-and-partnerships/partner-with-the-tepper-school/student-projects/index.html
21. https://www.aboutamazon.com/news/innovation-at-amazon/amazon-invests-25-million-in-a-10-year-research-collaboration-to-advance-ai
22. https://hdsr.mitpress.mit.edu/pub/gylaxji4/release/6
23. https://carnegieclassifications.acenet.edu
24. https://www.americanprogress.org/article/the-high-return-on-investment-for-publicly-funded-research
25. https://www.rdworldonline.com/top-15-rd-spenders-of-2024
26. Thompson, Bonnet and Ye (2019). "Open Innovation and the Rise of Digital"
27. https://pressroom.toyota.com/toyota-establishes-ai-research-centers-mit-stanford

28. https://pressroom.toyota.com/toyota-establishes-ai-research-centers-mit-stanford
29. www.rhventures.org
30. Theodore Maiman, physicist known for developing the first working laser.
31. https://www.esa.int/Science_Exploration/Space_Science/Planck/Max_Planck_Originator_of_quantum_theory#:~:text=These%20are%20small%20%27packets%27%20that%20can%20only,meeting%20of%20the%20Physikalische%20Gesellschaft%20in%20Berlin
32. https://engineering.oregonstate.edu/all-stories/equipment-donation-sparks-new-life-into-electrical-engineering-lab
33. https://www.clevelandmetroschools.org/site/Default.aspx?PageType=3&DomainID=109&PageID=9904&ViewID=6446ee88-d30c-497e-9316-3f8874b3e108&FlexDataID=1790
34. https://lz284.org/doc/Carnegie%20R1%20and%20R2%20Research%20Classifications%20Doctoral%20Universities.pdf
35. For examples of various agreements that can be used, visit innovationalchemy.net.

Part 2

1. https://ivmf.syracuse.edu/about-ivmf/history-timeline/
2. https://ivmf.syracuse.edu/
3. https://ivmf.syracuse.edu/fast-facts/
4. https://news.syr.edu/blog/2021/05/03/founding-partner-jpmorgan-chase-renews-commitment-to-ivmf-to-enhance-the-post-service-lives-of-veterans-and-their-families/
5. https://www.ut.edu/academics/sykes-college-of-business/centers-and-institutes/institute-for-sales-excellence/corporate-partners
6. https://en.wikipedia.org/wiki/Boundary_spanning
7. Impact for economic growth: Living MIT graduates who have started and built for-profit companies do not qualify as a nation but, if they did, they'd be the world's 10th largest economy, with gross revenue falling between the GDP of Russia ($2.097 trillion) and India ($1.877 trillion), 2015 https://exec.mit.edu/s/blog-post/mit-entrepreneurs-the-world-s-10th-largest-economy-MC5MBXKNFDD5H4PHHILGSXDBF4UY
8. https://en.wikipedia.org/wiki/Robert_S._Langer

9. https://www.sciencedirect.com/science/article/abs/pii/S0048733320301402
10. https://ethw.org/Frederick_Terman
11. https://www.ncbi.nlm.nih.gov/books/NBK45556/
12. https://www.ncbi.nlm.nih.gov/books/NBK45556/
13. https://www.nsf.gov/about/history/timeline70s.jsp
14. https://www.nsf.gov/statistics/directorate-profiles/
15. https://en.wikipedia.org/wiki/Bayh%E2%80%93Dole_Act#:~:text=7%20External%20links-,History,invested%20in%20government%2Dsponsored%20R%26D
16. https://autm.net/about-autm/mission-history
17. https://autm.net/surveys-and-tools/surveys/licensing-survey/2023-licensing-survey
18. https://hbswk.hbs.edu/item/open-source-software-the-nine-trillion-resource-companies-take-for-granted
19. https://www.hbs.edu/ris/Publication%20Files/24-038_51f8444f-502c-4139-8bf2-56eb4b65c58a.pdf
20. https://nam.org/study-manufacturing-in-u-s-could-need-up-to-3-8-million-workers-30626/
21. FAME National Website: http://fame-usa.com, FAME LinkedIn Showcase Page: http://www.linkedin.com/showcase/fame-usa
22. https://hbsp.harvard.edu/inspiring-minds/a-new-model-for-university-industry-partnerships
23. https://hbsp.harvard.edu/inspiring-minds/a-new-model-for-university-industry-partnerships
24. https://hbsp.harvard.edu/inspiring-minds/a-new-model-for-university-industry-partnerships
25. https://entrepreneurship.mit.edu/accelerator/program/
26. https://aiforimpact.github.io/
27. https://www.fedex.com/en-us/about/history.html
28. https://www.businessinsider.com/how-drew-houston-created-dropbox-2018-1#he-founded-dropbox-about-two-years-later-in-response-to-a-personal-technical-problem-4
29. https://backlinko.com/dropbox-users
30. https://about.att.com/newsroom/georgia_tech_launches_first_massive_online_degree_program.html#:~:text=AT&T%20Connected%20Learning%

20Center%20in%20Cleveland%20is,the%20AT&T%20Connected%20 Learning%20Center%20at%20Esperanza
31. https://www.bcg.com/press/23may2023-companies-rank-innovation-as-top-three-priority-2023
32. https://hbr.org/2019/11/what-kind-of-chief-innovation-officer-does-your-company-need
33. https://www.wellspring.com/news/ambitious-innovation-plans-despite-economic-uncertainty
34. https://www.technologyreview.com/2015/08/18/10816/the-past-and-future-of-kendall-square/
35. https://www.google.com/url?q=https://deshpande.mit.edu/impact/&sa=D&source=docs&ust=1731620819510084&usg=AOvVaw2uQWi5YLweJesHnzkUIl9u
36. https://www.usnews.com/best-colleges/rankings/business-entrepreneurship?_sort=rank&_sortDirection=asc
37. https://www.d-eship.com/
38. https://www.d-eship.com/articles/the-silicon-valley-entrepreneurship-model-can-be-toxic-fortunately-there-are-other-models/
39. https://www.bu.edu/law/experiential-learning/clinics/bu-mit-student-innovations-law-clinic/
40. https://venturecafecambridge.org/partners/cic/
41. https://www.massbio.org/innovation/
42. https://kendallsquare.org/
43. https://www.mtlc.co/mtlc-memberships/about-mtlc/
44. https://www.mtlc.co/
45. https://engine.xyz/
46. https://www.e14.vc/
47. https://news.mit.edu/2015/report-entrepreneurial-impact-1209
48. More tips and best practices for managing distance can be found at www.innovationalchemy.net
49. https://www.innovationleader.com/
50. https://newsroom.ibm.com/2024-04-04-Leading-Companies-Launch-Consortium-to-Address-AIs-Impact-on-the-Technology-Workforce
51. https://c3.ai/c3-ai-microsoft-and-leading-universities-launch-c3-ai-digital-transformation-institute/
52. https://innovation.nutrition.tufts.edu/what-we-do/
53. https://iucrc.nsf.gov/about/

54. https://iucrc.nsf.gov/about/
55. https://iucrc.nsf.gov/about/
56. https://www.nature.com/nature-index/news/how-to-be-part-of-a-research-consortium
57. https://www.twosigma.com/community/academic-partnerships/graduate-students/phd-fellowships/
58. https://www.bosch.com/research/about-bosch-research/working-at-bosch-research/industry-sabbatical-program/#:~:text=The%20Industry%20Sabbatical%20Program%20is%20specifically%20designed, intelligence%2C%20climate%20action%20and%20sustainability%2C%20 and%20healthcare
59. https://www.nvidia.com/en-us/industries/higher-education-research/academic-grant-program/#nv-accordion-57fe9a47bc-item-3ba00740aa
60. https://www.amazon.science/research-awards
61. https://www.sony.com/en/SonyInfo/research-award-program/
62. https://www.lilly.com/partners/research-award-program
63. https://research.adobe.com/data-science-research-awards/
64. https://news.3m.com/2013-06-13-Visionary-Meeting-of-the-Minds-Takes-Place-on-3M-Campus-as-the-Company-Hosts-Its-Science-and-Engineering-Faculty-Day-for-Young-University-Professors
65. https://create.roblox.com/docs/creator-fund
66. https://www.nature.com/nature-index/news/the-shifting-corporate-academic-relationship-in-pictures
67. https://www.natureindex.com/institution-outputs/netherlands/leiden-university/5139073734d6b65e6a002222
68. https://www.natureindex.com/country-outputs/Netherlands
69. https://www.nature.com/nature-index/news/the-shifting-corporate-academic-relationship-in-pictures
70. https://www.nature.com/nature-index/news/the-shifting-corporate-academic-relationship-in-pictures
71. https://journals.sagepub.com/doi/10.1177/09504222211064204
72. https://engineering.purdue.edu/JTRP
73. https://www.science.org/content/article/academic-consultant-why-2start-consultancy

74. https://sites.cs.ucsb.edu/~pconrad/talks/2019-03-01-sigcse-panel-sabbatical-in-industry/
75. https://www.cnbc.com/2024/10/14/honeywells-ceo-says-the-big-ai-payoff-wont-come-from-productivity.html
76. https://www.edx.org/masters/micromasters/mitx-principles-manufacturing?webview=false&campaign=Principles+of+Manufacturing&source=edx&product_category=micromasters&placement_url=https%3A%2F%2Fwww.edx.org%2Fmasters%2Fmicromasters
77. https://www.edx.org/masters/micromasters/purduex-quantum-technology-computing-and-sensin?webview=false&campaign=Quantum+Technology%3A+Computing+and+Sensing&source=edx&product_category=micromasters&placement_url=https%3A%2F%2Fwww.edx.org%2Fmasters%2Fmicromasters
78. https://mitsloan.mit.edu/action-learning/generative-ai-lab#welcome
79. https://www.wpi.edu/project-based-learning/project-based-education/interactive-qualifying-project
80. https://masschallenge.org/mission/
81. https://www.engineeringambassadorsnetwork.org/
82. https://www.eda.gov/funding/programs/build-to-scale
83. https://www.forbes.com/sites/homaycotte/2016/02/02/how-makerspaces-are-inspiring-innovation-at-startups/
84. https://sites.google.com/view/top100uni/home
85. https://ipwatchdog.com/2020/04/07/evolution-university-technology-transfer/id=120451/
86. https://ipwatchdog.com/2020/04/07/evolution-university-technology-transfer/id=120451/

Part 3

1. https://venturewell.org/industry-and-university-collaboration/
2. Starship is an organization I started at MIT in 2020. It involves many of the groups across campus working with industry. We meet monthly and share both internal and external resources to help each other, and the companies we work with.
3. https://news.mit.edu/2024/mit-takeda-program-completed-0618

4. https://venturewell.org/industry-and-university-collaboration/
5. https://cap.csail.mit.edu/sites/default/files/2023-04/Case%20Study_Inkbit23.pdf
6. Academic-Industry Collaborations: Why They Can Be Hard to Launch And What You Can Do About It jeffreybardzell August 11, 2023.
7. https://raeng.org.uk/media/wzqfaq4w/04-09-15-dowling-report-final-updated-contributors.pdf
8. https://www.startupblink.com/blog/top-20-countries-by-total-startup-output-in-2023/
9. https://theconversation.com/federal-funding-for-major-science-agencies-is-at-a-25-year-low-232582

Acknowledgments

I would like to acknowledge the many people who made this book possible. I am grateful for the support of my husband Joe for his patience with the process and his willingness to always be my sounding board; my boys Sam and Jake for their encouragement; my colleague Bill Aulet for his advice; and Prof. Daniela Rus for her support and friendship.

Additionally, I would like to acknowledge the contributions of Dr. Amitava "Babi" Mitra, Dr. Gregory Long, Christie Ko, Lucy Hattersly, Natascha Eckert, Dr. Michael Stonebraker, Prof. Daniela Rus, Daniel Dardani, Denis Dio Parker, Myron Kassabara, Rana Gupta, and Joseph Huang who all contributed insightful focus features and interviews to this book, as well as Julia Pallis whose artistic talent created the illustrations throughout the book.

A special thanks to my editors at Wiley for the guidance and wisdom provided on this journey.

And a huge thank-you to the many people who read and commented on the manuscript. Your insights were invaluable.

Last, I am grateful for the amazing faculty, staff, students, and especially my incredible team at MIT CSAIL Alliances, who were instrumental in shaping this book.

About the Author

Lori Glover, JD
Managing Director,
Global Strategic Alliances
MIT Computer Science Artificial
Intelligence Laboratory

Lori Glover leads global partnerships and alliances for MIT's Computer Science and Artificial Intelligence Lab (CSAIL) – the largest lab at MIT with over 1700 people and 60+ research groups.

She is responsible for corporate and organizational engagement with the lab through the CSAIL Alliance Program, research initiatives, the Visiting Industry Researcher program, start-ups and technology ecosystem, professional development programs and talent acquisition/recruiting within CSAIL. She serves as Executive Director of research initiatives MachineLearningApplications@CSAIL, NextGenerationSoftware Efficiency@CSAIL, FinTechAI@CSAIL and MIT''s Future of Data, Trust and Policy Initiative. Lori also serves as a a member of both non-profit and commercial Advisory Boards.

Her expertise spans strategic partnership development, computer science and AI research applications, finance, intellectual property, and law. She has led many innovative engagement programs bringing together world-renowned researchers with leading companies to address business challenges.

Drawing from her decades of experience, she often speaks on research advances and their impact on innovation at conferences and professional associations, as well as on the development of successful industry-academic partnerships, both nationally and internationally. She also consults on building successful engagement programs.

Lori also holds Bachelor of Arts and Juris Doctor degrees. She has practiced law as a member of the bar in both Massachusetts and Florida.

Index

3M nontenured faculty awards, 153
"16.84 Advanced Autonomous Robotic Systems," 23

A

Academia
  course cross-registration, 5–6
  industry, matchmakers, 97–98
Academic engagement, search, 18
Academic-industry engagement
  forms, 119
  partnerships, student stakeholder (involvement), 118
Academic-industry innovation engagement partnership, students (impact), 119–120
Academic institutions, idea incubation, 3
Academic organizations
  action items, 187–189
  innovation engagement partnership initiation, difficulty, 142f
Academic research, commercialization, 128
Academics
  Amazon research awards, 153
  audience, knowledge, 188
Academic sector
  advice, 208–210
  needs
    expression, 144–145
    requirement, 167–169
Academic technology transfer (AUTM infographic), 102, 103f
Acceleration, project feature, 45
Accelerators, 139–140
  presence, 8
Accessibility, increase, 184–185
Accountability, 183–184
  absence, 199
Adobe Data Science Research Awards, 153
Advanced Manufacturing Technician (AMT) program, 110, 111
Advisory boards (engagement model), 146, 155
Affiliate program, 231
Agility (gift/grant advantage), 30
Ahn, Luis von (entrepreneurial faculty member), 90

AI-Enabled Information and Communication Technology (ICT) Workforce Consortium, focus, 149
Algorithms, creation, 192–193
Alignment
　clarity, 173
　establishment, 14
　industry alignment worksheet, 216–221
　worksheet, 212
Alliances, search, 8
Amazon, research awards, 153
Amodei, Dario, 34
Analytics-based insights, 28
Ancillary connection points, 177
Apache License 2.0, permissive license, 17
Apprenticeships, effectiveness, 106
Aristotle, wisdom, 195
Artificial intelligence (AI)
　acceleration, 19, 53
　generative AI, usage, 33
　impact, 32, 179
　tools, application, 113
　usage, 29, 84–85, 165
Asano, Shintaro "Sam," 49
Askelos (technology), mission-driven impact, 134
Assessment worksheets, 211–223
Association of University Technology Managers (AUTM), 200, 202
AT&T, investment, 123–124
Audience, knowledge, 188
Aulet, Bill, 136

Aurora Flight Sciences/MIT NEET, collaboration, 20–27
AUTM infographic, 103f
Automatic Data Processing (ADP), interaction, 32

B

Bajpayee, Anurag, 134
Balakrishnan, Hari, 13
Balpayee, Anurag, 134
Banks-Hall, Regina (entrepreneurial faculty member), 90
Bardzell, Jeffrey, 186
Barzilay, Regina, 192
Bayh-Dole Act, 3, 37, 95, 97–98, 166
Benchmark online quiz (readiness quiz), 210
Berkeley Software Distribution Licence (BSD), permissive license, 16–17
Best practices, 205, 206–210
Bhatia, Sangeetha, 131–132
Bilateral seed-funded research engagements, 77
Biotechnology, boom, 98–99
Bosch Research Industry Sabbatical program, 151–152
Bose, Amar (entrepreneurial faculty member), 90
Boston University (BU) Law Clinic, legal help, 137
Bottom-up strategy, top-down strategy (balance), 76
Boudou, Justine, 3

Boundary spanners, 70, 71
  competence, importance, 76–77
  confessions, 71–78
  search, 182–183
Brin, Sergey, 102
British Telecom (BT), guidance, 80
Brooks, Rodney (entrepreneurial faculty member), 90
Buckets
  fees, 61–62
  types, 41–45
Build to Scale (B2S) program, 164
Burks, Luke, 25
Bush, Vannavar, 94
Business constraints, mutual understanding, 74
Business of Industry and Security (BIS), 60

C

C3.ai Digital Transformation Institute, 149
Call-oriented industry consortia, engagement, 191
Cambridge Innovation Center (CIC), space/connections (co-working), 138
Camp, Michael (entrepreneurial faculty member), 90
Capstone projects, 20, 27–28
  engagement model, 161–162
Capstones (engagement model), 147
Career Advising and Professional Development (CAPD) (MIT), 174
Career center, connection, 177–178
Carnegie Commission on Higher Education, classification framework development, 47
Catalyzers, search, 182–183
Center for Information Systems Research Research (CISR), 174
Center of Knowledge Interchange (CKI), 72
Charm, Leslie (entrepreneurial faculty member), 90
Chesbrough, Henry, 15
Cheung, Stephen, 158
Chief innovation officer (CINO), presence, 125
Cleveland Metropolitan School District, computer donation, 58
Co-authorship, benefits, 154
Code, sharing, 187
Cohen-Boyer recombinant DNA patent license, 98
Cold War tensions, 95
Collaboration
  kick-starting, 74–75
  opportunities, 79
College, connection, 216–221
Commercialization, 125
  financial impact, 130–131
  idea, expansion, 129–130
  impact, 128–135, 184
  objectives, 130
  statement, 133
  navigation, 100–101
  path, 7–10
  product impact, 130, 131
  research impact, 130, 131–133

253
Index

Communication, 175
  channels, clarity, 174
Community nonprofit support
    organizations, 138–139
Companies
  academic institution
    partnerships, 3
  involvement, research (impact),
    84–85, 88
  ongoing presence, absence, 7–8
  product creation, 53–54
  start-up location, 179
Competition, 124
  consideration, 194–197
  funding/resources, relationship,
    195
  internal competition, 195
  positioning, 195
Competitive advantage, 104–105
Computer Science and Artificial
    Intelligence Laboratory
    (CSAIL), 82
  BigData Initiative, 88
  building, experience, 12
  company, relationship, 231
  culture, defining, 231
  discretionary funding, need,
    232–233
  engagement
    broadening, 124
    consortium-like path, 36
  experience, 6
  Global Strategic Alliances, 232
  initiatives, 89
  interdisciplinary research lab,
    49–50
  landscape, appearance, 231
  mission, 232
  program
    fit, 231
    vision, clarity
      (determination), 232
  research
    areas, 231
    engagement, 67
  staffing decisions, 232
  stakeholders, identification, 232
  students, connection, 105
  Toyota, sponsored research
    engagement, 51–52
Computer Science and Artificial
    Intelligence Laboratory
    (CSAIL) Alliances, 123,
    174, 188
  building, 12, 229–237
  leveraging, 13
Computer Science and Artificial
    Intelligence Laboratory
    (CSAIL) Alliances
    Affiliates, 179–180
Conceiving, Designing,
    Implementing,
    Operating (CDIO)
    international initiative, 22
Confidential information
  absence, 54
  agreement terms, impact, 60
Connections
  leveraging, 191
  points, mapping, 126, 145–146,
    161, 222–223
Consortia
  engagement model, 146,
    148–151
  industry consortia, models,
    191–193

Constraints
    accounting, 194
    acknowledgement, 78–80
    understanding, 4–9
Consulting
    engagement model, 146, 158
    services, presence, 18
Continuous upskilling, long-term partnerships, 161
Control, trust (importance), 75
Co-ops (engagement model), 158–159
Coordination, absence, 198
Copyleft licences, 16
Core Technologies, 71
Corporate-academic relationships, shift, 154–155
Corporate alliance-building programs, 99
Corporate business units, 122–125
    stakeholder function, 80
Corporate engagement, 190
Corporate philanthropy offices, mapping, 144
Corporate relations, 190
    launch, 98
Corporate venture arms, 140–146
Corso, Jason (entrepreneurial faculty member), 90
Creativity
    independence, impact, 9
    project feature, 46
Crosby, Alfred, 130–131
Cultural divide, 10
Curriculum roles (engagement model), 146, 157
Custom programs (engagement model), 160–161
Cybersecurity, investments, 39

D

Dardani, Daniel, 96–102
Data capture, absence, 198
Data management
    faculty member/university, industry collaboration benefit, 83
    industry partners, collaboration, 87
Data-rich sectors, transformation, 165
Dawson, Joel, 133–134
Degree programs (engagement model), 160–161
Deliverables
    agreement terms, impact, 60
    list, 51
    setting out, 59
Deshpande Center for Technological Innovation (DCTI), 128–135, 162
    mission, 133–135
Deshpande, Gururaj/Jaishree, 128–135
Digital Economy Lab (Stanford), 28
Directorate of Defense Trade Controls (DDTC), 60
Disciplined Entrepreneurship (Aulet), 136
Discovery research, outsourcing, 155
Doudna, Jennifer A. (entrepreneurial faculty member), 90

Douglas, Dewayne, 3
DropBox, success, 117

E

E14. *See* Massachusetts Institute of Technology
Early-stage investment funds, operational support, 165
Eckert, Natascha, 71, 78
Economic development
　driving, 86, 88–89
　engagement model, 164–165
　partnering (engagement model), 147
Ecosystem, 190
　collaboration, 73–74
　creation, university-industry partners (impact), 86
　industry members, timing questions, 18
　seeding, 127
Edmonds, Jessica, 25
Education and innovation (E&I), 136
EdX (online MOOC), 160
Efficiency, focus, 183
Ekert, Natascha, 70
Embedded systems, 148–149
Employment, AI (impact), 32
Engagement
　exposure, relationship, 179–181
　framework, foundation, 141
　fruitfulness, 34
　gains (evaluation), MERIT chart (usage), 222
　high-level engagement, 68–69
　level, comfort, 172
　programs
　　commonalities, 173–174
　　student involvement, 105–106
　　reports, sample, 227–228
　　success, elements, 176f
　　time horizon, importance, 18–19
　　vehicle, industry sectors, 167–169
Engagement partnership
　building, 10–11
　challenges/support
　　faculty involvement, 120
　　human resource departments, assistance, 120–121
　　complication issues, avoidance, 121
　failure, reasons, 6
　initial planning structure, 175–176
　objectives, 173
　survival, 8
Engagement paths, 152, 172
　models, 146–147
　understanding, 146
Engagement Reports, usage, 42–43, 199
Engineering Ambassadors program, 163–164
Engineering centers (engagement model), 165–166
Entrepreneurial faculty, impact, 80, 82–86
Entrepreneurship, education/support, 135–137
Executive education programs (engagement model), 160–161

Expectations
  appropriation, 13
  management, 55–57
Expertise, leveraging, 5
Export Administration Regulations (EAR), 60
Export controls, agreement terms (impact), 60
External network, leveraging, 187–188
External relations, 190

F

Faculty
  career measurement, 11
  cooperation, need, 78–79
  network, access (importance), 4
  research start-up packages, equipment needs, 232–233
  sabbatical (engagement model), 158–159
Faculty member
  Advanced Manufacturing Technician (AMT) program, 110, 111
  benefits, 87
  industry partner collaboration, benefit, 83
Federal Express, student project, 117
Federation for Advanced Manufacturing Education (FAME), 106–112
  career pathway, 110
  competency level, 108
  comprehensive design/support, 111–112
  curriculum, 110
  design, 109
  differences, 110–112
  entry-level technicians, readiness (absence), 109
  extended programs, 110
  history, 108
  Lean-prepared graduates, 111
  Lean Program design, 111
  pathway scope, 111
  problem-solving, 108–109
  professional behaviors, 111
  quality, 109
Fellowships (engagement model), 146, 151–152
Financial accountability, 50
Flexibility (gift/grant advantage), 30
Flexibility/adaptability, project feature, 46
Food and Nutrition Innovation Institute, The, 150
Function-oriented checklists/templates, 224–227
Funding, 195
  amounts, agreement terms (impact), 60
  benefits, 38–39
  "color," 57
  money, involvement, 57–62
Funds (expenditure), explanation (requirement), 59
Future focused initiatives, 124

G

Galloway, Scott (entrepreneurial faculty member), 90
Game-changing ideas, 115–116
Gatorade, sales generation, 3

Generative AI Lab (GenAI-Lab), student/project pairing, 162
Generative AI, usage, 33
Gifts
  giving, impact, 57–59
  importance, 58
Git (GitHub), 17
GNU General Public License (GNU GPL), 16
Goals
  achievement, factors, 68–69, 172
  establishment, 65–68
  understanding, importance, 67
Goodwill, 7–8
  suffering, 8
Google, economic impact, 102
Go-Pro/Red Bull, market alignment, 5
Gradiant (technology), mission-driven impact, 134
Grant
  awards (engagement model), 146, 152–153
  writing, 132
Gupta, Rana K., 128, 135

H
Hadoop (Cloudera), 17
Hanrahan, Pat (entrepreneurial faculty member), 90
Harvard University, course cross-registration, 5–6
Hewlett, William, 91
High-impact research, conducting, 150
High-level engagement, 68–69
High-technology workforce, identification/mentoring/development, 150
Hoffman, Reid, 34
Holmes, Doug, 131
Houston, Drew, 117
Huang, Joseph, 200–201
Hunters, role, 186
Hynes, Tod, 116

I
Impractical theory, perception, 187
Incubators, 139–140
  presence, 8
Industrial partnering offices, launch, 98
Industry
  action items, 189–191
  alignment worksheet, 216–221
  benefits, innovation partnerships (impact), 181f
  calendar, usage, 14
  co-branding, 5
  collaboration, 83
    importance, 99
  commercialization, 19
  consortia, models, 191–193
  generation (success factor), 3
  growth, 196
  human resource departments, assistance, 120–121
  partnering, community college impact, 106–112
  partners, academic research project data source, 32

partnerships, impact, 11
pathways, 232
sector
   advice, 206–208
   needs, expression, 144–145
   university students, employment opportunities, 9–10
Industry-sponsored projects, business school usage, 28
Industry-sponsored research, investment, 104–105
Industry-University Cooperative Research Centers (IUCRCs), goals, 150
Information
   gathering, 188, 231–232
   sharing, 173
Ingredients worksheet, 211
Initiative-funded project, example, 39–40
Initiatives, 36
   company involvement, 38
   industry benefits, 38
   MIT benefits, 38–39
   projects, 38
Innovation, 200–202
   advancing, 194
   alchemy, 70, 197
   boom, catalyst, 97–98
   centers, presence, 8
   communities, fostering, 138
   economy, ideas (impact), 104
   ecosystem, professional associations (presence), 147–148
   elements, periodic table, 1, 8, 95, 127, 136–137, 173, 184, 206
   engine, 132
   equation, 49, 131, 192
   fostering, 125, 200
   ecosystem, creation, 86
   growth, 196
   open innovation, open mindset (requirement), 75–76
   partnerships, university/industry benefits, 181f
   process, 15
   programs (engagement model), 161
   project feature, 46
   research, impact, 47
   seeding, exploratory engagement, 41–42
   spurring, 193
   stories, 50
   strategy
      company roadmap, 155
      defining, 126–127
Innovation-based collaborations, 181
Innovation City USA, 91–92
Innovation engagement
   model, 147
   program development worksheet, 214–215
Innovation engagement partnership
   benefit, 159
   building, 57, 79
   charting, 56
   goals, 172
   initiation, difficulty, 142f
   inroads, 189–190
   mutual benefit, basis, 42

Innovation (*continued*)
  success, 81
  time/attention, 194–195
  win-win success, 52
Innovation-focus engagement partnership, stakeholders, 81f
Innovation supply chain, 166
  concept, 1–4
  fueling, 90
  harm, 15
  impact, 89–90
  industry/academia, role, 183
  operation, smoothness, 8
  traditional supply chain, comparison, 2f
Innovative insights, delivery, 28
Innovative technology development, driving, 150
In-residence model, 152
In-residence positions (engagement model), 146
Institute for Veterans and Military Families (IVMF)
  creation, 65
  pledge/partnership, 66
Intangible benefits, 37–38
Intangible bucket, 41–45
  list, 43–44
Intellectual property (IP), 80, 154
  agreement terms, impact, 60
  challenges, 75, 117–118
  creation, 34–35
  example, 54
  impact, 92–96
  obtaining, 54–55
  ownership, maintenance, 118
  protection, 99
  purposes, 119
  research, link, 52
Intentions, 73–74
Interdisciplinary Academic Center, 28–35
Interdisciplinary industry-university collaboration, case studies, 228–229
Interdisciplinary research project, collaboration, 75–76
Internal competition, 195
Internal network, usage, 188
International Traffic in Arms (ITAR), 60
Internet Protocol (IP) confusion, 117–122
Internet Systems Consortium (ISC) License, permissive license, 17
Internships
  effectiveness, 106
  engagement model, 146
Invisibles, rise, 52–55
Ivory tower, perception, 187

J

Jacobs, Irwin, 102
Joint researcher centers (engagement model), 146, 157
JPMorgan Chase (JPMC), Syracuse University (partnership), 65–66

K

Kassaraba, Myron (interview), 118–122
Katabi, Dina, 52–53
Kendall innovation ecosystem, 137

Kendall Square Association (KSA), 127
  community nonprofit support, 138–139
  foundational framework, 141–146
KeyBank, donations, 58
Keysight Technologies, equipment (donation), 58
Killian, John, 127
Knowledge, sharing, 29
Ko, Christie, 28–35
Koller, Daphne (entrepreneurial faculty member), 90
Kumar, Vijay, 27

L
Labor, division, 185–186
Langer, Robert, 89–91
Large language models (LLMs), 84–85
Layne, Rachel, 104
Lead generation, 188–189, 191
Lead scientists, access (importance), 4
Lean Continuous Flow model, 111
Legal departments
  blame, 92
  examination, 80
  impact, 92–96
Legal programs, cooperation (need), 78–79
Licenses, types, 16
Licensing
  fees, 99
  technology (engagement model), 166, 170

Lilly Research Award Program (LRAP), collaborations, 153
Linux (Red Hat), 17
Liquie AI (spinout), 84–85
Local business organizations, presence, 8
Longer-term time horizon/speed, 28–35
Long, Gregory L., 20–27
Long-term collaborations, 46
Long-term engagement
  commitment, 74–75
  industry perspective, 45–46
Long-term impact, project feature, 46
Long-term strategic engagement, 6
Long-term timelines, 39–40
Lutchen, Kenneth R., 113

M
Machine learning (ML)
  acceleration, 53
  technologies, usage, 165
Machine Learning for Pharmaceutical Development and Syntheses (MLPDS), 192
Maker spaces (fablabs) (hackerspaces)
  engagement model, 165–166
  presence, 8
Manyika, James, 34
Marini, Davide, 180
Market alignment, example, 5
Marketing, 188–189, 191
Marquee names, prioritization, 198

Martin Trust Center. *See*
　　Massachusetts Institute of
　　Technology (MIT)
Massachusetts College of Art and
　　Design (MassArt), course
　　cross-registration, 5–6
Massachusetts Institute of
　　Technology (MIT)
　Career Advising and Professional Development
　　(CAPD), 174
　course cross-registration, 5–6
　Delta V NYC, 116
　departments, industry
　　interaction, 143f
　E14, 140–146
　Engine, 139–140
　Industrial Liaison Program
　　(STEX25), 100
　initiatives, benefits, 38–39
　Martin Trust Center, 85, 116,
　　135–137
　Media Lab, 42
　mission, 21
　MIT-IBM Watson AI Lab,
　　collaboration, 86
　New Engineering Education
　　Transformation (NEET)
　Aurora Flight Sciences,
　　benefits, 25
　Aurora Flight Sciences,
　　collaboration, 20–27
　Boeing co-sponsorship,
　　23–24
　challenges, 23–25
　program, benefits, 25–27
　program, launch, 21

New Engineering Education
　　Transformation (NEET)
　Autonomous Machines,
　　25–26
　launch, 22
　Senior Capstone Project/
　　evolution, 22–23
　open-source license, 38
　permissive license, 17
　Sloan School of Management,
　　162
Massachusetts Institute of
　　Technology Energy
　　Initiative (MITEI), 31–33, 48
Massachusetts Technology
　　Leadership Council
　　(MTLC), community
　　nonprofit support,
　　138, 139
MassBio, community nonprofit
　　support, 138–139
MassChallenge, 163
Massive Online Open Courseware
　　(MOOC), 160
Master Research Agreements
　　(MRAs), usage, 75
Matusik, Wojciech, 10, 180
MBA projects (engagement
　　model), 161–162
McCarthy, J. Michael, 27
Measure, Exposure, Reach,
　　Impact, Tangible (MERIT)
　　chart, usage, 222
Membership (engagement model),
　　146, 147–148
MERIT chart, usage, 222
Metrics, partnership metric, 40

Micro-credentials (engagement model), 160–161
MicroMasters, 160
Mid-term time horizon/speed, 36–38
Mid-term timelines, 39–40
Milestones, meeting, 176
Mistakes, learning, 197–199
Mitra, Amitava "Babi," 20–27
Moderna, COVID-19 vaccine, 89
Monetary losses, subcontrol failures (links), 39
Monetary transaction, 163
Money
  color, 57–62
  importance, 74–75
Moniz, Ernest, 31
Moss Kanter, Rosabeth, 6
"Most Innovative Square Mile on the Planet" Kendall square, 126f
Motivation metrics, 10
Myomo (technology), mission-driven impact, 134
MySQL (Oracle), 17

N

Nagle, Frank, 104
Narendran, Kailas, 134
National Association of Colleges and Employers (NACE), 200
National Association of Manufacturers, workforce partner, 107–108
National Employment Report, production, 32
National Science Foundation (NSF)
  funding, 150–151
  university research support, 94
Nature, pre-competitiveness, 148
Near-term research, university focus (absence), 55
Network
  building, 184
  external network, leveraging, 187–188
  internal network, usage, 188
  leveraging, 190
Network of Academic Corporate Relations Officers (NACRO), professional connections (value), 200–202
New Engineering Education Transformation (MIT NEET). *See* Massachusetts Institute of Technology
"New Model for Industry-Academic Partnerships, A," 113
New talent, acquisition, 18
Next generation pipeline programs (engagement model), 163–164
Nixon, Richard, 95
Nonexclusive royalty free license (NERF)
  granting, 53–54
  sponsor, granting, 60
Nongovernmental organizations (NGOs)
  neighbors, 8
  presence, 8

Nonprofit organizations, innovation engagement partnership initiation difficulty, 142f
Nonprofits, Amazon research awards, 153
NVIDIA
  AI research/workforce development, 36
  faculty grants, 152

O

Obama, Barack, 3
Objectives, attention, 190
Obligations, 16
Ocado Group plc, CSAIL engagement, 179–180
Office of Research Administration Services (RAS), 93
Office of Science and Technology, abolishment, 95
Office of Sponsored Programs (OSP), 93
Open innovation, 71
  meaning, 15
  open mindset, requirement, 75–76
Open-source capabilities, 104
Open source code (engagement model), 166, 170
Open-source community
  code, sharing, 187
  licence types, 16
Open-source licenses
  component, usage, 16
  shares, representation, 17f
Open-source movement, contributions, 15–16
Open-source project, 17–18
Open-source software, 104
Open-source, term (requirement), 16
Opinion leaders, access (importance), 4
Optical coherence tomography (OCT) scanner, development, 10
Orange Umbrella, 114
Oregon State University, equipment (availability), 58
Organic growth, personal contacts (impact), 178
Organization
  academic/corporate partners, involvement, 140–141
  culture, impact, 9–14, 79–80
  partner search, 5
  pathways, 232
Organizational structure, 68–69
Ownership, 183–184

P

Packard, David, 91
Page, Larry, 102
Pan Himalayan Grossroots Development Foundation, 26
Parker, Dennis Dio, 106–108
Partnering, timing questions, 18
Partnership
  complication issues, avoidance, 121
  development, hampering, 12–13
  experience, sharing, 121–122
  formation, 106
  goals/benefits, recognition, 64f
  ingredients, 70

innovation-focus engagement partnership, stakeholders, 81f
leadership support, 83–84
opportunities, legal department blame, 92
pursuit, reasons, 1–4
research partnership, case study, 7–8
resources, requirement, 69
strategic partnership, uniqueness, 72–73
strategy
  accountability/ownership, 183–184
  ingredients, 70
  success, benefit/measurement, 66
Partnership team
  building, 182–186
  structure, 185–186
  visibility/accessibility, increase, 184–185
Partners, understanding, 74
Patent and Trademark Act Amendments, 3
Patents
  filing, 120
  securing, 10
Paul, Richard, 27
Performance, fixed time, 51
Permissive licenses, 16–17
Personnel
  dedication, 194
  space, relationship, 195–196
Philanthropy
  engagement model, 147, 162–163
  presence, 173

Pipeline programs (engagement model), 147, 163. *See also* Next generation pipeline programs
Plan
  creation, 171
  questions, 172
  execution, 186–197
  failure, 172
  impact, 193
  initiation, 187–193
Planck, Max, 56
Playing for Change Foundation, 62
Point of contact (POC), 79–80, 184, 199
Positioning, 195
Possibilities, exploration, 4–9
Post-quantum applications, expansion, 56
Pratt & Whitney, support, 163–164
President's Science Advisory Committee, abolishment, 95
Principal investigator (PI), research, 120
Principles of Manufacturing (MIT), 160
Problem-solving, enhancement (project feature), 46
Problem statements, 36–37
Process-specific consultancy, 54–55
Procter & Gamble Company (P&G), University of Cincinnati (UC) partnership, 6
Product
  creation, 53–54
  delivery, 19

Product (*continued*)
  development (success factor), 3
  donation, 75
  enhancement, 104–105
  impact, 130, 131
Professional education, engagement partnership objective, 173
Professional programs (engagement model), 147, 160–161
Professional sabbatical (engagement model), 158–159
Professional training centers, 144
Project-based learning, 162
Project performance, fixed time, 51
Project-sponsored research, 59
Proposals
  learning/information exchange, 38
  receiving, 37
Proprietary data, agreement terms (impact), 60
Proprietary derivative works, permission, 16
Proprietary information, example, 54
Proximity, benefits, 146
Publication
  agreement terms, impact, 59–60
  allowance, refusal, 14–15
Purdue University, The Joint Transportation Research Program, 157

Q

Qualcomm, economic impact, 102
Quantum reality, 56

R

Ramos, Javier, 180
Raskar, Ramesh, 116
Readiness quiz, 12, 210
Recruitment
  audience knowledge, 115
  considerations, 114–115
  timing, 114
  undergraduate/graduate recruitment, campus visits, 114
  university partner leveraging, 115
Red Bull/Go-Pro, market alignment, 5
Relational database management systems, usage, 87
Relationships
  building, 7
  commitment, 174
  depth, 46
Research
  access/visibility, project feature, 46
  commercialization, impact, 128–135
  connection points, visualization, 178f
  focus, 179
  impact, 47, 130, 131–133
  partnership, case study, 7–8
  publishing, importance, 59–60
  seeded research, 37–38

shaping, ability (increase), 46
sponsored research, aspects, 50–51
Research and development (R&D), 47–49, 148, 184
engagement partnership objective, 173
infrastructure, cost (struggle), 86
unit, discipline (need), 144
Research-based conferences, value, 87–88
Researchers
commercialization, impact, 128–135
problem-solving, 42
talent pool, access, 84
Reserve Officers Training Corps (ROTC), creation, 65
Resources, 195, 205
requirement, 69
Return on investment (ROI)
measurement, 173
metrics, 13
partnership measurement, 40
positive ROI, 41
understanding, 174
worksheet, 213
measurement, 222
Reward metrics, 10
Roblox Creator Fund, 153
Roboticist, mathematician (teamwork), 49–50
Roche, Maria, 3
Roosevelt, Franklin D., 94
Rose-Hulman Institute of Technology (Rose-Hulman Ventures), 52

Rus, Daniela, 180
interview, 80, 82–86

S

Sabbatical (engagement model), 146, 158–159
Salesforce, customized version (usage), 199
Samueli, Henry (entrepreneurial faculty member), 90
Sarofim, Adel F., 26
Science Advisory Boards, enactment, 155
"Science, The Endless Frontier" (Bush report), 94
Scientific discovery, role (success factor), 3
Scientific publications, corporate contributions, 156f
Scorsese, Martin, 57
Secure Cyber Risk Aggregation and Management (SCRAM), 192
FinTech@CSAIL Initiative funding, 39–40
Security measures, adoption rates (benchmarks), 39
Seeded research, 37–38
Seed-funded research engagements, 77
Self-competition, avoidance, 114
Senior project, delivery (changes), 24
Set budget, inclusion, 59
Shared industrial needs, meeting, 150
Shared knowledge, impact, 7

Shareholders, value (delivery), 4
Sharing, importance/difficulty, 14–18
Short-term time horizon/speed, 20–28
Short-term timelines, 39–40
Siemens Global Academic partnerships, 70
Siemens Research and Innovation Ecosystem (RIE)
  components, 72–73
  growth, 77
  operating processes, 73–74
  organization examination, 73
  scheme, 77
Size (gift/grant advantage), 30
Societal impact (engagement model), 147, 164–165
Socrates, wisdom, 42
Sony Interactive Entertainment (SIE), academic engagement case study, 45–46
Sony research awards, 153
Southard Institute for Sales Excellence, University of Tampa (UT) establishment, 66–67
Spinouts
  support/resources, access, 85–86, 88
  university (nurturing process), 85
Sponsored programs, cooperation (need), 78–79
Sponsored research, 80
  aspects, 50–51
  engagement
    model, 146, 154–155
    scope, dependence, 154–155
  usage, 59–61
Sponsored research agreements (SRAs)
  structure, 61
  timeframe coverage, 60
Sponsored research (OSP/RAS), examination, 92–96
Staffing decisions, 232
Stakeholders
  corporate business units, 80
  identification, 172, 232
  knowledge, 80
  misreading, 197–198
  student function, 80, 105–106
Stakeholders Group, 79
Stanford Digital Economy Lab (S-DEL), 32, 35
  Advisory Group, The, 34
Stanford Industrial Park (Stanford Research Park), creation, 91–92
Start-ups
  disruption, 50
  impact, 11
  mentoring/advice, 137
  nimbleness, 100
  organic growth, 231
  output (global country ranking), 196f
  product creation, 53–54
  programs (engagement model), 147, 161, 173
  R&D infrastructure cost, struggle, 86

support, ecosystem (creation), 86, 88–89
support/resources, access, 85–86, 88
tech transfer engine, 99–100
university, nurturing process, 85
Statement of work (SOW), crafting, 59
Status quo, disruption, 163
Steenbock, Harry, 3
STEM education, support (initiative), 58
STEM fields, 113, 151
STEM-interested students, decisions, 110
STEM-oriented pathway, creation, 107
STEM program, 164
Stonebraker, Mike (interview), 80, 87–89
Strategic advisor roles (engagement model), 146, 157
Strategic alliances, 190
Strategic engagements, industry perspective, 71–78
Strategic partnership
  initiation, issues, 76
  uniqueness, 72–73
Strategic value, knowledge (absence), 12
Strategy
  assessment, 68–70
  defining, 63
"Strong communication," 176–177
Student-focused events, 67–68
Students
  academic work/contributions, boundaries (maintenance), 120–121
  challenges, 118–119
  low-cost investments, 74
  employment arrangement, 119
  opportunities, 9–10
  entrepreneurs, 115–117
  floating, 117–122
  funding, providing, 39
  internships
    engagement model, 158–159
    IP checklist, 224–226
    preparation, 21
  stakeholder function, 80, 105–106
  talent pool, access, 84
  work, 118
Students Army Training Corps, establishment, 65
Success
  defining/measuring, determination, 175
  groundwork, 4–9
  measure, 194
  secrets, 176–178
  tracking, 197–199
Sustainability, neglect, 199
Syracuse University, JPMorgan Chase (JPMC) partnership, 65–66

T

Takeda Pharmaceutical Co., MIT School of Engineering (engagement), 179
Talent
 acquisition, 165
  engagement partnership objective, 173
 attracting/retaining, 106
 connection points, visualization, 177f
 development, 124
 growth, 196
 projects, 75
 recruitment, 114–115
 training, 38
Tangible benefits, 37–38
 alignment, 41
Tangible bucket, 40–41
 list, 43–44
Tangible positive impact, yield, 193
Team. *See* Partnership team
Technical workers, retirement range, 109
Technicians, development programs, 109
Technological innovation, role (success factor), 3
Technology
 commercialization, 10
 development (engagement model), 165
 engagement partnership objective, 173
 entrepreneurship, 164–165
 faculty member/university, industry collaboration (benefit), 83
 industry partners, collaboration, 87
 licensing technology (engagement model), 166, 170
 Readiness Level, 71
 research and development, university-industry partnership success factors, 83–84, 87–88
Technology Licensing Office (TLO), 55, 93–96
Technology licensing/Transfer Office (TLO/TTO), 92–96, 102, 166
Technology transfer
 commercial impact, 96–102
 future, 100–102
 license transaction, contrast, 101
 start-ups, relationship, 99–100
 success story, 98–99
Technology Transfer Office (TTO), 55, 93–96
 appearance, 97–98
Terman, Frederick, 91
Texas A&M, capstone projects, 27–28
ThemisAI, 84–85
The Routable Company (TRC), 84
Thiel, Peter (entrepreneurial faculty member), 90
Thompson, Neil, 48

Time
  commitment, 147
  speed, 18
  table, establishment, 59
Timeframe, agreement terms (impact), 60
Time horizon, 18
  importance, 18–19
Timeline
  defining, 18
  planning, 175
Toyota-CSAIL joint Research center, initiation, 85
Toyota Motor Engineering & Manufacturing, 106–112
Toyota Research Institute (TRI), 51–52
Transactional one-off engagements, impact, 174
Trilateral seed-funded research engagements, 77
Trust
  increase, 46
  suffering, 8

U

Udacity (platform), 123
Unbiased expert opinions/ knowledge, on-call service, 29
Undergraduate/graduate recruitment, campus visits, 114
United States
  energy crisis, 94–95
  Office of Scientific Research and Development (OSRD), 94

United States R&D to GDP ratio (National Center for Science and Engineering Statistics), 48f
Universities
  benefits, innovation partnerships (impact), 181f
  connection, 216–221
  industry partner collaboration, benefit, 83
  industry partners, collaboration, 87
  partners, leveraging, 115
  students, employment opportunities, 9–10
University-industry collaborations, 71, 157
  examples/lessons, 85
  support/resources, access, 85–86, 88
University Industry Demonstration Partnership (UIDP), 200, 202
University Industry Innovation Network (UIIN), 200, 202
University-industry partnerships
  opportunities, 4
  process, 88–89
  success, factors, 83–84, 87–88
University of Cincinnati (UC), Procter & Gamble Company (P&G) partnership, 6
University of Tampa (UT), Southard Institute for Sales Excellence, 66–67

US-EU Trade and Technology Council's (TTC) Talent for Growth Task Force, 149
U.S. global leadership, enhancement, 150

V

Value, assigning, 222–223
Venti Technologies, 84
Venture Cafe, space/connections (co-working), 138
Venture capital (VC) firms, 140–146
  presence, 8
Venture Mentoring Service (VMS), 137
Venture Well report, 4
Vertica (Hewlett Packard acquisition), 128
"Virtuous circle," 176–177
Virtuous cycle, 132
Visibility, increase, 184–185
Visiting Industry Researchers (VIRs), 159
Visiting researchers/fellows (engagement model), 147
Visualizations, 141–142
Viterbi, Andrew (entrepreneurial faculty member), 90

W

Weak points, acknowledgement, 78–80
Wellesley College, course cross-registration, 5–6
Whitacker, Steve, 80
Wins, attention, 198
Win-win engagement model, creation, 45
Wi-vi technology, usage, 52–53, 93
Worcester Polytechnic Institute's (WPI) Interactive Qualifying Project (IQP), 162
Workforce
  development organizations, 144
  developments education, 8
Working Knowledge (Harvard Business), 104
Work, scope, 50
Work study programs, effectiveness, 106
World Food Programme (WFP), food ration supply, 62